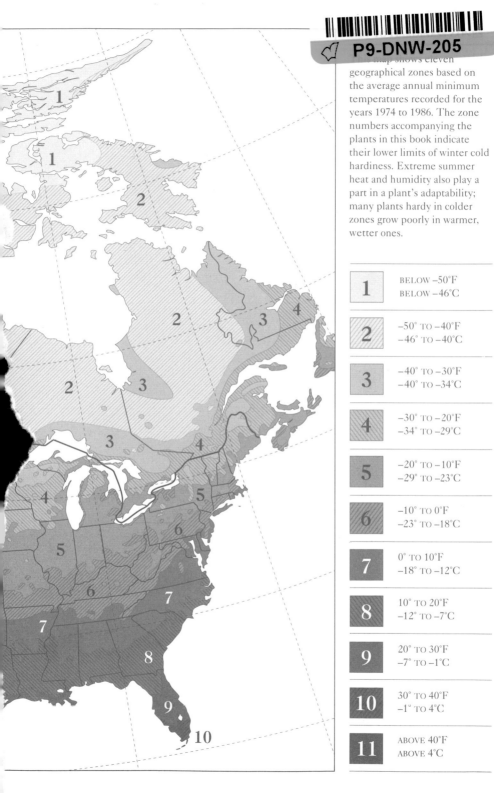

map shows eleven geographical zones based on the average annual minimum temperatures recorded for the years 1974 to 1986. The zone numbers accompanying the plants in this book indicate their lower limits of winter cold hardiness. Extreme summer heat and humidity also play a part in a plant's adaptability; many plants hardy in colder zones grow poorly in warmer, wetter ones.

Zone	Temperature
1	BELOW −50°F BELOW −46°C
2	−50° TO −40°F −46° TO −40°C
3	−40° TO −30°F −40° TO −34°C
4	−30° TO −20°F −34° TO −29°C
5	−20° TO −10°F −29° TO −23°C
6	−10° TO 0°F −23° TO −18°C
7	0° TO 10°F −18° TO −12°C
8	10° TO 20°F −12° TO −7°C
9	20° TO 30°F −7° TO −1°C
10	30° TO 40°F −1° TO 4°C
11	ABOVE 40°F ABOVE 4°C

allegan
Pachapandra
for mt Cuba

GARDEN HANDBOOKS

GARDEN
TREES

EYEWITNESS
GARDEN HANDBOOKS

GARDEN
TREES

A DK PUBLISHING BOOK

Produced for DK Publishing by
Cooling Brown (*Book Packaging*)
Hampton, Middlesex, England TW12 2SA

MANAGING EDITOR Francis Ritter
MANAGING ART EDITOR Derek Coombes

First American Edition, 1996
2 4 6 8 10 9 7 5 3

Published in the United States by
DK Publishing, Inc.
95 Madison Avenue
New York, New York 10016

Library of Congress Cataloging-in-Publication Data
Garden trees. –– 1st American ed.
    p.   cm. –– (Eyewitness garden handbooks)
Includes index.
ISBN 0-7894-0428-1
    1. Ornamental trees –– Handbooks, manuals, etc.
    2. Ornamental trees –– Pictorial works. I. Series.
SB435.G375 1996   95-43913
635.9' 77 –– dc20   CIP

Color reproduction by Colourscan, Singapore
Printed and bound in Singapore by Star Standard Industries

CONTENTS

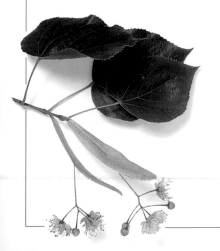

CONIFERS

CONTRIBUTORS

ALLEN J. COOMBES
*Hardy Trees, Magnolias
and Guide to Tree Care*

KENNETH A. BECKETT
Tender Trees

KEITH RUSHFORTH
Conifers and Dwarf Conifers

SUSYN ANDREWS
Hollies

HOW TO USE THIS BOOK

THIS BOOK PROVIDES the ideal quick reference guide to selecting and identifying trees for the garden.

The **Trees in the Garden** section is a helpful introduction to trees and gives advice on choosing a suitable tree for a particular site or purpose, such as for a container, as a screen, or simply as a specimen plant.

To choose or identify your tree, turn to the **Catalog of Garden Trees**, where photographs are accompanied by concise plant descriptions. The entries are grouped by size and season of interest. In addition, if you have a color preference, the trees are also grouped by color (see the Color Wheel below) for easy selection. Clear descriptions and cultivation requirements are to be found under each plant entry.

For additional information on tree cultivation, routine care, and propagation, turn to the **Guide to Tree Care**, where comprehensive information on all aspects of caring for your tree can be found.

The Color Wheel

All the trees featured in the book are grouped according to the color of their main feature of interest.

They are always arranged in the same order, indicated by the Color Wheel below, from white through reds and blues, to yellows and oranges.

Variegated trees are categorized by the color of their variegation, that is, white or yellow.

THE SYMBOLS

The symbols below are used throughout the **Catalog of Garden Trees** to indicate a tree's preferred growing conditions and hardiness. However, both the climate and soil conditions of your particular site should also be taken into account, since they may affect a tree's growth.

☼	Prefers full sun	◊	Prefers well-drained soil
☼	Prefers partial shade	◖	Prefers moist soil
☀	Tolerates full shade	●	Prefers wet soil

pH Needs acid soil

❄ Half-hardy – can withstand temperatures down to 0°C (32°F)

❄❄ Frost hardy – can withstand temperatures down to -5°C (23°F)

❄❄❄ Fully hardy – can withstand temperatures down to -15°C (5°F)

The range of winter temperatures that each tree is able to withstand is shown by the USDA plant hardiness zone numbers that are given in each entry. The temperature ranges for each zone are shown on the endpaper map in this book.

Tree size categories

The trees featured in the Catalog are divided according to the average height they attain. However, heights may vary from the ones given, according to site, climate, and age.

The categories are as follows:

LARGE
Over 50ft (15m)
MEDIUM
30–50ft (10–15m)
SMALL
Up to 30ft (10m)

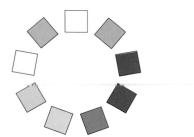

HOW TO USE THE CATALOG OF TREES

HEADINGS
Each chapter is subdivided into sections, according to the average size of the trees and their main season of interest.

The tree's *family name* appears here.

The tree's *common name(s)* appear here.

The tree's *botanical name* appears here.

TREE PORTRAITS
The color photographs show the main features of the tree (see THE COLOR WHEEL on previous page).

ENTRIES
Each tree's growing habit, flowers, fruits, and leaves are described. Details of the tree's native habitat, cultivation, and propagation, together with any other botanical names, are also provided.

SYMBOLS
The symbols indicate the sun, soil, and temperature requirements (see THE SYMBOLS on previous page).

Autumn | TREES SMALL/Winter • 113

Simaroubaceae | QUASSIA

PICRASMA AILANTHOIDES
Habit Spreading. *Flowers* Insignificant. *Fruits* Small, pea-like, in early summer. Red. *Leaves* Deciduous, with 9–13 sharply toothed leaflets. Glossy bright green, turning brilliant yellow, orange, and red in autumn.
• NATIVE HABITAT Japan, N. China, and Korea.
• CULTIVATION Tolerates semi-shade and lime-rich soil, but grows best in fertile, moisture-retentive, neutral to acid, loamy soils.
• PROPAGATION By seed in autumn.
• OTHER NAMES *P. quassioides.*

❀ ❀ ❀
Z 5–8
HEIGHT 30ft (10m)
SPREAD 22ft (7m)

Leguminosae

BAUHINIA VARIEGATA 'Candida'
Habit Dense, rounded, spreading with age. *Flowers* Fragrant, large, in short, few-flowered racemes from winter to early summer. Pure white. *Leaves* Deciduous, broadly oval, deeply notched. Dark green.
• NATIVE HABITAT Garden origin.
• CULTIVATION Best grown in a conservatory in cooler climates. Grow in fertile soil or soil mix. Water freely in growth, then moderately.
• PROPAGATION By leafless cuttings of semi-ripe wood in summer.

❀ ❀ ❀
Z 10–11
HEIGHT 25ft (8m)
SPREAD 30ft (10m)

Rosaceae | CRAB APPLE

MALUS 'Golden Hornet'
Habit Broadly pyramidal. *Flowers* Large, cup-shaped, in profusion in late spring. White, flushed pink, deep pink in bud. *Fruits* Small, rounded crab apples. Golden-yellow. *Leaves* Deciduous, broadly oval. Dark green, then yellow in autumn.
• NATIVE HABITAT Garden origin.
• CULTIVATION Tolerates dappled shade, but flowers and fruits best in sun. Grow in any but waterlogged soil.
• PROPAGATION By budding in summer or by grafting in winter.

Leguminosae | ORCHID TREE, MOUNTAIN EBONY

BAUHINIA VARIEGATA
Habit Dense, rounded, spreading with age. *Flowers* Fragrant, large, in short, few-flowered racemes from winter to early summer. Magenta to lavender. *Leaves* Deciduous, broadly oval, deeply notched. Dark green.
• NATIVE HABITAT Tropical mountain forests of E. Asia.
• CULTIVATION Best grown in a conservatory in cooler climates. Water freely when in growth.
• PROPAGATION By seed in spring.
• OTHER NAMES *B. purpurea* of gardens.

❀ ❀ ❀
Z 4–8
HEIGHT 30ft (10m)
SPREAD 25ft (8m)

❀ ❀ ❀
Z 10–11
HEIGHT 25ft (8m)
SPREAD 30ft (10m)

DWARF CONIFERS • 155

DWARF CONIFERS
Slow-growing and dwarf conifers are invaluable in small gardens, offering year-round interest with an enormous range of color, form, and habit. The compact cultivars are ideal for rock gardens, while spreading and prostrate forms are invaluable when used as ground cover. Nearly all tolerate a range of growing conditions, thriving on acid to neutral soil, and yew

and junipers tolerate lime. Some are not wind-tolerant and need a sheltered site. They may grow to exceed their stated height after 15–20 years but replacement plants can be propagated. *Cupressocyparis* root easily with heeled, greenwood, or softwood cuttings, but *Cedrus, Picea, Pseudotsuga,* and *Tsuga* require hardwood cuttings. *Pinus* and *Abies* are usually grafted.

PICEA PUNGENS 'Montgomery'
Habit Dense, rounded-conical. *Leaves* Rigid, stout, needle-like, sharply spine-tipped, 3in (2cm) long. Bright gray-blue.
• HEIGHT 3ft (1m).
• SPREAD 3ft (1m).

Picea pungens 'Montgomery'

PINUS SYLVESTRIS 'Doone Valley'
Habit Irregularly conical, compact, upright. *Leaves* In pairs, straight, or slightly twisted, needle-like, 1½–2in (4–5cm) long. Dark blue-green.
• HEIGHT 3ft (1m).
• SPREAD 3ft (1m).

Pinus sylvestris 'Doone Valley'

☼ ◐ ❀ ❀ ❀ Z 3–7

☼ ◐ ❀ ❀ ❀ Z 2–8

ABIES LASIOCARPA 'Arizonica Compacta'
Habit Slow-growing, dense, regular, broadly conical. *Leaves* Linear, forward-pointing on top of the shoots, spreading below. Silvery-blue, with broad, white bands beneath. *Bark* Corky.
• HEIGHT 12–15ft (4–5m).
• SPREAD 5–6ft (1.5–2m).

Abies lasiocarpa 'Arizonica Compacta'

JUNIPERUS SCOPULORUM 'Springbank'
Habit Narrowly columnar, with overlapping branch tips. *Leaves* Aromatic, scale-like, pressed closely to shoots. Intense silvery-blue.
• HEIGHT 12ft (4m).
• SPREAD 3ft (1m).

Juniperus scopulorum 'Springbank'

◑ ◐ ❀ ❀ ❀ Z 5–6

JUNIPERUS SQUAMATA 'Holger'
Habit Low, prostrate, wide-spreading, with nodding branchlets. *Leaves* Aromatic, needle-like, with turning sulphur-yellow in spring, giving beautiful contrast with older foliage.
• HEIGHT 6ft (2m).
• SPREAD 6ft (2m).

Juniperus squamata 'Holger'

Juniperus scopulorum 'Springbank'

☼ ◐ ❀ ❀ ❀ Z 4–8

☼ ◐ ❀ ❀ Z 3–7

SILHOUETTES
The shape and proportions of the tree are indicated by the silhouette.

SIZES
The average height and spread of the trees are given, although these may vary according to site, climate, and age.

FEATURE BOXES
Plant groups or genera of special interest to the gardener are presented in separate feature boxes.

TREES IN THE GARDEN

MORE THAN ANY other feature in the garden, trees form the structural framework of a design, with their distinctive silhouettes providing a foil of contrasting elements against the softer lines of other plantings.

Trees offer an enormous diversity of shape and form, as well as color and texture of foliage, flowers, and bark. They may be grown in many ways: informally in a woodland setting, underplanted with bulbs and shade-loving perennials, or formally in avenues or as pleached (interlaced) hedging. Some are so beautiful in bloom that, if sited alone, they make a beautiful, eye-catching garden feature.

Choosing trees

Trees are generally the largest, longest-lived and most expensive of plants in the garden, so selecting and siting them are primary design decisions. In smaller gardens or in a "one-tree garden," careful choice and siting are vital. Although a tree's overall appearance and special features are important, it is also essential to consider its suitability for the garden's soil, climate, and exposure, and to take account of its rate of growth and final height and spread.

Garden centers usually carry a limited range of the most popular ornamental trees, but specialist nurseries and mail-order services offer a much wider choice.

Trees as design elements

Trees are the living equivalent of hard landscaping features, creating a strong visual impact in much the same way as walls and paving. If used structurally, trees can define or enclose space: they can mark boundaries or separate one part of the garden from another. If used as hedging, they can create effective screens; when used in pairs they can frame a distant view; or when in rows, may be used to create an arch.

Long-lasting designs

Grouped together in a planned design, trees create a strong impact, developing over the years, with their varied colors and forms.

Shape and form

A tree's form and shape are important to the style of a garden. Many trees can be used in formal or informal settings, but some, especially those that are cone-shaped, such as *Carpinus betulus* 'Fastigiata', almost demand formal use. Trees with a strong shape fit well in small, paved gardens. In contrast, mountain ashes (*Sorbus aucuparia*) and crab apples (*Malus*) are typically informal trees. For gardens with an oriental theme, Japanese maples (*Acer palmatum*) and *Salix babylonica* var. *pekinensis* 'Tortuosa' are ideal.

While round-headed or spreading trees often have an informal appearance, they cast shade and rain shadow, making

TREE SHAPES

SPREADING
Prunus x *yedoensis*
(Yoshino cherry)

WEEPING
Prunus x *subhirtella* 'Pendula Rubra'

PYRAMIDAL
Carpinus betulus
'Fastigiata'

ROUND–HEADED
Fagus sylvatica
(Common beech,
European beech)

CONICAL
Pseudotsuga menziesii
var. *glauca*
(Blue Douglas fir)

ARCHING
Archontophoenix alexandrae
(Alexandra palm)

COLUMNAR
Acer rubrum
'Columnare'

Planning garden color

Although most gardens look their best in summer, successional planting can create year-round interest. Spring and autumn-flowering trees, as well as those grown for their foliage, bark, berries, and winter outline, provide color and variety throughout the year.

underplanting difficult. Trees with an irregular, open-branch framework cast little shade, and may be underplanted with bulbs and small perennials.

Successional interest

In many gardens, the glorious but short-lived flowers of spring and summer leave little to lift the spirits in the dark days of winter. But with planning and careful selection from a palette of flowers, foliage, berries, and bark, color and interest can be maintained throughout the year. Choose trees with successive flowering, such as *Cercis siliquastrum* for spring, *Stewartia pseudocamellia* for summer, and *Magnolia campbellii* and its forms which flower from late winter. The beautiful silvery foliage of *Sorbus aria* 'Lutescens' appears in spring, while in autumn the maples (*Acer*) give displays of brilliant golds and reds. Autumn highlights are provided by berrying species of *Sorbus*, *Cotoneaster*, *Crataegus*, and *Malus*, some persisting well into winter, which is the best time to appreciate the bark of species of *Acer*, *Betula*, *Eucalyptus*, and *Prunus*.

Specimen trees

A specimen tree is grown on its own and so can develop its full natural beauty without competition from other trees. It is important to select a specimen that is in scale with its setting – small trees look lost in wide, open areas and, conversely, large trees overwhelm confined spaces.

In formal gardens, specimen trees are usually planted in the center of the lawn. In less formal settings an offset tree adds a dynamic sense of movement to a design, and can lead the eye to the view down the garden. Specimens can mark the transition from one area of the garden to another, and providing a foil for a specimen enhances its effect – for example, by planting it in a swath of gravel, among groundcover plants, or by still water where it can be reflected.

Trees contrasted with plants

As well as providing a contrast of texture with other plants, trees can also be planted to enhance the perspective of the garden.

Using specimen trees

Specimens are trees with a particularly attractive or well-shaped outline. They look their best when sited on their own, so that they stand out against the rest of the garden. Magnolia × kewensis 'Wada's Memory' makes a magnificent specimen tree, with its profusion of large, fragrant, white flowers that appear before the leaves from mid- to late spring.

Features of interest

A tree's form provides a framework to display other features of interest at different times of the year. Foliage is the most important, by virtue of its mass and duration. The shape, color, and texture of leaves provide infinite variation, from the delicate, fern-like foliage of *Gleditsia triacanthos* 'Sunburst' to the large, architectural leaves of *Paulownia tormentosa*. Plants with dark or variegated foliage offer the potential of subtle or dramatic associations with plain, green-leaved species. Surface texture adds another dimension: glossy leaves give glittering reflections and can be contrasted with leaves of a matte texture.

Even the most transient of flowers can create memorable effects, ranging from the delicate profusion of the spring cherries (*Prunus* species) to the tropical opulence of the jacarandas. Trees that bloom in autumn, winter, and early spring are among the most valuable, providing interest in the darkest seasons. Choose flower colors to complement the overall design, and provide shelter for those with scent so that the still air captures their fragrance.

Fruits, berries, and pods often rival flowers in beauty, and many berrying trees attract wildlife. Do not overlook more subtle fruits, such as the pods of magnolias or the colored keys of maples.

Trees in containers
Container-grown trees have a striking look and can be moved to vary the garden design or for their own protection in winter.

The color and texture of bark can be fully appreciated in winter. Choose from the stark whites of the birches, the mahogany-reds of some *Prunus*, the striations of the snake-bark acers, or the peeling mosaics of *Eucalyptus*.

Trees for screens and windbreaks
Large-scale tree planting can be used to screen unsightly buildings and roads, while also deadening noise and filtering dust. They can provide shelter from wind and frost for other plants nearby. Tree selection is very important. Lombardy poplars (*Populus nigra* 'Italica') are often planted as screens, but their height and narrow outline not only highlight what they are intended to conceal, but also offer little protection from wind at ground level. Stands of mixed deciduous and evergreen trees provide a more effective barrier.

Hedges are the most dense and compact form of screening, and a number of trees tolerate close clipping into formal hedging. English yew (*Taxus baccata*) is the classic backdrop in many traditional gardens; English hornbeam (*Carpinus betulus*), English holly (*Ilex aquifolium*), and European beech (*Fagus sylvatica*) also create visually impenetrable but very effective wind-filtering screens. For informal flowering hedges try cherries (*Prunus* spp.) or strawberry tree (*Arbutus unedo*).

Trees in containers
Growing trees in large pots or tubs greatly extends their design potential. On patios, in courtyards – anywhere where soil space is at a premium – containerized trees create a verdant and colorful effect, and give height and structure to the design. Trees in large containers may be used to frame an entrance or to flank wide steps, while tender trees may be grown in containers, displayed outdoors in summer, then moved to a light, frost-free place as cold weather approaches.

Dwarf conifers
As a group, dwarf conifers are unique in their diversity of shape and form. They range from globose to spire- and cone-shaped, with habits including prostrate, erect, and weeping. Textures vary from soft and feathery to firm and spiky, and their colors encompass almost metallic shades of gold, silver, bronze, and steel blues, as well as rich blue-greens and dark greens.

Their compact form is well suited to small, modern gardens, where larger trees are impractical. Adaptable and easy to grow – in raised beds and borders, as well as in rock gardens – dwarf conifers are a garden essential. Even the tiniest of them may be used effectively to create miniature landscapes in troughs or other containers.

Adaptable dwarf conifers
Dwarf conifers are invaluable in the garden and are available in a wide variety of shapes, sizes, colors, and textures.

PLANTER'S GUIDE TO TREES

FOR EXPOSED SITES
Acer pseudoplatanus 'Simon
Louis Frères',
A. pseudoplatanus
f. *erythrocarpum*
Betula pendula 'Tristis'
Crataegus laevigata 'Paul's
Scarlet', *C.* × *lavallei*
'Carrierei'
Fagus sylvatica, F. sylvatica
f. *pendula, F. sylvatica*
f. *purpurea*
Fraxinus excelsior
Juniperus communis
'Hibernica'
Laburnum alpinum,
L. × *watereri* 'Vossii'
Picea abies
Pinus contorta, P. nigra,
P. ponderosa, P. sylvestris
'Fastigiata'
Populus × *canadensis* and cvs.
Quercus robur f. *fastigiata*
Salix alba
Sorbus aria 'Lutescens'
S. aucuparia
Taxus baccata 'Aurea',
T. baccata 'Dovastonii
Aurea'
Tilia cordata 'Rancho'

FOR SMALL GARDENS
Acer capillipes, A. griseum,
A. palmatum 'Koreanum'
Arbutus × *andrachnoides*
Betula albosinensis, B. ermanii
B. pendula 'Tristis'
B. utilis var. *jacquemontii*
Catalpa bignonioides 'Aurea'
Cercis siliquastrum
Cornus florida

Crataegus laevigata 'Paul's
Scarlet', *C.* × *lavallei*
'Carrierei'
Eucryphia × *nymansensis*
Gleditsia triacanthos
'Sunburst'
Laburnum × *watereri* 'Vossii'
Malus (many)
Pinus halepensis
Prunus (many)
Pyrus calleryana
'Chanticleer', *P. salicifolia*
'Pendula'
Sorbus cashmiriana,
S. commixta, S. vilmorinii

FOR CONTAINERS
Abies koreana
Acer negundo 'Variegatum'
A. palmatum 'Coreanum'
Chamaecyparis lawsoniana
'Gnom', *C. lawsoniana*
'Minima', *C. obtusa* 'Nana
Pyramidalis'
Cordyline australis
'Atropurpurea'
Ficus benjamina 'Variegata'
Ilex compact species and cvs.
Juniperus chinensis 'Stricta'
J. scopulorum 'Skyrocket'
Pinus mugo 'Gnom'
Prunus 'Kiku-shidare-zakura',
P. subhirtella 'Pendula
Rubra'
Taxus baccata 'Dovastonii
Aurea'
Thuja orientalis 'Aurea
Nana', *T. occidentalis*
'Caespitosa'

SPECIMEN TREES
Araucaria araucana
Abies procera 'Glauca'
Acer griseum, A. rubrum
Alnus cordata
Betula albosinensis
Carpinus betulus 'Fastigiata'
Cedrus atlantica f. *glauca,*
C. libani

Ginkgo biloba
Liquidambar styraciflua
Liriodendron tulipifera
Magnolia campbellii 'Charles
Raffill'
Metasequoia glyptostroboides
Nyssa sylvatica
Picea breweriana, P. omorika,
P. bungeana
Prunus maackii
Salix × *sepulcralis* var.
chrysocoma
Sequoiadendron giganteum
Tsuga heterophylla

POLLUTION TOLERANT
Acer (not Japanese maples)
Aesculus (all)
Ailanthus altissima
Alnus cordata, A. glutinosa
'Imperialis', *A. incana*
Amelanchier (all)
Betula papyrifera
Carpinus betulus and cvs.
Catalpa bignonioides
Crataegus (most)
Davidia involucrata
Fraxinus (all)
Laburnum (all)
Liriodendron tulipifera
Malus (all)
Morus nigra
Platanus (all)
Populus (most)
Prunus avium, P. padus and
cvs.
Prunus (all Japanese
cherries)
Quercus ilex,
Q. × *hispanica*
'Lucombeana'

Salix (most)
Sorbus aria
'Lutescens' and variants,
S. aucuparia and variants

CATALOG OF
GARDEN
TREES

Hippocastanaceae	COMMON HORSE-CHESTNUT

AESCULUS HIPPOCASTANUM

Habit Vigorous, spreading. **Flowers** Tubular, flared at the mouth. They appear in large, conical, upright panicles in mid- to late spring. White, flushed with pink, yellow at the center.
Fruits Rounded, spiny, green husk, enclosing 1 or 2 glossy brown seeds. **Leaves** Deciduous, divided into 5–7 narrowly oval, pointed leaflets. Dark green, turning yellow and orange-brown in autumn.
• NATIVE HABITAT Mountain woods of N. Greece and Albania.
• CULTIVATION Grow in sun or semi-shade in any fertile, well-drained soil. Very old trees sometimes develop downward-growing branches that turn sharply upward where they meet the ground, thus forming natural layers. It is a reliably flowering species, often grown as a park tree and suitable as a specimen in larger gardens.
• PROPAGATION By seed in autumn.

Z 3–8

HEIGHT
To 80ft
(25m)

SPREAD
70ft (20m)

Hippocastanaceae	

AESCULUS × CARNEA 'Briotii'

Habit Broadly columnar or round-headed.
Flowers Tubular, flared at mouth, in upright,
conical spires in late spring. Rich bright red.
Fruits Smooth or slightly spiny husks enclosing
glossy brown nuts. **Leaves** Deciduous, divided,
with 5–7 twisted, sharply toothed leaflets. Dark green.
• NATIVE HABITAT Garden origin.
• CULTIVATION Grow in sun or semi-shade in any
fertile, well-drained soil.
• PROPAGATION By budding in late summer or by
grafting in winter.

Z 4–7

HEIGHT
To 70ft
(20m)

SPREAD
50ft (15m)

Hippocastanaceae	CHINESE HORSE-CHESTNUT

AESCULUS CHINENSIS

Habit Slow-growing, spreading. **Flowers** Small,
tubular, in long, slender spires in mid-summer.
White. **Leaves** Deciduous, divided into 7 long,
narrow, oblong-oval leaflets. Glossy bright green.
• NATIVE HABITAT Forests of N. China.
• CULTIVATION Grow in sun or semi-shade in any
fertile, well-drained soil.
• PROPAGATION By seed in autumn.

Z 6–8

HEIGHT
70ft (20m)
or more

SPREAD
30ft (10m)

Aceraceae	BIG LEAF MAPLE, OREGON MAPLE

ACER MACROPHYLLUM

Habit Broadly columnar. **Flowers** Small, fragrant,
in long, pendent clusters in spring. Yellow.
Fruits 2 seeds, fused together, each with a wing.
Leaves Deciduous, deeply lobed. Dark green,
turning orange and gold in autumn.
Bark Vertically fissured. Gray-brown.
• NATIVE HABITAT Damp woodland and canyons of
W. North America.
• CULTIVATION Grow in full sun or light, dappled
shade in fertile, moisture-retentive soil.
• PROPAGATION By seed in autumn.

Z 5–7

HEIGHT
To 70ft
(20m)

SPREAD
50ft (15m)

Salicaceae	WHITE POPLAR, ABELE, SILVER-LEAVED POPLAR

POPULUS ALBA

Habit Broadly columnar. **Flowers** Drooping
catkins, with male and female on separate plants.
Fruits Small capsules enclosing tiny seeds in
white cotton. **Leaves** Deciduous, wavy-margined,
3–5 lobes. Dark green above, silvery-white beneath,
turning yellow in autumn.
• NATIVE HABITAT Woods of Europe, N. Africa,
C. and W. Asia.
• CULTIVATION Grow in deep, fertile, moisture-
retentive soil. Plant away from buildings and drains.
• PROPAGATION By hardwood cuttings in winter.

Z 3–9

HEIGHT
To 70ft
(20m)

SPREAD
50ft (15m)
or more

Salicaceae	JAPANESE POPLAR

POPULUS MAXIMOWICZII

Habit Vigorous, upright, conical. *Flowers* Male and female catkins on separate plants. *Fruits* Pendent, female catkins bear seeds clothed in silky hair in late summer. *Leaves* Deciduous, oval, heart-shaped at base. Balsam-scented. Bright green, white beneath, turning yellow in autumn.
• NATIVE HABITAT Woodlands of E. Asia.
• CULTIVATION Grow in deep, fertile, moisture-retentive soil. Plant at least 100ft (30m) away from buildings and drains.
• PROPAGATION By hardwood cuttings in winter.

Z 3–8

HEIGHT
To 70ft
(20m)

SPREAD
30ft (10m)

Fagaceae	SPANISH CHESTNUT, SWEET CHESTNUT

CASTANEA SATIVA 'Albomarginata'

Habit Broadly columnar. *Flowers* Tiny, in clustered catkins, in summer. Creamy-yellow. *Fruits* Prickly husks enclosing edible nuts. Brown. *Leaves* Deciduous, lance-shaped. Dark green, margined white, turning yellow in autumn.
• NATIVE HABITAT Species occurs in woodlands of S. Europe, N.W. Africa, S.W. Asia. Garden origin.
• CULTIVATION Grow in sun or semi-shade, in fertile, well-drained soil.
• PROPAGATION By budding in summer or by grafting in late winter.

Z 5–6

HEIGHT
80ft (25m)

SPREAD
50ft (15m)

Magnoliaceae	TULIP TREE

LIRIODENDRON TULIPIFERA' 'Aureomarginatum

Habit Vigorous, broadly columnar, spreading with age. *Flowers* Tulip-shaped, carried at branch tips of mature trees in mid-summer. Pale green, with orange markings at the base. *Leaves* Deciduous, lobed. Dark green, with yellow margins above, blue-white beneath, turning butter-yellow in autumn.
• NATIVE HABITAT Garden origin.
• CULTIVATION Tolerates semi-shade. Grow in deep, moist but well-drained, slightly acid soil.
• PROPAGATION By budding in late summer.

Z 5–9

HEIGHT
To 70ft
(20m)

SPREAD
To 30ft
(10m)

Rosaceae	BLACK CHERRY, RUM CHERRY

PRUNUS SEROTINA

Habit Broadly columnar, irregularly spreading. *Flowers* Small, fragrant, in upright or drooping spikes at branch tips, in early summer. White. *Fruits* Small, edible cherries. Black when ripe. *Leaves* Deciduous, elliptic to lance-shaped. Glossy dark green, turning yellow in autumn.
• NATIVE HABITAT Pasture and woods of North America.
• CULTIVATION Grow in any but waterlogged soil.
• PROPAGATION By seed in autumn or by softwood cuttings in summer.

Z 3–9

HEIGHT
To 70ft
(20m)

SPREAD
40ft (10m)
or more

Sterculiaceae	FLAME BOTTLE TREE, FLAME TREE

BRACHYCHITON ACERIFOLIUS

Habit Spreading, with a rounded crown.
Flowers Small, in dense clusters, on bare branches from spring to late summer. Brilliant scarlet.
Leaves Deciduous, 3–7 lobes, heart-shaped at the base. Lustrous dark green.
• NATIVE HABITAT Tropical forests of Australia.
• CULTIVATION Grown as a house or conservatory plant. Grow in a free-draining, sandy soil or soil mix. Prune after flowering to restrict size.
• PROPAGATION By seed in spring.
• OTHER NAMES *Sterculia acerifolia.*

Z 10–11

HEIGHT
To 80ft
(20m)

SPREAD
80ft (20m)

Aceraceae	

ACER PLATANOIDES 'Crimson King'

Habit Vigorous, spreading. *Flowers* Tiny, in dense clusters in mid-spring. Yellow, tinged red.
Fruits Small, round seed, with large papery wings.
Leaves Deciduous, large, palmately lobed, each lobe with long, slender points. Deep red-purple, turning orange in autumn.
• NATIVE HABITAT Garden origin.
• CULTIVATION Tolerates semi-shade and almost any fertile, well-drained soil.
• PROPAGATION By grafting in late winter or early spring or by budding in summer.

Z 3–7

HEIGHT
60ft (18m)

SPREAD
50ft (15m)
or more

Fagaceae	PURPLE BEECH, COPPER BEECH

FAGUS SYLVATICA Purple Group

Habit Round-headed, broadly spreading.
Leaves Deciduous, oval, with wavy margins. Purple and silky when young, turning rich copper in autumn. *Bark* Smooth. Pale gray.
• NATIVE HABITAT Species grows in woodlands of Europe. Garden origin.
• CULTIVATION Tolerates alkaline and acid soils, provided they are well drained. Excellent for hedging. Trim in summer.
• PROPAGATION By budding in late summer or by seed in autumn. Seed-raised plants are variable.

Z 4–7

HEIGHT
100ft (30m)

SPREAD
80ft (25m)

Salicaceae	GRAY POPLAR

POPULUS X *CANESCENS*

Habit Vigorous, broadly columnar.
Flowers Catkins, in spring. Male: grayish-red; female: green, on separate plants
Leaves Deciduous, rounded to oval, toothed. Gray when young, later glossy dark green and gray beneath, turning yellow in autumn.
Bark Diamond-shaped markings. Gray.
• NATIVE HABITAT A natural hybrid occurring in river valleys from C. Europe to Russia.
• CULTIVATION Grow in moist, fertile soil.
• PROPAGATION By hardwood cuttings in winter.

Z 3–8

HEIGHT
To 80ft
(25m)

SPREAD
To 50ft
(15m)

Salicaceae	

POPULUS x CANADENSIS 'Robusta'

Habit Fast-growing, conical, with upright branches. **Flowers** Long, male catkins in spring. Red. **Leaves** Deciduous, broadly triangular. Bronze-red on emergence, later glossy dark green. **Bark** Vertically fissured. Pale gray.
• NATIVE HABITAT Garden origin.
• CULTIVATION Grow in deep, fertile, moisture-retentive soil. Excellent for windbreaks. As with most species of poplar, the deeply penetrating root system may cause extensive damage, so plant at least 100ft (30m) away from buildings, walls, and

drains, especially on clay soils. This, and other *Populus* species, are susceptible to bacterial canker and fungal diseases. A male clone, *P.* x *canadensis* 'Robusta' does not produce the fruits that in female clones such as 'Regenerata' or 'Marylandica' give rise to woolly litter as they ripen.
• PROPAGATION By hardwood cuttings in winter.

Z 3–9

HEIGHT
To 100ft
(30m)

SPREAD
40ft (12m)
or more

Salicaceae	

POPULUS × CANADENSIS
'Serotina de Selys'

Habit Vigorous, columnar. *Flowers* Catkins in spring. Red. *Leaves* Deciduous, broadly triangular. Pale green when young, later gray-green, turning yellow in autumn.
• NATIVE HABITAT Garden origin.
• CULTIVATION Grow in deep, fertile, moisture-retentive soil. Plant at least 100ft (30m) away from buildings, walls, and drains, especially on clay soils.
• PROPAGATION By hardwood cuttings in winter.
• OTHER NAMES *P. × canadensis* 'Serotina Erecta'.

Z 3–9

HEIGHT
To 80ft (25m) or more

SPREAD
20ft (6m)

Betulaceae	GRAY ALDER

ALNUS INCANA

Habit Open, with a conical crown. *Flowers* Upright catkins, on bare branches in early spring. Male: drooping, reddish; female: small, red, on same plant. *Fruits* Small, woody, cone-like. *Leaves* Deciduous, oval, pointed, toothed. Dull dark green, gray-downy beneath.
• NATIVE HABITAT Mountains of Europe and the Caucasus.
• CULTIVATION Tolerates wet or waterlogged soil.
• PROPAGATION By seed in autumn or by hardwood cuttings in early winter.

Z 2–6

HEIGHT
55ft (17m)

SPREAD
22ft (7m)

Fagaceae	

QUERCUS MACRANTHERA

Habit Broadly spreading, with a dense, rounded crown. *Fruits* Acorns, to 1in (2.5cm) long. Cups clothed in hairy scales. *Leaves* Deciduous, oval, to 6in (15cm) long, with deeply cut, rounded lobes. Dark green above, paler and hairy beneath.
• NATIVE HABITAT Dry, mountain woodlands in the Caucasus.
• CULTIVATION Tolerates semi-shade and lime-rich soils. Grow in deep, fertile, well-drained soil.
• PROPAGATION By seed in autumn.

Z 6–9

HEIGHT
To 70ft (20m)

SPREAD
50ft (15m)

Fagaceae	WEEPING BEECH

FAGUS SYLVATICA 'Pendula'

Habit Weeping. *Leaves* Deciduous, oval, wavy-margined. Bright green and silky when young, turning rich yellow and old gold in autumn. *Bark* Smooth. Pale gray.
• NATIVE HABITAT Woodlands, often on limestone soils, in Europe.
• CULTIVATION Tolerates alkaline and acid soils, provided they are well drained. A beautiful specimen for large gardens.
• PROPAGATION By budding in late summer or by seed in autumn. Seed-raised plants are variable.

Z 4–7

HEIGHT
50ft (15m) or more

SPREAD
70ft (20m)

Fagaceae	

QUERCUS ROBUR f. FASTIGIATA

Habit Upright, columnar, dense. **Fruits** Acorns, to 1½in (4cm) long, one-third enclosed by a cup. **Leaves** Deciduous, elliptic to broadly oval, lobed. Dark green above, bluish-green beneath. **Bark** Fissured. Pale gray.
• NATIVE HABITAT Woodlands of Europe.
• CULTIVATION Tolerates semi-shade and lime-rich soils. Grow in deep, fertile, well-drained soil.
• PROPAGATION By budding in late summer or by seed in autumn. Seed-raised plants are variable.

Z 4–8

HEIGHT
70ft (20m)
or more

SPREAD
20ft (6m) or
more

Betulaceae	ITALIAN ALDER

ALNUS CORDATA

Habit Fast-growing, broadly conical. **Flowers** Upright catkins, on bare branches, in early spring. Male: drooping, reddish; female: small, red. **Fruits** Small, woody, cone-like. **Leaves** Deciduous, broadly oval to rounded, heart-shaped at the base, leathery. Glossy dark green.
• NATIVE HABITAT Deciduous, mountain woodlands of C. and S. Italy and Corsica.
• CULTIVATION Tolerates dry, wet soils.
• PROPAGATION By seed in autumn or by hardwood cuttings in early winter.

Z 5–7

HEIGHT
80ft (25m)

SPREAD
35ft (11m)

Fagaceae	ALGERIAN OAK, MIRBECK'S OAK

QUERCUS CANARIENSIS

Habit Dense, columnar when young, becoming broader with age. **Fruits** Acorns, one-third enclosed by a cup. **Leaves** Deciduous or semi-evergreen, broadly oval to elliptic, shallowly lobed. Dark green above, paler beneath. **Bark** Fissured.
• NATIVE HABITAT Woodlands of N. Africa and S.W. Europe.
• CULTIVATION Tolerates semi-shade, clay, and lime-rich soils. Grow in deep, well-drained soil.
• PROPAGATION By seed in autumn.
• OTHER NAMES Q. mirbeckii.

Z 8–9

HEIGHT
70ft (20m)

SPREAD
50ft (15m)

Salicaceae	LOMBARDY POPLAR

POPULUS NIGRA 'Italica'

Habit Very fast-growing, narrowly columnar, with strongly upright branches. **Flowers** Male catkins in mid-spring. Red. **Leaves** Deciduous, rounded, diamond-shaped. Bright green.
• NATIVE HABITAT Garden origin.
• CULTIVATION Grow in deep, fertile, moisture-retentive soil. Plant at least 100ft (30m) away from buildings, walls, and drains, especially on clay soils. Good for screens and windbreaks. Susceptible to bacterial canker and fungal diseases.
• PROPAGATION By hardwood cuttings in winter.

☼ ◐
❀❀❀

Z 3–9

HEIGHT
To 100ft
(30m)

SPREAD
15ft (5m)

Aceraceae	LOBEL'S MAPLE

ACER LOBELII

Habit Upright, narrowly columnar. **Flowers** Tiny, in erect clusters, in late spring. Yellow-green. **Fruits** 2 seeds, fused together, each with a green wing. **Leaves** Deciduous, with 5 wavy-edged, pointed lobes. Glossy dark green, turning yellow in autumn.
• NATIVE HABITAT Mountain woods of S. Italy.
• CULTIVATION Tolerates semi-shade and almost any fertile, well-drained soil. Excellent for planting in confined spaces.
• PROPAGATION By seed in autumn.

☼ ◐
❀❀

Z 6–8

HEIGHT
To 70ft
(20m)

SPREAD
15ft (5m)

Juglandaceae	ENGLISH WALNUT, PERSIAN WALNUT

JUGLANS REGIA

Habit Slow-growing, dense, broadly spreading. **Flowers** Catkins, with male and female on same plant, in late spring. Yellow-green. **Fruits** Smooth husks, enclosing edible, creamy-white nuts. **Leaves** Deciduous, aromatic, with 5–7 elliptic leaflets. Bronzed when young, later dark green.
• NATIVE HABITAT Stream sides and valleys from S.E. Europe to China.
• CULTIVATION Grow in deep, fertile soil. Needs long, hot summers to ripen fruits.
• PROPAGATION By seed in autumn.

☼ ◐
❀❀❀

Z 3–9

HEIGHT
100ft (30m)

SPREAD
70ft (20m)

Tiliaceae	LINDEN

TILIA OLIVERI

Habit Open, spreading, with broadly rounded crown. **Flowers** Small, fragrant, cup-shaped, in clusters in summer. Greenish-yellow, with pale green bracts. **Fruits** Round, smooth, winged, to ½in (1cm) across. Gray-green. **Leaves** Deciduous, heart-shaped, pointed. Dark green above, silvery-white beneath.
• NATIVE HABITAT Woodlands of C. China.
• CULTIVATION Tolerates semi-shade. It does best when grown in deep, fertile soil that is moisture-retentive but well drained. Unlike many lindens, it is usually unaffected by aphids and so does not cause problems with dripping honeydew and the unsightly mold that this subsequently causes. It makes a stately specimen tree and is shown to its best advantage when planted alone as a specimen in large gardens. It is distinguished among all the lindens by its very handsome foliage.
• PROPAGATION By seed in autumn.

Z 6–8

HEIGHT
50ft (15m)
or more

SPREAD
30ft (10m)

Fagaceae	CHINKAPIN OAK, YELLOW CHESTNUT OAK

QUERCUS MUEHLENBERGII

Habit Dense, round-headed. **Fruits** Acorns to ¾in (2cm) long, half enclosed in a cup with downy scales. **Leaves** Deciduous, oblong to lance-shaped, sharply toothed. Bright green, coloring well in autumn. **Bark** Flaky. Gray.
• NATIVE HABITAT Woodlands of North America.
• CULTIVATION Tolerates semi-shade and lime-rich soils. Grow in deep, fertile, well-drained soil.
• PROPAGATION By seed in autumn.

Z 5–7

HEIGHT
60ft (18m)

SPREAD
50ft (15m)

Ulmaceae	MEDITERRANEAN HACKBERRY, SOUTHERN NETTLE TREE

CELTIS AUSTRALIS

Habit Broadly columnar, spreading with age. **Flowers** Insignificant. **Fruits** Small, round, berry-like. Purple-black. **Leaves** Deciduous, lance-shaped to oval, pointed, sharply toothed. Dark green above, gray-green beneath, and hairy.
• NATIVE HABITAT Dry, rocky slopes of S. Europe and S.W. Asia.
• CULTIVATION Grow in any fertile soil. Performs best in areas with long, hot summers.
• PROPAGATION By seed in autumn.

Z 6–8

HEIGHT
To 70ft (20m)

SPREAD
50ft (15m)

Platanaceae	LONDON PLANE

PLATANUS × HISPANICA

Habit Vigorous, broadly columnar, the crown spreading with age. **Flowers** Insignificant, with male and female on same plant. **Fruits** Spherical, bristly, in clusters of 2–4. **Leaves** Deciduous, with 3–5 large, sharply toothed lobes. Bright green. **Bark** Flaky. Cream, pink-gray, and brown.
• NATIVE HABITAT Garden origin.
• CULTIVATION Grow in deep, fertile soil.
• PROPAGATION By hardwood cuttings in early winter.
• OTHER NAMES *P. × acerifolia.*

Z 6–9

HEIGHT
95ft (28m)

SPREAD
70ft (20m)

Fagaceae	RAULI BEECH

NOTHOFAGUS PROCERA

Habit Broadly conical. **Leaves** Deciduous, oval to lance- or trowel-shaped, regularly toothed and veined. Bronzed when young, later matte dark green, turning orange, red, and gold in autumn.
• NATIVE HABITAT Forests of Argentina and Chile.
• CULTIVATION Grow in deep, fertile, neutral to acid soil. Shelter from strong winds. Makes an elegant specimen in woodland gardens and other sheltered sites.
• PROPAGATION By seed in autumn.
• OTHER NAMES *N. nervosa.*

Z 7–9

HEIGHT
80ft (25m)

SPREAD
50ft (15m)

Lauraceae

SASSAFRAS ALBIDUM

Habit Upright, open, later spreading, suckering.
Flowers Insignificant, in spring. Yellowish.
Fruits Small, egg-shaped berries. Blue.
Leaves Deciduous, aromatic, elliptic to oval, often
2- or 3-lobed. Bright green above, blue-green
beneath, turning yellow, red, or purple in autumn.
• NATIVE HABITAT Woodlands and thickets of
E. North America.
• CULTIVATION Grow in deep, fertile, preferably
neutral to acid soil. Young growth is susceptible to
late frosts. An elegant and unusual specimen for the
large garden. The leaves emit a curious fragrance
of orange and vanilla when crushed. Sassafras roots
are used commercially in the making of perfumes
and root beer.
• PROPAGATION By seed or suckers in autumn or
by root cuttings in winter.
• OTHER NAMES *S. officinale.*

Z 4–9

HEIGHT
75ft (22m)

SPREAD
50ft (15m)
or more

Juglandaceae	BLACK WALNUT

JUGLANS NIGRA

Habit Fast-growing, dense, broadly spreading. **Flowers** Catkins, male and female on same plant, in late spring. Yellow-green. **Fruits** Smooth husks enclosing edible nuts. **Leaves** Deciduous, large, aromatic, with 11–17 slender, pointed leaflets. Glossy dark green.
• NATIVE HABITAT Rich woodlands of C. and S. United States.
• CULTIVATION Grow in deep, fertile soil. Needs long, hot summers to ripen fruits.
• PROPAGATION By seed in autumn.

☼ ◑
❄ ❄ ❄

Z 4–9

HEIGHT
To 100ft
(30m)

SPREAD
65ft (20m)

Juglandaceae	HEARTNUT, JAPANESE WALNUT

JUGLANS AILANTIFOLIA var. CORDIFORMIS

Habit Spreading, with a broad-domed crown. **Flowers** Catkins. Male: to 12in (30cm) long; female: 4in (10cm), on the same plant in late spring. Greenish. **Fruits** Slightly hairy, poisonous husks enclosing edible nuts. **Leaves** Deciduous, large, with 11–17 elliptic, short-pointed, hairy leaflets. Dark green above, paler beneath.
• NATIVE HABITAT Damp areas in Japan.
• CULTIVATION Grow in any deep, fertile soil.
• PROPAGATION By seed in autumn.
• OTHER NAMES *J. cordiformis.*

☼ ◑
❄ ❄ ❄

Z 5–9

HEIGHT
50ft (15m)
or more

SPREAD
50ft (15m)

Fagaceae	WATER OAK

QUERCUS NIGRA

Habit Spreading, with a narrowly dome-shaped crown. **Fruits** Acorns, to ¾in (1.5cm) long, half enclosed by scaly cups. **Leaves** Deciduous or semi-evergreen, variably lobed, especially on young plants. Glossy rich green.
• NATIVE HABITAT Damp habitats in S.E. United States.
• CULTIVATION Grow in deep, fertile, moisture-retentive soil.
• PROPAGATION By seed in autumn.
• OTHER NAMES *Q. aquatica.*

☼ ◑
❄ ❄ ❄

Z 6–9

HEIGHT
60ft (18m)
or more

SPREAD
40ft (12m)

Fagaceae	ROBLE BEECH

NOTHOFAGUS OBLIQUA

Habit Fast-growing, broadly columnar, with slender, arching branches. **Leaves** Deciduous, oval, toothed, smooth. Deep green above, blue-green beneath, turning orange and red in autumn.
• NATIVE HABITAT Forests of Argentina and Chile.
• CULTIVATION Tolerates semi-shade. Grow in deep, fertile, preferably neutral to acid soil. Shelter from strong winds. Grows rapidly to make a handsome specimen in woodland gardens and in other sheltered sites.
• PROPAGATION By seed in autumn.

☼ ◐
❄ ❄ ❄

Z 7–9

HEIGHT
80ft (25m)
or more

SPREAD
50ft (15m)

Sterculiaceae	CHINESE PARASOL TREE

FIRMIANA SIMPLEX

Habit Robust, vigorous, rounded. *Flowers* Small, bell-shaped, in long, showy panicles in summer. Lemon-yellow. *Fruits* Leaf-like, with seeds at the edges.
Leaves Deciduous, large, 3–5 lobes. Dark green.
• NATIVE HABITAT Forests of Japan to Vietnam.
• CULTIVATION Tolerates partial shade. Grow in a fertile, moisture-retentive soil or soil mix. Water freely when in growth, otherwise sparingly.
• PROPAGATION By seed when ripe or in spring.
• OTHER NAMES *F. platanifolia*, *Sterculia platanifolia*.

☼ ◊

Z 7–9

HEIGHT
60ft (18m)
less in cult.

SPREAD
30ft (10m)

Fagaceae	

QUERCUS PETRAEA 'Columnea'

Habit Dense, slender, upright. *Fruits* Acorns, to 1¼in (3cm) long, one-third enclosed by a cup.
Leaves Deciduous, large, wavy-edged. Bronze when young, later a leathery, dark green.
Bark Vertically ridged. Gray.
• NATIVE HABITAT Garden origin.
• CULTIVATION Tolerates semi-shade, coastal conditions, and a wide range of soil types.
• PROPAGATION By grafting in late winter.

☼ ◊
❀❀❀

Z 4–8

HEIGHT
70ft (20m)
or more

SPREAD
30ft (6m)

Tiliaceae	PENDENT SILVER LINDEN, WEEPING LINDEN

TILIA 'Petiolaris'

Habit Broadly columnar, with pendent branches.
Flowers Toxic to bees. Small, fragrant, cup-shaped, in drooping clusters in mid-summer. Creamy-yellow. *Fruits* Rounded, woody. Gray-green. *Leaves* Deciduous, heart-shaped, pointed. Dark green above, silver beneath.
• NATIVE HABITAT Origin uncertain.
• CULTIVATION Tolerates semi-shade. Grow in deep, fertile soil. Prone to aphid infestation.
• PROPAGATION By grafting in late summer.
• OTHER NAMES *T. petiolaris*, *T. tomentosa* 'Petiolaris'.

☼ ◊
❀❀❀

Z 5–7

HEIGHT
90ft (28m)

SPREAD
60ft (18m)

Fagaceae	

QUERCUS CASTANEIFOLIA

Habit Broadly spreading. *Fruits* Acorns, to 1in (2.5cm) long, half enclosed in a cup with long scales. *Leaves* Deciduous, oblong to narrowly oval, with sharp, triangular teeth. Very glossy, dark green above, gray beneath. *Bark* Smooth. Gray.
• NATIVE HABITAT Forests of the Caucasus and N. Iran.
• CULTIVATION Tolerates semi-shade and lime-rich soils. Grow in fertile soil.
• PROPAGATION By seed in autumn.

☼ ◊
❀❀❀

Z 7–9

HEIGHT
80ft (25m)

SPREAD
60ft (18m)

Fagaceae	EUROPEAN BEECH, COMMON BEECH

FAGUS SYLVATICA

Habit Broadly spreading. **Fruits** Small, bristly husks enclosing 2 edible nuts. **Leaves** Deciduous, oval, with wavy margins. Brilliant green on emergence, later mid- to dark green, turning copper-gold in autumn. **Bark** Smooth. Silver-gray.
• NATIVE HABITAT Woodlands, usually on chalk, in Europe.
• CULTIVATION Tolerates semi-shade and thrives in well-drained, acid and alkaline soils. Excellent for hedging. Trim in summer.
• PROPAGATION By seed in autumn.

Z 4–7

HEIGHT
100ft (30m)

SPREAD
50ft (15m)

Fagaceae	HUNGARIAN OAK

QUERCUS FRAINETTO

Habit Fast-growing, spreading, with a large, domed crown. **Fruits** Acorns, to ¼in (2cm) long, half enclosed in a cup. **Leaves** Deciduous, long, oval-oblong, with deeply cut, rounded lobes. Dark green above, gray-green beneath. **Bark** Deeply fissured. Dark gray.
• NATIVE HABITAT Woodlands of S.E. Europe.
• CULTIVATION Tolerant of almost any well-drained soils, including alkaline ones.
• PROPAGATION By seed in autumn.
• OTHER NAMES *Q. conferta, Q. pannonica.*

Z 6–9

HEIGHT
To 80ft
(25m)

SPREAD
70ft (20m)

Salicaceae	

POPULUS ALBA 'Raket'

Habit Narrow, upright. **Flowers** Catkins; male and female on separate plants. **Fruits** Small capsules enclosing seeds in white cotton. **Leaves** Deciduous, wavy-margined, 3–5 lobes. Dark green above, silvery-white beneath, yellow in autumn.
• NATIVE HABITAT Garden origin.
• CULTIVATION Tolerates coastal conditions. Grow in deep, fertile, moisture-retentive soil. Plant at least 100ft (30m) away from buildings and drains.
• PROPAGATION By hardwood cuttings in winter.
• OTHER NAMES *P. alba* 'Rocket'.

Z 3–9

HEIGHT
To 70ft
(20m) or
more

SPREAD
15ft (5m) or
more

Fagaceae	PIN OAK

QUERCUS PALUSTRIS

Habit Fast-growing, spreading, with slender branches, pendulous at the tips. **Fruits** Acorns, to ⅝in (1.5cm) long, up to one-third enclosed in a broad, shallow cup. **Leaves** Deciduous, deeply lobed. Shining deep green above, turning scarlet in autumn. **Bark** Smooth. Gray-brown.
• NATIVE HABITAT Swampy woodlands of S.E. Canada and N.E. United States.
• CULTIVATION Tolerates semi-shade and very moist soils. Grow in deep, fertile soil.
• PROPAGATION By seed in autumn.

Z 4–9

HEIGHT
70ft (20m)

SPREAD
40ft (12m)

Juglandaceae	SHAGBARK HICKORY

CARYA OVATA

Habit Broadly columnar. **Flowers** Catkins, in late spring. Male: clusters of 3, to 5in (13cm) long, green-yellow; female: inconspicuous, on same plant. **Fruits** Green husk enclosing edible, white nut. **Leaves** Deciduous, with 5 taper-pointed, toothed leaflets. Dark yellow-green, golden yellow in autumn. **Bark** Peeling in strips. Gray-brown.
• NATIVE HABITAT Woodland and valleys of E. North America.
• CULTIVATION Grow in deep, fertile soil.
• PROPAGATION By seed in autumn.

Z 4–8

HEIGHT
76ft (22m)

SPREAD
60ft (18m)

Fagaceae	HOLM OAK

QUERCUS ILEX

Habit Broadly spreading, with a rounded crown. **Fruits** Acorns, to ¾in (2cm) long, one-third enclosed in a cup. **Leaves** Evergreen, elliptic to narrowly oval. Glossy dark green above, silvery-gray and hairy beneath. **Bark** Rugged. Black.
• NATIVE HABITAT Woodland and dry scrub on hillsides around the Mediterranean.
• CULTIVATION Tolerates both dry and alkaline soils, and coastal exposure, but grows best in deep, fertile soils in mild areas.
• PROPAGATION By seed in autumn.

Z 8–10

HEIGHT
80ft (25m)

SPREAD
To 70ft
(20m)

Fagaceae	RED OAK

QUERCUS RUBRA

Habit Fast-growing, broadly spreading. **Fruits** Acorns, to 1¼in (3cm) long, one-quarter enclosed in a shallow cup. **Leaves** Deciduous, long, elliptic-oval, sharply lobed, with slender teeth. Dark green, paler beneath, turning red in autumn.
• NATIVE HABITAT Woodlands of E. North America.
• CULTIVATION Tolerant of urban pollution and almost any well-drained soil, including alkaline soils.
• PROPAGATION By seed in autumn.
• OTHER NAMES Q. borealis **var.** maxima.

Z 4–8

HEIGHT
80ft (25m)

SPREAD
60ft (18m)

Fagaceae	LAUREL OAK

QUERCUS LAURIFOLIA

Habit Broadly conical, becoming increasingly round-headed with age. *Fruits* Acorns, almost round, flattish at the base, to ⅝in (1.5cm) long, one-third enclosed in a cup. *Leaves* Deciduous or semi-evergreen, narrowly oblong to lance-shaped, shallowly lobed or unlobed, smooth. Glossy green, bronze-tinted when young. *Bark* Scaly. Gray.
• NATIVE HABITAT Woodland on sandy soils, and at the edges of coastal swamps in E. United States.
• CULTIVATION Tolerates semi-shade and moist but not waterlogged soils. Grow in deep, fertile soil.

A handsome tree that retains its leaves well into winter, giving a semi-evergreen appearance. This, and other semi-evergreen oaks, thrives best if given shelter from cold, dry, winter winds. The leaves resemble those of *Laurus nobilis*, the bay laurel, hence the common name.
• PROPAGATION By seed in autumn.

Z 6–9

HEIGHT
60ft (18m)

SPREAD
40ft (12m)

Magnoliaceae	TULIP TREE

LIRIODENDRON TULIPIFERA

Habit Broadly columnar, spreading with age.
Flowers Tulip-shaped, at branch tips, in mid-summer. Pale green, tepals banded orange at the base. **Leaves** Deciduous, lobed, with middle lobe cut off or notched at the tip. Dark green above, paler beneath, turning butter-yellow in autumn.
• NATIVE HABITAT Deciduous woods of E. North America.
• CULTIVATION Tolerates semi-shade. Grow in fertile, moisture-retentive, slightly acid soil.
• PROPAGATION By seed in autumn.

Z 5–9

HEIGHT
95ft (28m)

SPREAD
70ft (20m)

Juglandaceae	

PTEROCARYA × REHDERIANA

Habit Very fast-growing, broadly spreading, suckering. **Flowers** Tiny catkins, with male and female on same plant. Greenish. **Fruits** Winged, in long pendulous catkins, to 18in (45cm) long.
Leaves Deciduous, divided into 11–21 oblong leaflets, with winged leaf stalks. Dark green.
Bark Purple-brown; pale orange within fissures.
• NATIVE HABITAT Garden origin.
• CULTIVATION Grow in any deep, fertile soil.
• PROPAGATION By softwood cuttings in summer or by suckers in autumn.

Z 5–8

HEIGHT
80ft (25m)

SPREAD
65ft (20m)

Simaroubaceae	TREE OF HEAVEN

AILANTHUS ALTISSIMA

Habit Fast-growing, broadly columnar.
Flowers Small, in large panicles, from mid- to late summer. Male and female usually on separate plants. Yellowish-green. **Fruits** Winged, pink-tinted. **Leaves** Deciduous, with 15–30 paired, lance-shaped to oval, pointed leaflets. Dark green.
• NATIVE HABITAT Mountain woodlands of China.
• CULTIVATION Grow in deep, fertile soil.
• PROPAGATION By seed in autumn or by suckers or root cuttings in winter.
• OTHER NAMES *A. glandulosa.*

Z 4–8

HEIGHT
To 80ft
(25m) or
more

SPREAD
52ft (15m)

Fagaceae	

FAGUS SYLVATICA 'Dawyck Gold'

Habit Dense, columnar. **Leaves** Deciduous, oval, with wavy margins. Bright yellow on emergence, later yellow-green, turning copper-gold in autumn.
Bark Silver-gray. Smooth.
• NATIVE HABITAT Garden origin.
• CULTIVATION Thrives in light shade and in well-drained soils, both acid and alkaline.
• PROPAGATION By budding in late summer.

Z 4–7

HEIGHT
60ft (18m)

SPREAD
15ft (5m)

Tiliaceae	CAUCASIAN LINDEN

TILIA 'Euchlora'

Habit Broadly columnar. **Flowers** Small, fragrant, cup-shaped, in drooping clusters in mid-summer. Creamy-yellow. **Leaves** Deciduous, broadly oval, pointed, unequally heart-shaped at the base. Dark green above, paler beneath.
• NATIVE HABITAT Origin uncertain.
• CULTIVATION Tolerates semi-shade. Grow in deep, fertile soil. Usually resistant to aphids and free of honeydew.
• PROPAGATION By grafting in late summer.
• OTHER NAMES *Tilia* × *euchlora*.

☼ ◊
❀❀❀
Z 3–7

HEIGHT
70ft (20m)

SPREAD
30ft (10m)

Tiliaceae	EUROPEAN LINDEN

TILIA × *EUROPAEA*

Habit Vigorous, broadly columnar. **Flowers** Small, fragrant, cup-shaped, in drooping clusters in mid-summer. Pale yellow. **Leaves** Deciduous, broadly oval with heart-shaped base, with a short-pointed tip. Dark green above, paler below.
• NATIVE HABITAT Woodlands of Europe.
• CULTIVATION Tolerates semi-shade. Grow in deep, fertile soil. Often infested with aphids, which drip honeydew on the ground beneath.
• PROPAGATION By grafting in late summer.
• OTHER NAMES *Tilia* × *vulgaris*.

☼ ◊
❀❀❀
Z 3–7

HEIGHT
120ft (35m)

SPREAD
50ft (15m)

Bombacaceae	SILK-FLOSS TREE

CHORISIA SPECIOSA

Habit Fast-growing. Trunk covered with stout spines and swollen at the base. **Flowers** Large, cup-shaped. Pink to burgundy, petals creamy and spotted at the base in autumn. **Fruits** Capsules enclosing seeds in silky floss. **Leaves** Deciduous, lance-shaped, toothed. Pale green. **Bark** Thorny.
• NATIVE HABITAT Tropical Brazil and Argentina.
• CULTIVATION Grow as a house or conservatory plant. Water moderately when in growth, sparingly when leafless. Prune in spring to restrict growth.
• PROPAGATION By seed in spring.

☼ ◊
Z 9–10

HEIGHT
50ft (15m)

SPREAD
30ft (10m)

Aceraceae	

ACER RUBRUM 'Scanlon'

Habit Broadly columnar. **Flowers** Small, in dense clusters on bare branches, in spring. Red. **Fruits** Small, round seed, with papery wings. Red. **Leaves** Deciduous, 3–5 lobes. Dark green, turning brilliant red in autumn.
• NATIVE HABITAT Garden origin.
• CULTIVATION Tolerates some lime, but grow in fertile, moisture-retentive, neutral to acid soil for best autumn color.
• PROPAGATION By grafting in late winter or early spring or by budding in summer.

☼ ◊
❀❀❀
Z 3–9

HEIGHT
50ft (15m)

SPREAD
15ft (5m)

Hamamelidaceae	SWEET GUM

LIQUIDAMBAR STYRACIFLUA

Habit Broadly conical, spreading with age.
Leaves Deciduous, alternate, palmate, with 5–7
pointed, finely toothed lobes. Glossy green, turning
brilliant orange, red, and purple in autumn.
• NATIVE HABITAT Damp woodlands of E. United
States.
• CULTIVATION Tolerates semi-shade. Does not
thrive on shallow alkaline soil. Grow in fertile,
moist but well-drained soil.
• PROPAGATION By softwood cuttings in summer or
by seed in autumn.

☼ ◑
❀❀❀

Z 5–9

HEIGHT
80ft (25m)

SPREAD
60ft (18m)

Fagaceae	SCARLET OAK

QUERCUS COCCINEA

Habit Broadly spreading. *Fruits* Acorns, to 1in
(2.5cm) long, up to one half enclosed in a shiny cup.
Leaves Deciduous, elliptic, deeply lobed, with
bristly teeth, persisting for several weeks. Glossy
dark green above, paler beneath, turning brilliant
scarlet in autumn,
• NATIVE HABITAT Sandy woods of E. North
America.
• CULTIVATION Tolerates semi-shade, but colors
best in sun. Grow in deep, fertile soil.
• PROPAGATION By seed in autumn.

☼ ◊
❀❀❀

Z 4–9

HEIGHT
To 70ft
(20m)

SPREAD
50ft (15m)

Fagaceae	NORTHERN PIN OAK

QUERCUS ELLIPSOIDALIS

Habit Broadly spreading. *Fruits* Acorns, to ¾in
(2cm) long, one-third to one-half enclosed in a cup.
Leaves Deciduous, elliptic, deeply lobed, each
lobe with slender, pointed teeth. Glossy dark green
above, paler beneath, turning deep purplish-red,
then crimson in autumn.
• NATIVE HABITAT Dry woodlands of E. and C.
North America.
• CULTIVATION Tolerates semi-shade, but colors
best in sun. Grow in deep, fertile soil.
• PROPAGATION By seed in autumn.

☼ ◊
❀❀❀

Z 4–7

HEIGHT
70ft (20m)

SPREAD
60ft (18m)

Aceraceae	SYCAMORE MAPLE

ACER PSEUDOPLATANUS 'Erythrocarpum'

Habit Vigorous, broadly columnar, spreading with
age. *Flowers* Tiny, in pendulous clusters in spring.
Fruits Small, round seed, with papery, bright red
wings. *Leaves* Deciduous, with 5 coarsely toothed
lobes. Dark green.
• NATIVE HABITAT Mountain woods from Europe
to S.W. Asia.
• CULTIVATION Grow in any but waterlogged soil.
• PROPAGATION By grafting in late winter or early
spring, by budding in summer, or by seed in
autumn. Seed-raised plants are variable.

☼ ◊
❀❀❀

Z 4–7

HEIGHT
70ft (20m)

SPREAD
50ft (15m)

Aceraceae		

ACER RUBRUM 'Schlesingeri'

Habit Round-headed, broadly columnar.
Flowers Small, in dense clusters, on bare branches in spring. Red. *Fruits* 2 seeds, fused together, each with a red wing. *Leaves* Deciduous, 3–5 lobes. Dark green, turning brilliant scarlet in early autumn.
• NATIVE HABITAT Garden origin.
• CULTIVATION Tolerates some lime, but grow in fertile, moisture-retentive, neutral to acid soil for best autumn color.
• PROPAGATION By grafting in late winter or early spring or by budding in summer.

Z 3–9

HEIGHT
70ft (20m)

SPREAD
35ft (11m)

Aceraceae	RED MAPLE, SWAMP MAPLE

ACER RUBRUM

Habit Round-headed, broadly columnar.
Flowers Small, in dense clusters on bare branches in spring. Red. *Fruits* 2 seeds, fused together, each with a red wing. *Leaves* Deciduous, 3–5 lobes. Dark green, turning brilliant red and scarlet in autumn.
• NATIVE HABITAT Damp soils in E. North America.
• CULTIVATION Tolerates some lime, but grow in fertile, moisture-retentive, neutral to acid soil for best autumn color.
• PROPAGATION By seed in autumn.

Z 3–9

HEIGHT
70ft (20m)

SPREAD
30ft (10m)

Cercidiphyllaceae	KATSURA TREE

CERCIDIPHYLLUM JAPONICUM

Habit Fast-growing, open, spreading.
Leaves Deciduous, rounded, heart-shaped at the base. Fallen leaves smell like burnt sugar. Bronze when young, turning smooth, bluish-green, then yellow, bronze-purple, and red in autumn.
• NATIVE HABITAT Mountain woods of the Himalayas and Japan.
• CULTIVATION Tolerates dappled shade. Grow in any deep, fertile soil. Autumn color is best on acid soils. Young leaves may be damaged by late frosts.
• PROPAGATION By seed in autumn.

Z 4–8

HEIGHT
70ft (20m)

SPREAD
50ft (15m)

Nyssaceae	BLACK GUM, SOUR GUM

NYSSA SYLVATICA

Habit Slow-growing, broadly conical-columnar.
Leaves Deciduous, oval to elliptic, blunt-pointed. Glossy dark green above, blue-green beneath, turning yellow, orange, and scarlet in autumn.
• NATIVE HABITAT Swamps and damp woods of E. North America.
• CULTIVATION Tolerates semi-shade. Grow in fertile, neutral to acid soil. Resents transplanting. Performs best in areas with long, hot summers.
• PROPAGATION By softwood cuttings in summer or by seed in autumn.

Z 3–9

HEIGHT
70ft (20m)

SPREAD
35ft (11m)

Fagaceae	WHITE OAK

QUERCUS ALBA

Habit Broadly spreading. **Fruits** Acorns, to 1in (2.5cm) long, one-quarter enclosed in a cup. **Leaves** Deciduous, broadly oval, tapered at the base, deeply and irregularly lobed. Pink-tinted when young, turning glossy bright green, then rich purple-red in autumn.
• NATIVE HABITAT Dry woodlands of S.E. Canada and E. United States.
• CULTIVATION Unsuitable for alkaline soils. Grow in deep, fertile soil.
• PROPAGATION By seed in autumn.

Z 3–9

HEIGHT
50ft (15m)

SPREAD
35ft (11m)

Ulmaceae	JAPANESE ZELKOVA, KEAKI

ZELKOVA SERRATA

Habit Broadly spreading, with a rounded crown, branches ascending. **Leaves** Deciduous, oval, sharply pointed, and toothed. Dark green, turning yellow, orange, or red in autumn.
• NATIVE HABITAT Stream sides in woodlands of China, Japan, and Korea.
• CULTIVATION Grow in fertile, moist, but well-drained soil. Best with shelter from strong, cold winds.
• PROPAGATION By seed in autumn.
• OTHER NAMES *Z. acuminata, Planera acuminata.*

Z 5–8

HEIGHT
70ft (20m)

SPREAD
40ft (12m)

Bignoniaceae	AFRICAN TULIP TREE, FLAME-OF-THE-FOREST

SPATHODEA CAMPANULATA

Habit Dense, with a rounded crown. **Flowers** Tulip-shaped, in dense clusters, throughout the year. Scarlet. **Fruits** Woody capsules with poisonous seeds. **Leaves** Evergreen, with 4–9 pairs of oblong-oval leaflets. Dark green.
• NATIVE HABITAT Forests of tropical Africa.
• CULTIVATION Container-grown plants seldom bloom. Grow in fertile soil or soil mix. Water freely when in growth, otherwise moderately.
• PROPAGATION By seed in spring or by semi-ripe cuttings in summer.

Z 10–11

HEIGHT
70ft (20m)

SPREAD
30ft (10m)

Fagaceae	FERN-LEAF BEECH

FAGUS SYLVATICA var. HETEROPHYLLA 'Aspleniifolia'

Habit Dense, broadly columnar. **Leaves** Deciduous, narrowly lance-shaped, deeply cut into long, slender lobes. Dark green, turning copper-gold in autumn. **Bark** Smooth. Silver-gray.
• NATIVE HABITAT Garden origin.
• CULTIVATION Thrives in light shade and in well-drained soils, both acid and alkaline.
• PROPAGATION By budding in late summer.

Z 4–7

HEIGHT
80ft (25m)

SPREAD
50ft (15m)

Rosaceae	SWEET CHERRY, GEAN, MAZZARD

PRUNUS AVIUM

Habit Broadly columnar. **Flowers** Cup-shaped, in clusters in spring with, or just before, the leaves. White, pinkish when in bud. **Fruits** Small, edible, sweet or bitter cherries. Red. **Leaves** Deciduous, elliptic to oblong, pointed, sharply toothed. Bronze when young, turning matte dark green, then yellow and red-crimson in autumn.
• NATIVE HABITAT Woods throughout Europe.
• CULTIVATION Grow in any but waterlogged soil. A beautiful specimen for the wild garden.
• PROPAGATION By seed in autumn.

Z 5–8

HEIGHT
70ft (20m)

SPREAD
30ft (10m)

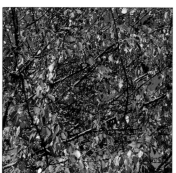

Aceraceae	

ACER PLATANOIDES 'Lorbergii'

Habit Vigorous, spreading. **Flowers** Tiny, in dense clusters in mid-spring. Yellow. **Fruits** Small, round seed, with large, papery wings. **Leaves** Deciduous, deeply divided, with 5 slender, long-pointed lobes. Pale green, turning yellow and orange in autumn.
• NATIVE HABITAT Species grows in mountain woods of Europe and S.W. Asia. Garden origin.
• CULTIVATION Tolerates semi-shade and almost any fertile, well-drained soil.
• PROPAGATION By grafting in late winter or early spring or by budding in summer.

Z 3–7

HEIGHT
70ft (20m)

SPREAD
35ft (11m)

Ulmaceae	WILLOW OAK

QUERCUS PHELLOS

Habit Broadly spreading. **Fruits** Acorns, to ⅝in · (1.5cm) long, one-quarter enclosed in a shallow cup. **Leaves** Deciduous, long, narrow, willow-like, smooth. Bright green, turning yellow, orange, and brown in autumn.
• NATIVE HABITAT Moist soils and swamps of E. United States.
• CULTIVATION Unsuitable for alkaline soils. Grow in deep, fertile soil.
• PROPAGATION By seed in autumn. Acorns mature in their second year.

Z 5–9

HEIGHT
70ft (20m)

SPREAD
35ft (11m)

Oleaceae	EUROPEAN ASH

FRAXINUS EXCELSIOR

Habit Vigorous, broadly columnar.
Flowers Small, purple, apetalous. Male and female appear before the leaves on the same or separate plants in spring. **Fruits** Winged keys. in large, dense clusters. **Leaves** Deciduous, divided into 9–13 lance-shaped, sharply toothed leaflets. Dark green.
• NATIVE HABITAT Damp woodland and hedgerows of Europe.
• CULTIVATION Grow in any fertile, well-drained but not-too-dry soil.
• PROPAGATION By seed in autumn.

Z 5–7

HEIGHT
100ft (30m)

SPREAD
65ft (20m)

Leguminosae	

SOPHORA JAPONICA 'Violacea'

Habit Broadly spreading, with a rounded crown.
Flowers Small, fragrant, pea-like, in large sprays in late summer and early autumn. White, flushed lilac-pink. *Fruits* A pod, approximately 3in (8cm) in length. *Leaves* Deciduous, with 7–17 oval, pointed leaflets. Dark green, turning yellow in autumn.
• NATIVE HABITAT Woodlands in dry mountain valleys of China.
• CULTIVATION Tolerant of poor, dry soils and urban pollution. Grow in any fertile, well-drained soil. Plants do not flower until reaching maturity, which may be at about 30 years of age. Although the tree grows vigorously, it needs long, hot summers to flower profusely and prefers a warm climate. The pod is rarely set in cool temperate climates.
• PROPAGATION By grafting in late winter to early spring.

Z 4–8

HEIGHT
70ft (20m)

SPREAD
70ft (20m)

Myrtaceae	MOUNTAIN GUM

EUCALYPTUS DALRYMPLEANA

Habit Vigorous, fast-growing, open, columnar.
Flowers Small, in clusters of 3, in late summer-autumn. **Leaves** Evergreen; juvenile: rounded, without stalks; adult: lance-shaped. Bronze on emergence, then blue-green.
Bark Peeling. Pinkish-gray, creamy-white beneath.
• NATIVE HABITAT Mountains of S.E. Australia and Tasmania.
• CULTIVATION Grow in fertile, well-drained soil and provide shelter from cold winds.
• PROPAGATION By seed in spring or autumn.

Z 9–10

HEIGHT
70ft (20m)

SPREAD
25ft (8m)

Betulaceae	PAPER BIRCH, CANOE BIRCH

BETULA PAPYRIFERA

Habit Vigorous, open, broadly conical.
Flowers Catkins. Males to 4in (10cm) long; females shorter, on same plant. Greenish.
Leaves Deciduous, oval, with tapering points, toothed. Dark green, turning golden yellow in autumn. **Bark** Peeling. White.
• NATIVE HABITAT Woods and mountains of North America.
• CULTIVATION Grow in moist, well-drained soil.
• PROPAGATION By softwood cuttings in summer or by seed in autumn. Seed-raised plants variable.

Z 2–7

HEIGHT
70ft (20m)

SPREAD
25ft (8m)

Betulaceae	GOLD BIRCH, ERMAN'S BIRCH, RUSSIAN ROCK BIRCH

BETULA ERMANII

Habit Elegant, open, broadly conical.
Flowers Upright catkins. Male: to 4in (10cm) long; female: shorter, on same plant. Greenish.
Leaves Deciduous, oval, heart-shaped at the base, pointed, toothed. Glossy green, turning yellow in autumn. **Bark** Peeling in strips. Creamy-white.
• NATIVE HABITAT Forests of N.E. Asia and Japan.
• CULTIVATION Grow in moist, well-drained soil.
• PROPAGATION By softwood cuttings in early summer or by seed in autumn. Seed-raised plants are variable.

Z 5–8

HEIGHT
70ft (20m)

SPREAD
25ft (8m)

Myrtaceae	CIDER GUM

EUCALYPTUS GUNNII

Habit Vigorous, fast-growing, conical.
Flowers Small, in clusters of 3, in late spring-summer. White. **Leaves** Evergreen. Juvenile: rounded, stalkless. Gray-blue. Adult: oval to lance-shaped. Silvery, turning smooth, gray-green.
Bark Peeling. Gray, greenish, and orange, creamy-white beneath.
• NATIVE HABITAT Mountain forests of Tasmania.
• CULTIVATION Grow in fertile, well-drained soil. Shelter from cold winds.
• PROPAGATION By seed in spring or autumn.

Z 9–10

HEIGHT
70ft (20m)

SPREAD
25ft (8m)

Moraceae	BANYAN TREE

FICUS BENGHALENSIS

Habit Spreading, with stilt-like prop roots.
Flowers Insignificant. **Fruits** Small, fig-like. Brown. **Leaves** Evergreen, oval, to 8in (20cm) long, leathery. Rich green, with paler veins.
• NATIVE HABITAT Humid tropical forests of S. Asia.
• CULTIVATION Grow as a house or conservatory plant in cooler climates. Tolerates partial shade. Grow in a fertile, free-draining soil or soil mix. Water freely when in growth.
• PROPAGATION By leaf-bud cuttings, stem-tip cuttings, or air-layering in summer.

Z 10–11

HEIGHT
60ft (18m)

SPREAD
76ft (22m)

Moraceae	

FICUS ELASTICA 'Doescheri'

Habit Vigorous, upright, then spreading.
Leaves Evergreen, large, oblong to oval, leathery. Lustrous dark green, splashed with gray-green and yellow.
• NATIVE HABITAT Garden origin.
• CULTIVATION Grow as a house or conservatory plant. Tolerates partial shade. Grow in a fertile, free-draining soil or soil mix. Water freely when in growth and sparingly in low temperatures.
• PROPAGATION By leaf-bud, stem-tip cuttings, or air-layering in summer.

Z 10–11

HEIGHT
55ft (17m)

SPREAD
30ft (10m)
or more

Myrtaceae	TASMANIAN SNOW GUM, MOUNT WELLINGTON PEPPERMINT

EUCALYPTUS COCCIFERA

Habit Vigorous, fast-growing, broadly spreading.
Flowers Small, in clusters of 3–7 in early summer. White. **Leaves** Evergreen. Juvenile: rounded, without stalks. Adult: aromatic, lance-shaped, hooked at the tip, smooth. Green to gray-green.
Bark Peeling. Blue-gray, creamy-white beneath.
• NATIVE HABITAT Mountains of Tasmania.
• CULTIVATION Grow in fertile, well-drained soil and provide shelter from freezing winds.
• PROPAGATION By seed in spring or autumn.

Z 9–10

HEIGHT
60ft (18m)

SPREAD
25ft (8m)

| Palmae | ALEXANDRA PALM, NORTHERN BANGALOW PALM |

ARCHONTOPHOENIX ALEXANDRAE

Habit Erect, unbranched. **Flowers** In sprays on mature trees. Cream to yellow. **Leaves** Evergreen, feather-shaped, arching, to 11ft (3.5m) long.
• NATIVE HABITAT Rainforests of E. Australia.
• CULTIVATION Grown as a conservatory plant in cooler climates. Tolerant of some shade. Grow in a humus-rich, free-draining soil or soil mix. Provide good light, but shade from hot summer sun to avoid foliage scorch. Water moderately when in growth but sparingly when temperatures are low. The tree will not reach its full height potential when grown in cultivation. In cooler climates the young plants make handsome specimens for display in the home or conservatory, although these palms will seldom reach a sufficient size to enable flowering.
• PROPAGATION By seed in spring at not less than 75°F (24°C).

Z 10–11

HEIGHT
To 80ft
(25m)

SPREAD
22ft (7m)

Fagaceae	TURNER'S OAK

QUERCUS × *TURNERI*

Habit Dense, rounded, broadly spreading.
Fruits Acorns, to ¾in (2cm) long, one-half enclosed in a cup. **Leaves** Semi-evergreen, oblong to broadly oval, tapering at the base, with 3–5 triangular teeth on each side. Glossy dark green.
• NATIVE HABITAT Garden origin.
• CULTIVATION Tolerates lime-rich soils and semi-shade. Grow in deep, fertile soil.
• PROPAGATION By grafting in late winter.

Betulaceae	WEEPING BIRCH

BETULA PENDULA 'Tristis'

Habit Slender, elegant, open, with pendulous branchlets. **Flowers** Catkins, drooping or upright. Male: to 2½in (6cm) long; female: shorter, on the same plant. Greenish. **Leaves** Deciduous, triangular to diamond-shaped. Bright green, turning yellow in autumn. **Bark** White. Black fissures with age.
• NATIVE HABITAT Garden origin.
• CULTIVATION Grow in moist, well-drained soil.
• PROPAGATION By softwood cuttings in summer.

☼ ◊
❀❀❀

Z 7–9

HEIGHT
70ft (20m)

SPREAD
60ft (18m)

☼ ◊
❀❀❀

Z 2–6

HEIGHT
70ft (20m)

SPREAD
22ft (7m)

Fagaceae	

NOTHOFAGUS DOMBEYI

Habit Open-branched, broadly columnar.
Leaves Evergreen, small, narrowly oval, finely and sharply toothed. Sometimes loses its leaves in very cold winters. Glossy dark green.
• NATIVE HABITAT Mountain forests of Argentina and Chile.
• CULTIVATION Grow in deep, fertile, neutral to acid soil, ensuring shelter from cold and strong winds. Makes an exceptionally elegant specimen in woodland gardens and other sheltered sites.
• PROPAGATION By seed in autumn.

☼ ◑
❀❀

Z 9–10

HEIGHT
70ft (20m)

SPREAD
30ft (10m)

Fagaceae	CORK OAK

QUERCUS SUBER
Habit Broadly spreading, with a rounded crown.
Fruits Acorns, to 1¼in (3cm) long, one-half
enclosed in a cup. **Leaves** Evergreen, oval to
oblong, stiff, usually toothed. Glossy dark green
above, gray-felted beneath. **Bark** Thick, rugged,
corky. Pale gray. Cork is used commercially.
• NATIVE HABITAT Woodlands on hillsides around
W. Mediterranean.
• CULTIVATION Tolerates dry soils but grows best
on deep, fertile soils and in mild areas.
• PROPAGATION By seed in autumn.

☼ ◊
❀ ❀

Z 8–10

HEIGHT
70ft (20m)

SPREAD
70ft (20m)

Palmae	QUEEN PALM

SYAGRUS ROMANZOFFIANA
Habit Upright, unbranched. **Flowers** Small, in
huge clusters on mature plants. Yellow.
Fruits Egg-shaped, berry-like. Orange.
Leaves Arching, feather-shaped, with leaflets to
10–15ft (3–5m) long. Lustrous dark green.
• NATIVE HABITAT Dry, open forests of Brazil.
• CULTIVATION Grow as a house or conservatory
plant in cooler climates. Tolerates partial shade.
Grow in a humus-rich soil or soil mix.
• PROPAGATION By seed in spring.
• OTHER NAMES *Arecastrum romanzoffianum.*

☼ ◊

Z 10–11

HEIGHT
52ft (16m)

SPREAD
30ft (10m)

Palmae	SOUTHERN WASHINGTONIA

WASHINGTONIA ROBUSTA
Habit Fast-growing, upright, unbranched.
Flowers Tiny, in large, long-stalked sprays in
summer. Creamy-white. **Fruits** Small, spherical
berries. Black. **Leaves** Evergreen, fan-shaped, leaf-
blade and petioles both to 3ft (1m) long. Mid-green.
• NATIVE HABITAT Baja California to Mexico.
• CULTIVATION Grow as a conservatory plant in
cooler climates. Grow in a fertile soil or soil mix
with sharp sand added. Water moderately in
summer, otherwise sparingly.
• PROPAGATION By seed in spring.

☼ ◊

Z 9–10

HEIGHT
50ft (15m)

SPREAD
10ft (3m)

Fagaceae	LUCOMBE OAK

QUERCUS × HISPANICA 'Lucombeana'
Habit Broadly conical or with a dense, rounded,
billowing crown. **Fruits** Acorns, to 1in (2.5cm)
long, one-third enclosed in a cup. **Leaves** Semi-
evergreen, oval-elliptic or oblong, coarsely toothed.
Glossy dark green above, downy-gray beneath.
Bark Slightly corky. Gray.
• NATIVE HABITAT Garden origin.
• CULTIVATION Tolerates lime-rich soils and semi-
shade. Grow in deep, fertile soil. A very beautiful
specimen for large gardens.
• PROPAGATION By grafting in late winter.

☼ ◊
❀ ❀ ❀

Z 6–9

HEIGHT
80ft (30m)

SPREAD
70ft (20m)

Proteaceae	MACADAMIA NUT

MACADAMIA INTEGRIFOLIA

Habit Spreading. *Flowers* Small, in panicles in spring. Creamy-yellow. *Fruits* Edible nuts. Brown. *Leaves* Evergreen, oblong to broadly oval, leathery, in whorls of 3. Dark green.
• NATIVE HABITAT Tropical highland forests of E. Australia.
• CULTIVATION Tolerates semi-shade. Grow in humus-rich, moisture-retentive soil or soil mix. Water freely when in growth, otherwise moderately. Prune if necessary in autumn. The tree rarely bears fruit when cultivated in cool temperate zones. It makes an interesting foliage specimen when grown in a warm conservatory. In tropical and sub-tropical regions it is grown as an ornamental shade tree and also on a commercial basis for its crisp, oil-rich, sweet nuts. Large trees are susceptible to damage in strong winds.
• PROPAGATION By seed in autumn or spring.

Z 10–11

HEIGHT
70ft (20m)

SPREAD
50ft (15m)

Platanaceae	ORIENTAL PLANE TREE, ORIENTAL SYCAMORE

PLATANUS ORIENTALIS

Habit Vigorous, broadly columnar, the crown spreading with age. **Flowers** Tiny, insignificant. Male and female on same plant. **Fruits** Spherical, bristly, in pendent clusters of up to 6. Brown. **Leaves** Deciduous, palmately lobed, with sharply cut, slender, toothed lobes. Glossy bright green. **Bark** Flaky. Cream, pinkish-brown, and gray.
• NATIVE HABITAT Mountain woodlands and riversides in S.E. Europe.
• CULTIVATION Grow in deep, fertile soil.
• PROPAGATION By seed in autumn.

Z 7–9

HEIGHT
80ft (25m)

SPREAD
80ft (25m)

Betulaceae	CHINESE RED BIRCH

BETULA ALBOSINENSIS

Habit Elegant, open-branched, with a broadly conical crown. **Flowers** Catkins. Male: to 2½in (6cm) long, yellow; female: upright, green, on same plant. **Leaves** Deciduous, oval, sharply toothed with tapering point. Glossy green, turning yellow in autumn. **Bark** Peeling in strips. Coppery-red to orange-red, shining, cream color beneath.
• NATIVE HABITAT Mountain woods of W. China.
• CULTIVATION Grow in moist, well-drained soil.
• PROPAGATION By softwood cuttings in summer. Birches hybridize freely; seed-raised plants variable.

Z 5–8

HEIGHT
60ft (18m)

SPREAD
28ft (9m)

Fagaceae	

NOTHOFAGUS BETULOIDES

Habit Narrowly columnar, broadening with age, sometimes shrubby. **Leaves** Evergreen, oval to elliptic, to 1in (2.5cm) long, blunt-toothed at margins. Glossy, very dark green, paler and conspicuously veined beneath.
• NATIVE HABITAT Evergreen forests in Chile and Argentina.
• CULTIVATION Tolerates dappled shade. Grow in deep, fertile, well-drained soil. Shelter from cold, dry winds. Unsuitable for alkaline soils.
• PROPAGATION By seed in autumn.

Z 9–10

HEIGHT
70ft (20m)

SPREAD
20ft (6m)

Lauraceae	CALIFORNIA LAUREL, HEAD-ACHE TREE, OREGON MYRTLE

UMBELLULARIA CALIFORNICA

Habit Broadly spreading. **Flowers** Small, apetalous, in clusters in late winter-early spring. Yellow-green sepals. **Fruits** Egg-shaped berries. Deep purple. **Leaves** Evergreen, aromatic, elliptic to oblong. Glossy bright green or yellow-green.
• NATIVE HABITAT Scrub and evergreen forest in canyons of S.W. Oregon and California.
• CULTIVATION Grow in fertile, moist but well-drained soil. Provide shelter from cold, dry winds. Leaves emit poisonous vapor when crushed.
• PROPAGATION By seed in autumn.

Z 9–10

HEIGHT
70ft (20m)

SPREAD
40ft (12m)

Salicaceae	GOLDEN WILLOW

SALIX ALBA var. VITELLINA
Habit Fast-growing, broadly spreading.
Leaves Deciduous, lance-shaped. Green, paler beneath. **Bark** Young twigs yellow.
• NATIVE HABITAT Riversides and damp meadows from Europe to W. Asia.
• CULTIVATION Grow in any but very dry soil. Often grown for bright winter twigs. Pollard annually in early spring or every other year. Do not plant within 100ft (30m) of buildings.
• PROPAGATION By semi-ripe cuttings in summer or by hardwood cuttings in winter.

Z 2–9

HEIGHT
70ft (20m)

SPREAD
30ft (10m)

Rosaceae	TEA CRAB APPLE, HUPEH CRAB

MALUS HUPEHENSIS
Habit Vigorous, broadly spreading, with ascending branches. **Flowers** Large, fragrant, shallowly cup-shaped, in profusion in mid-spring. White, pink in bud. **Fruits** Round, red crab apples, to ⅜in (1cm) across, in red-stalked clusters.
Leaves Deciduous, elliptic to oval, taper-pointed, finely toothed. Dark green.
• NATIVE HABITAT Mountain woodlands of China.
• CULTIVATION Tolerates some shade, but blooms best in sun. Grow in any but waterlogged soil.
• PROPAGATION By seed in autumn.

Z 5–8

HEIGHT
40ft (12m)

SPREAD
40ft (12m)

Salicaceae	GOLDEN WEEPING WILLOW

SALIX × SEPULCRALIS var. CHRYSOCOMA
Habit Weeping, broadly spreading.
Leaves Deciduous, narrowly lance-shaped. Bright green, later dark green; blue-green beneath.
• NATIVE HABITAT Garden origin.
• CULTIVATION Grows in any but very dry soil, but seen to best effect near water. Do not plant within 100ft (30m) of buildings. Prone to fungal cankers.
• PROPAGATION By semi-ripe cuttings in summer or by hardwood cuttings in winter.
• OTHER NAMES S. alba 'Tristis', S. 'Chrysocoma'.

Z 5–8

HEIGHT
70ft (20m)

SPREAD
50ft (15m)

Salicaceae	VIOLET WILLOW

SALIX DAPHNOIDES
Habit Fast-growing, broadly conical. **Flowers** Male catkins in spring. Silvery, with yellow anthers.
Leaves Deciduous, narrowly elliptic. Glossy dark green above, blue-green beneath. **Bark** Young shoots dark purple, bloomed white.
• NATIVE HABITAT Damp woodlands in Europe.
• CULTIVATION Grow in any but very dry soil. Often grown for winter twigs. Pollard annually in early spring or every other year.
• PROPAGATION By semi-ripe cuttings in summer or by hardwood cuttings in winter.

Z 5–8

HEIGHT
30ft (10m)

SPREAD
22ft (7m)

Rosaceae	SIBERIAN CRAB APPLE

MALUS BACCATA var. *MANDSCHURICA*

Habit Vigorous, broadly spreading, with a rounded crown. *Flowers* Fragrant, shallowly cup-shaped, in profusion in mid-spring. White. *Fruits* Small, egg-shaped, long-persistent. Red or yellow.
Leaves Deciduous, elliptic to oval, taper-pointed, finely toothed. Dark green above, paler beneath.
• NATIVE HABITAT Scrub and woodlands of N.E. Asia.
• CULTIVATION Tolerates some shade, but blooms best in sun. Grow in any but waterlogged soil.
• PROPAGATION By budding in summer or by grafting in late winter.

Z 4–7

HEIGHT
50ft (15m)

SPREAD
35ft (11m)

Rosaceae	CALLERY PEAR

PYRUS CALLERYANA 'Chanticleer'

Habit Narrowly conical, symmetrical.
Flowers Small, 5-petaled, in sprays in spring.
White. *Leaves* Deciduous, oval to elliptic. Glossy dark green, turning purplish or scarlet in autumn.
• NATIVE HABITAT Garden origin.
• CULTIVATION Tolerant of urban conditions. Grow in any fertile, well-drained soil. Resistant to fireblight. A beautiful tree for confined spaces.
• PROPAGATION By budding in summer or by grafting in winter.
• OTHER NAMES *P. calleryana* 'Cleveland Select'.

Z 5–9

HEIGHT
43ft (13m)

SPREAD
20ft (6m)

Rosaceae	ST. LUCIE CHERRY

PRUNUS MAHALEB

Habit Bushy, round-headed. *Flowers* Small, fragrant, cup-shaped, in clusters from mid- to late spring. White. *Fruits* Small, bitter cherries. Black.
Leaves Deciduous, broadly oval to rounded, toothed. Dark green, turning yellow in autumn.
• NATIVE HABITAT In woods and thickets on dry hillsides of C. and S. Europe.
• CULTIVATION Grow in any but waterlogged soil.
Flowers may not be freely carried on young plants, but become more profuse with age.
• PROPAGATION By seed in autumn.

Z 6–7

HEIGHT
30ft (10m)

SPREAD
25ft (8m)

Styraceae	MOUNTAIN SILVER BELL

HALESIA MONTICOLA

Habit Fast-growing, conical or spreading.
Flowers Small, bell-shaped, in a profusion of pendent clusters in late spring. White. *Fruits* Four papery wings. *Leaves* Deciduous, elliptic to broadly oval-oblong, pointed. Bright green, later mid-green.
• NATIVE HABITAT North Carolina and Arkansas.
• CULTIVATION Grow in moist but well-drained, neutral to acid soil. Shelter from cold winds.
• PROPAGATION By softwood cuttings in summer or by seed in autumn.
• OTHER NAMES *H. carolina* var. *monticola*.

Z 5–9

HEIGHT
40ft (12m)

SPREAD
28ft (8m)

| Cornaceae | PACIFIC DOGWOOD, MOUNTAIN DOGWOOD |

CORNUS NUTTALLII

Habit Broadly conical. **Flowers** Tiny, in hemispherical clusters, in late spring and sometimes again in autumn. Green, surrounded by 4–7 large, conspicuous, creamy-white bracts, flushed pink with age. **Leaves** Deciduous, oval, to 6in (15cm) long, pointed. Dark green, turning yellow or red in autumn.
• NATIVE HABITAT Lowland forests and mountain forests of W. North America.
• CULTIVATION Tolerates light, dappled shade. Grow in fertile, freely draining soil. Dislikes

shallow, alkaline soils. An elegant and beautiful specimen tree, it is also well suited to open areas in woodland gardens. It is notable for its beautiful habit, having an open crown of ascending branches arising from a straight, fluted bole. The flower buds are clearly visible at the branch tips in winter.
• PROPAGATION By seed in autumn.

Z 6–9

HEIGHT
40ft (12m)

SPREAD
25ft (8m)

Rosaceae	

PRUNUS AVIUM 'Plena'

Habit Round-headed, spreading.
Flowers Double, cup-shaped, in large clusters in spring with or just before leaves. Pure white.
Fruits Small, edible, sweet or bitter cherries. Red.
Leaves Deciduous, elliptic to oblong, pointed, sharply toothed. Bronze when young, turning matte dark green, then yellow and red-crimson in autumn.
• NATIVE HABITAT Garden origin.
• CULTIVATION Grow in any but waterlogged soil. One of the most beautiful of the flowering cherries.
• PROPAGATION By softwood cuttings in summer.

Z 5–8	
HEIGHT	40ft (12m)
SPREAD	40ft (12m)

Rosaceae	BIRD CHERRY

PRUNUS PADUS

Habit Conical when young, spreading with age.
Flowers Small, fragrant, in upright or drooping spikes in mid- to late spring. White. *Fruits* Small, rounded to egg-shaped cherries. Glossy black.
Leaves Deciduous, elliptic, pointed, finely toothed. Dark green, turning yellow or red in autumn.
• NATIVE HABITAT Stream sides in open areas and in woods throughout Europe.
• CULTIVATION Grow in any but waterlogged soil. A beautiful specimen for the wild garden.
• PROPAGATION By seed in autumn.

Z 3–6	
HEIGHT	50ft (15m)
SPREAD	30ft (10m)

Oleaceae	FLOWERING ASH, MANNA ASH

FRAXINUS ORNUS

Habit Broadly spreading, round-headed.
Flowers Tiny, fragrant, in large, conical clusters from late spring to early summer. Creamy-white.
Fruits Seeds, with papery wings, in clusters.
Leaves Deciduous, divided into 5–9, oblong to oval, pointed leaflets. Matte dark green.
• NATIVE HABITAT Woodland on dry slopes from S. Europe to S.W. Asia.
• CULTIVATION Grow in any fertile soil, provided it is not too dry.
• PROPAGATION By seed in autumn.

Z 5–6	
HEIGHT	50ft (15m)
SPREAD	43ft (13m)

Ericaceae	MADRONA

ARBUTUS MENZIESII

Habit Broadly columnar, spreading with age.
Flowers Small, urn-shaped, in upright panicles in late spring. White. *Fruits* Small, strawberry-like berries. Orange-red. *Leaves* Evergreen, elliptic. Glossy dark green above, bluish beneath.
Bark Peeling. Red-brown, golden-olive beneath.
• NATIVE HABITAT Forests of W. North America.
• CULTIVATION Tolerates dappled shade. Grow in fertile, humus-rich soil. Shelter from winds.
• PROPAGATION By seed in autumn or by semi-ripe cuttings in summer.

Z 7–9	
HEIGHT	50ft (15m)
SPREAD	50ft (15m)

Meliaceae	CHINABERRY, BEAD TREE

MELIA AZEDARACH

Habit Round-headed, spreading. **Flowers** Small, fragrant, star-shaped, in spring. Pinkish-lilac. **Fruits** Small, round, berry-like. Orange-yellow. **Leaves** Deciduous, divided into many oval to elliptic leaflets. Dark green.
• NATIVE HABITAT N. India and China.
• CULTIVATION Tolerant of very dry soil and coastal conditions. Grow in any well-drained soil. Flowers best in areas with long, hot summers.
• PROPAGATION By seed in autumn.

Rosaceae	KWANZAN CHERRY

PRUNUS 'Kanzan'

Habit Vigorous, vase-shaped, with ascending branches, spreading with age. **Flowers** Large, double, in dense clusters, carried with the emerging leaves from mid- to late spring. Bright purplish-pink. **Leaves** Deciduous, oval, long-pointed. Coppery-bronze on emergence, then dark green.
• NATIVE HABITAT Garden origin.
• CULTIVATION Grow in any but waterlogged soil.
• PROPAGATION By softwood cuttings in summer, by budding in summer, or by grafting in winter.
• OTHER NAMES P. 'Sekiyama'.

☀ ◊
✿ ✿

Z 7–10

HEIGHT
30ft (10m)

SPREAD
30ft (10m)

☀ ◊
✿ ✿ ✿

Z 5–7

HEIGHT
To 30ft
(10m)

SPREAD
28ft (9m)

Rosaceae	HILL CHERRY

PRUNUS SERRULATA var. SPONTANEA

Habit Broadly spreading. **Flowers** Cup-shaped, in profusion from mid- to late spring. White to pale pink. **Fruits** Cherries, to 1in (2.5cm) long. Dark purplish-red. **Leaves** Deciduous, oblong to oval-elliptic, pointed, toothed. Bronze when young, then dark green, turning yellow through red in autumn.
• NATIVE HABITAT Woods, in the hills and mountains of China, Japan, and Korea.
• CULTIVATION Grow in any but waterlogged soil.
• PROPAGATION By seed in autumn.
• OTHER NAMES P. jamasakura.

☀ ◊
✿ ✿ ✿

Z 5–7

HEIGHT
40ft (12m)

SPREAD
40ft (12m)

Rosaceae	CRAB APPLE

MALUS 'Profusion'

Habit Vigorous, spreading. **Flowers** Cup-shaped, in profuse clusters from mid- to late spring. Deep purplish-red. **Fruits** Tiny, rounded crab apples. Red-purple. **Leaves** Deciduous. Bronze-purple on emergence, later dark green, veined crimson.
• NATIVE HABITAT Garden origin.
• CULTIVATION Tolerates semi-shade. Grow in any but waterlogged soil. Susceptible to fireblight.
• PROPAGATION By budding in late summer or by grafting in mid-winter.
• OTHER NAMES *M.* × *moerlandsii* 'Profusion'.

Z 5–7

HEIGHT
To 30ft
(10m)

SPREAD
28ft (9m)

Scrophulariaceae	

PAULOWNIA TOMENTOSA

Habit Broadly columnar. **Flowers** Fragrant, foxglove-like, in large, upright panicles in spring. Pinkish-lilac. **Leaves** Deciduous, broadly oval, heart-shaped at the base, sometimes lobed, hairy. Dark green above, densely hairy beneath.
• NATIVE HABITAT Mountains of China.
• CULTIVATION Grow in any fertile soil. Flowers best in regions with long, hot summers.
• PROPAGATION By seed in autumn or spring or by root cuttings in winter.
• OTHER NAMES *P. imperialis*.

Z 5–9

HEIGHT
46ft (14m)

SPREAD
30ft (10m)

Leguminosae	

GLEDITSIA TRIACANTHOS 'Sunburst'

Habit Spreading. **Leaves** Deciduous, finely divided into many slender leaflets. Bright golden-yellow on emergence, becoming dark green. Young and mature leaves make effective contrasts.
• NATIVE HABITAT Garden origin.
• CULTIVATION Tolerates urban pollution. Grow in any well-drained soil.
• PROPAGATION By budding in late summer.
• OTHER NAMES *G. triacanthos* 'Inermis Aurea'.

Z 3–9

HEIGHT
To 30ft
(10m)

SPREAD
30ft (10m)

MAGNOLIAS

Magnolias are a genus of deciduous, evergreen, or semi-evergreen shrubs and trees. They are usually found in woodland and forests, often in mountainous areas, and mainly in the northern hemisphere. Some have been known in cultivation in China for over 1400 years.

Magnolias are usually exceptionally long-lived, and are much valued for their elegant habit and beautiful, often intensely fragrant, flowers. These range from the tough but delicate-looking, star-shaped blooms of *M. stellata* to the exotic, goblet-shaped blooms of *M.* x *soulangeana*.

Magnolias are among the most handsome of plants when grown as free-standing specimens; they are not only gloriously beautiful in flower, they often offer an architectural branch framework in winter. Some also produce interesting fruits. The buds and flowers of early-flowering species may be damaged by

frosts, so avoid planting in frost pockets. Most also need shelter from strong winds, since their branches can be brittle. All grow best on deep, fertile, moisture-retentive but well-drained soils that are humus-rich, and preferably neutral or acid. Some, such as *M. kobus*, *M. wilsonii*, and *M. grandiflora*, tolerate lime, provided that the soil is deep and humus-rich. Grow in sun or light, dappled shade.

Magnolias generally require little pruning, other than to remove dead wood and badly placed branches, although overgrown specimens can be cut back hard. This should be done after flowering for early-flowering deciduous species, and in early spring for late-flowering evergreens.

Propagate species by seed in autumn or by semi-ripe cuttings in summer. Cultivars, hybrids, and variants are propagated by semi-ripe cuttings in summer or by grafting in winter.

M. KOBUS 'Norman Gould'
Habit Slow-growing, spreading, sometimes shrubby.
Flowers Fragrant, star-shaped, opening from silky buds in mid-spring. White.
Leaves Deciduous, narrowly oblong-oval. Dark green.
• HEIGHT 15ft (5m).
• SPREAD 15ft (5m).

M. kobus 'Norman Gould'

☼ ◊ ❋ ❋ ❋   Z 4–8

M. x KEWENSIS 'Wada's Memory'
Habit Dense, broadly conical.
Flowers Fragrant, large, on bare branches from mid- to late spring. Creamy-white to pure white. *Leaves* Aromatic. Deciduous, oval. Red-purple, then dark green.
• OTHER NAMES
M. 'Wada's Memory'.
• HEIGHT 30ft (9m).
• SPREAD 20ft (6m).

M. x *kewensis* 'Wada's Memory'

☼ ◊ ❋ ❋ ❋   Z 4–7

M. KOBUS
Habit Broadly conical.
Flowers Fragrant, up to 4in (10cm) across, in profusion in spring. Creamy-white tepals, flushed pink at the base.
Leaves Slightly aromatic. Deciduous, elliptic to oval, tapering at the base, smooth. Dark green.
• CULTIVATION
Blooms at about 10–15 years of age.
• HEIGHT To 70ft (20m), often less.
• SPREAD 30ft (10m).

M. kobus

☼ ◊ ❋ ❋ ❋   Z 4–8

M. CYLINDRICA
Habit Spreading, sometimes shrubby.
Flowers Fragrant, upright, opening on bare branches in spring. Narrow, creamy-white tepals and sepals.
Leaves Deciduous, broadly to elliptic. Dark green above, paler and downy beneath.
• HEIGHT 28ft (9m).
• SPREAD 20ft (6m).

M. cylindrica

☼ ◊ ❁❁❁   Z 4–9

M. SALICIFOLIA
Habit Broadly conical.
Flowers Fragrant, large, opening on bare branches in early spring. Narrow, white tepals and sepals.
Leaves Aromatic. Deciduous, oval to lance-shaped or elliptic. Reddish when young, then dark green above, blue-green beneath.
• HEIGHT 30ft (10m).
• SPREAD 15ft (5m).

M. salicifolia
Anise magnolia

☼ ◊ ❁❁❁   Z 4–8

M. × WIESNERI
Habit Open, bushy, spreading.
Flowers Fragrant, large, saucer-shaped, opening from tight, round buds in late spring. White, with crimson stamens.
Leaves Deciduous, broadly oval, leathery. Dark green.
• OTHER NAMES
M. × watsonii.
• HEIGHT 22ft (7m).
• SPREAD 22ft (7m).

M. × wiesneri

☼ ◊ ❁❁❁   Z 8–9

M. WILSONII
Habit Open, spreading.
Flowers Fragrant, large, pendent, cup- then saucer-shaped, in late spring–early summer. White; crimson stamens.
Leaves Deciduous, elliptic-oblong to lance-shaped. Matte green, silky beneath.
• CULTIVATION
Tolerates semi-shade.
• HEIGHT 25ft (8m).
• SPREAD 20ft (6m).

M. wilsonii

☼ ◊ ❁❁❁   Z 6–8

M. DENUDATA
Habit Rounded, spreading, sometimes shrubby.
Flowers Fragrant, very large, goblet-shaped, on bare branches from mid- to late spring. White.
Leaves Deciduous, oval. Mid-green, softly hairy beneath.
• OTHER NAMES
M. heptapeta.
• HEIGHT 30ft (10m) or more.
• SPREAD 30ft (10m).

M. denudata
Lily tree, Yulan

☼ ◊ ❁❁   Z 5–8

M. 'Charles Coates'
Habit Rounded, open, spreading. **Flowers** Very fragrant, carried with the emerging leaves in late spring and early summer. Creamy-white with an inner ring of red stamens.
Leaves Deciduous, oval, wedge-shaped at base, to 10in (25cm) long. Light green.
• HEIGHT To 20ft (6m).
• SPREAD 15ft (5m).

M. 'Charles Coates'

☼ ◊ ❁❁❁   Z 6–8

M. 'Manchu Fan'
Habit Vigorous, upright.
Flowers Fragrant, large, goblet-shaped, in late spring. Creamy-white; innermost tepals flushed purple-pink at base.
Leaves Deciduous, elliptic. Pale green when young, turning darker.
• HEIGHT 30ft (10m) or more.
• SPREAD 30ft (10m).

M. 'Manchu Fan'
Gresham hybrid

☼ ◊ ❁❁❁   Z 6–8

M. FRASERI
Habit Broadly
spreading, open-
branching.
Flowers Fragrant,
saucer-shaped, opening
from vase-shaped buds at
the branch tips in late
spring–early summer.
Rich creamy-white.
Leaves Deciduous,
large, heart-shaped at
base, soft. Bronzed at
first, then pale green.
• HEIGHT To 56ft (14m).
• SPREAD To 40ft (12m).

M. fraseri

☼ ◊ ❀❀❀   Z 6–8

M. HYPOLEUCA
Habit Vigorous,
pyramidal.
Flowers Very fragrant,
large, cup-shaped, in
early summer. Creamy-
white, pink-flushed, with
crimson stamens.
Leaves Deciduous, very
large, broadly oval. Deep
green.
• OTHER NAMES
M. obovata.
• HEIGHT 52ft (16m).
• SPREAD 25ft (8m).

M. hypoleuca

☼ ◊ ❀❀❀   Z 5–8

M. SPRENGERI
Habit Open, spreading.
Flowers Fragrant. Large,
bowl-shaped, on bare
branches in mid-spring.
White, sometimes tinted
red or pink.
Leaves Deciduous,
broadly oval, wedge-
shaped at base. Dark
green.
• HEIGHT 40ft (12m).
• SPREAD 30ft (10m).

M. sprengeri

☼ ◊ ❀❀   Z 6–9

**M. GRANDIFLORA
'Exmouth'**
Habit Dense, broadly
conical *Flowers* Very
fragrant, large, cup-
shaped. Appear
intermittently from mid-
summer to early autumn.
Creamy-white.
Leaves Evergreen,
narrow, elliptic, glossy.
Soft green above, with
red-brown felt beneath.
• HEIGHT To 80ft (25m).
• SPREAD 40ft (12m).

M. grandiflora
'Exmouth'
Southern magnolia

☼ ◊ ❀❀❀   Z 7–9

M. TRIPETALA
Habit Conical, open,
broadly spreading with
age. *Flowers* Large, from
slender buds at branch
tips in late spring to early
summer. Creamy-white,
with narrow tepals.
Leaves Deciduous, oval
to elliptic, pointed. Dark
green above, hairy; gray-
green beneath.
• HEIGHT 40ft (12m).
• SPREAD 30ft (10m).

M. tripetala
Umbrella tree

☼ ◊ ❀❀❀   Z 4–8

**M. x VEITCHII
'Peter Veitch'**
Habit Very vigorous,
spreading.
Flowers Fragrant, large,
goblet-shaped, on bare
branches in spring.
Waxy-white, flushed
pink-purple.
Leaves Deciduous,
broadly oval-oblong,
pointed. Bronzed when
young, then dark green.
• HEIGHT To 80ft (25m).
• SPREAD 25ft (8m).

M. x veitchii
'Peter Veitch'
Gresham hybrid

☼ ◊ ❀❀❀   Z 6–8

M. *CAMPBELLII*
Habit Upright, broadly
conical. **Flowers** Slightly
fragrant, very large, cup-
shaped, on bare branches
from late winter to early
spring. Pale pink to deep
pink.
Leaves Deciduous,
oblong-oval, pointed.
Dark green, paler below,
flushed purple when
young.
• HEIGHT 52ft (16m).
• SPREAD 35ft (11m).

M. campbellii

☼ ◊ ❀❀   Z 5–7

M. *CAMPBELLII*
subsp. *MOLLICOMATA*
Habit Upright, broadly
conical. **Flowers** Slightly
fragrant, large, cup-
shaped, in late winter to
early spring. Pale lilac-
pink. **Leaves** Deciduous,
oblong-oval, pointed.
Dark green, often hairy
beneath, flushed purple
when young.
• HEIGHT 52ft (16m) or
more.
• SPREAD 35ft (11m).

M. campbellii subsp.
mollicomata

☼ ◊ ❀❀❀   Z 5–7

M. 'Heaven Scent'
Habit Vigorous,
spreading. **Flowers** Very
fragrant, narrowly cup-
shaped, in late spring.
Pale pink, flushed deep
pink at base; tepal
reverse-striped magenta.
Leaves Deciduous,
oblong-oval. Dark green.
• HEIGHT 30ft (10m) or
more.
• SPREAD 30ft (10m).

M. 'Heaven Scent'
Gresham hybrid

☼ ◊ ❀❀❀   Z 6–8

M. *CAMPBELLII*
'Wakehurst'
Habit Open, spreading.
Flowers Fragrant, large,
narrowly bowl-shaped, on
bare branches in mid-
spring. Purplish-pink,
rich pink within.
Leaves Deciduous, oval
to lance-shaped or
elliptic. Dark green.
• HEIGHT 50ft (15m).
• SPREAD 30ft (10m).

M. campbellii
'Wakehurst'

☼ ◊ ❀❀   Z 5–7

M. *CAMPBELLII*
'Charles Raffill'
Habit Vigorous, upright,
later spreading.
Flowers Fragrant, large,
cup-shaped, in mid-
spring. Rose-purple,
white within. Margins
flushed pink-purple.
Leaves Deciduous,
oblong-oval, pointed.
Mid-green.
• HEIGHT 52ft (16m) or
more.
• SPREAD 35ft (11m).

M. campbellii
'Charles Raffill'

☼ ◊ ❀❀❀   Z 5–7

M. *CAMPBELLII*
'Darjeeling'
Habit Upright, broadly
conical. **Flowers** Slightly
fragrant, large, cup-
shaped, on bare branches
in late winter to early
spring. Rose-pink.
Leaves Deciduous,
oblong-oval, pointed.
Dark green, paler below.
Purplish when young.
• HEIGHT 52ft (16m).
• SPREAD 35ft (11m).

M. campbellii
'Darjeeling'

☼ ◊ ❀❀   Z 5–7

Styraceae	JAPANESE SNOWBELL

STYRAX JAPONICA

Habit Open, broadly spreading. **Flowers** Slightly fragrant, small, pendent, bell-shaped, carried beneath the branches in early to mid-summer. White. **Leaves** Deciduous, elliptic to oval. Rich glossy green, turning yellow or red in autumn.
• NATIVE HABITAT Open areas, usually on damp ground, in China, Japan, and Korea.
• CULTIVATION Tolerates dappled shade. Grow in neutral to acid soil and shelter from cold winds.
• PROPAGATION By softwood cuttings in summer or by seed in autumn.

Z 5–8

HEIGHT
30ft (10m)

SPREAD
25ft (8m)

Betulaceae	EASTERN HOP HORNBEAM, IRONWOOD

OSTRYA VIRGINIANA

Habit Broadly conical-rounded. **Flowers** Catkins. Male: to 2in (5cm) long, yellow; female: small, green, on same plant in spring. **Fruits** Nuts, enclosed in pale, bladder-like husks, carried in short, pendent clusters. **Leaves** Deciduous, ovate, toothed. Dark green, turning rich yellow in autumn.
• NATIVE HABITAT Woodlands of E. North America.
• CULTIVATION Tolerates dappled shade. Grow in any fertile, well-drained soil.
• PROPAGATION By seed in autumn.

Z 3–9

Height
50ft (15m)

SPREAD
40ft (12m)

Rosaceae	HIMALAYAN WHITEBEAM

SORBUS VESTITA

Habit Broadly conical. **Flowers** Small, flattened clusters in late spring-early summer. White. **Fruits** Small, rounded to pear-shaped, berry-like. Green, flecked brown. **Leaves** Deciduous, elliptic, veined. Dark gray-green above, silvery-white and downy beneath.
• NATIVE HABITAT Forests in the Himalayas.
• CULTIVATION Fertile, moisture-retentive soil.
• PROPAGATION By softwood cuttings in summer or by seed in autumn.
• OTHER NAMES *S. cuspidata.*

Z 7–8

HEIGHT
50ft (15m)

SPREAD
30ft (10m)

Nyssaceae	DOVE TREE, GHOST TREE, POCKET-HANDKERCHIEF TREE

DAVIDIA INVOLUCRATA

Habit Broadly conical. **Flowers** Tiny, in rounded heads, with conspicuous purple anthers, surrounded by large, white, papery bracts of unequal size, in late spring. **Fruits** Rounded berry, 1in (2.5cm) across. Green, ripening to purple.
Leaves Deciduous, heart-shaped, with slender, pointed tip. Bright green, felted beneath.
Bark Peeling vertically in small flakes. Orange-brown.
• NATIVE HABITAT Moist, mountain woods in China.

• CULTIVATION Tolerates semi-shade. Grow in any moisture-retentive soil. Provide shelter from strong winds. Flowers only when mature. The numerous papery bracts give the appearance of handkerchiefs hanging from the tree.
• PROPAGATION By semi-ripe cuttings in early summer or by seed in autumn.

Z 6–8

HEIGHT
46ft (14m)

SPREAD
30ft (10m)

Bignoniaceae	INDIAN BEAN TREE, EASTERN CATALPA

CATALPA BIGNONIOIDES

Habit Broadly spreading. **Flowers** Trumpet-shaped, 2-lipped, in upright panicles in mid- to late summer. White, yellow- and purple-spotted. **Fruits** Long, pendent pods. **Leaves** Deciduous, heart-shaped, pointed at the tip. Light green.
• NATIVE HABITAT Woods and stream sides of S.E. United States.
• CULTIVATION Grow in fertile, well-drained soil. Shelter from strong winds. Flowers only when mature. Thrives in areas with long, hot summers.
• PROPAGATION By seed in autumn.

Z 5–9

HEIGHT
50ft (15m)

SPREAD
50ft (15m)

Bignoniaceae	WESTERN CATALPA, NORTHERN CATALPA

CATALPA SPECIOSA

Habit Broadly columnar. **Flowers** Trumpet-shaped, 2-lipped, in upright panicles in mid-summer. White, purple-spotted. **Fruits** Long, narrow, pendent pods. **Leaves** Deciduous, broadly oval, taper-pointed at the tip. Dark green.
• NATIVE HABITAT Damp woods, swamps, and riverbanks of C. United States.
• CULTIVATION Grow in deep, fertile, well-drained soil. Provide shelter from strong winds. Thrives in areas with long, hot summers.
• PROPAGATION By seed in autumn.

Z 4–8

HEIGHT
50ft (15m)

SPREAD
50ft (15m)

Theaceae	JAPANESE STEWARTIA

STEWARTIA PSEUDOCAMELLIA

Habit Broadly columnar. **Flowers** Shallowly cup-shaped, opening from silky buds in mid-summer. Glistening white, with golden stamens. **Leaves** Deciduous, oval to elliptic, finely toothed. Dark green, turning yellow and red in autumn. **Bark** Peeling. Red-brown, gray-pink beneath.
• NATIVE HABITAT Mountain woods of Japan.
• CULTIVATION Grow in rich, neutral to acid soil. Shelter from cold winds. Prefers shade at the roots.
• PROPAGATION By softwood cuttings in summer or by seed in autumn.

Z 4–7

HEIGHT
50ft (15m)

SPREAD
30ft (10m)

Fagaceae	VARIEGATED TURKEY OAK

QUERCUS CERRIS 'Argenteovariegata'

Habit Broadly spreading, with a rounded crown. **Fruits** Acorns to 1in (2.5cm) long, half enclosed in a cup clothed with long, slender scales. **Leaves** Deciduous, elliptic to oblong, deeply lobed. Glossy dark green, margined yellow, fading to cream.
• NATIVE HABITAT Garden origin.
• CULTIVATION Tolerates semi-shade, alkaline soils, and coastal conditions. Grow in deep, fertile, well-drained soil.
• PROPAGATION By grafting in late winter.
• OTHER NAMES Q. cerris 'Variegata'.

Z 5–7

HEIGHT
50ft (15m)

SPREAD
30ft (10m)

Rosaceae

SORBUS ARIA 'Lutescens'

Habit Dense crown, conical when young, later spreading. *Flowers* Small, in flattened clusters in late spring. White. *Fruits* Small, rounded berries, in clusters. Orange-red. *Leaves* Deciduous, elliptic to oval, toothed, densely clothed in creamy down when young. Gray-green, turning russet and gold in autumn.
• NATIVE HABITAT Garden origin.
• CULTIVATION Tolerant of heavy clay soils, semi-shade, urban pollution, and exposed, coastal conditions. Thrives in both acid and alkaline soils.

Grow in fertile, moisture-retentive but well-drained soil. It makes a beautiful and adaptable specimen tree, well suited to town gardens and having a long season of interest.
• PROPAGATION By softwood cuttings or budding in summer or by grafting in winter.

☀ ◊
❄ ❄ ❄

Z 5–6

HEIGHT
43ft (13m)

SPREAD
25ft (8m)

| Hippocastanaceae | INDIAN HORSE-CHESTNUT |

AESCULUS INDICA 'Sydney Pearce'

Habit Vigorous, upright, broadly columnar, later spreading. *Flowers* Tubular to bell-shaped, flared at the mouth, carried freely in narrow, upright panicles in mid-summer. White, flushed pink, marked red and yellow. *Fruits* Scaly, spineless husk enclosing a single, small, shiny seeds ("conkers"). *Leaves* Deciduous, with 5–7 lance-shaped, stalked leaflets. Bronze when young, turning dark olive green.
• NATIVE HABITAT Garden origin.
• CULTIVATION Tolerates dappled shade. Grow in fertile, moisture-retentive but well-drained soil. This elegant, low-branching tree flowers much later than the common horse-chestnut and bears its blooms near ground level where they can be seen more clearly.
• PROPAGATION By budding in late summer or by grafting in late winter.

Z 7–8

HEIGHT
43ft (13m)

SPREAD
43ft (13m)

Aceraceae	SYCAMORE MAPLE

ACER PSEUDOPLATANUS 'Simon Louis Frères'

Habit Broadly spreading, with a domed crown.
Leaves Deciduous, with 5 coarsely toothed lobes.
Pink on emergence, later streaked yellowish and
pale green above, green beneath.
• NATIVE HABITAT Garden origin.
• CULTIVATION Tolerates exposure and almost
any soil. Smaller and slower-growing than the
species. An attractive specimen for open sites.
• PROPAGATION By grafting in late winter or early
spring or by budding in summer.

Z 4–7

HEIGHT
40ft (12m)
or more

SPREAD
30ft (10m)

Bignoniaceae	

JACARANDA MIMOSIFOLIA

Habit Vigorous, rounded. **Flowers** Narrowly bell-
shaped, in large panicles in spring and early
summer. Vivid blue-purple, white at throat. Seldom
flowers at less than 10ft (3m) tall. **Leaves**
Deciduous, fern-like, elliptic. Green.
• NATIVE HABITAT Dry forests of Argentina, Bolivia.
• CULTIVATION Grow under glass as a foliage pot
plant. Water freely in growth, otherwise sparingly.
• PROPAGATION By seed in spring or by semi-ripe
cuttings in summer.
• OTHER NAMES *J. acutifolia, J. ovalifolia.*

Z 10–11

HEIGHT
43ft (13m)

SPREAD
25ft (8m)

Aceraceae	VARIEGATED BOX ELDER

ACER NEGUNDO 'Variegatum'

Habit Fast-growing, broadly columnar.
Leaves Deciduous, with 3–5 lance-shaped to
oblong, toothed, pointed, sometimes lobed leaflets.
Bright green, irregularly margined creamy-white.
• NATIVE HABITAT Garden origin.
• CULTIVATION Grow in any fertile, moisture-
retentive but well-drained soil. Prune out any
branches with all-green leaves.
• PROPAGATION By grafting in late winter or early
spring or by budding in summer.
• OTHER NAMES *A. negundo* 'Argenteovariegatum'.

Z 5–8

HEIGHT
46ft (14m)

SPREAD
22ft (7m)

Rosaceae	MOUNTAIN ASH

SORBUS THIBETICA 'John Mitchell'

Habit Vigorous, broadly conical, rounded with
age. **Flowers** Tiny, in small clusters in late spring.
Creamy-white. **Fruits** Small, round berries.
Orange-brown. **Leaves** Deciduous, large, rounded-
elliptic. Green above, densely silver-downy beneath.
• NATIVE HABITAT Garden origin.
• CULTIVATION Grow in fertile, moisture-
retentive soil.
• PROPAGATION By softwood cuttings or budding
in summer or by grafting in winter.
• OTHER NAMES *S.* 'Mitchellii'.

Z 6–8

HEIGHT
43ft (13m)

SPREAD
22ft (7m)

Meliaceae	

TOONA SINENSIS

Habit Broadly columnar. **Flowers** Small, fragrant, in large, drooping panicles in mid-summer. White. **Leaves** Deciduous, with 10–24 oblong to lance-shaped leaflets. Pinkish-bronze on emergence, later dark green, turning yellow in autumn. **Bark** Shaggy, peeling in strips.
• NATIVE HABITAT Woodlands in China.
• CULTIVATION Grow in any fertile soil.
• PROPAGATION By seed in autumn or by root cuttings in winter.
• OTHER NAMES *Cedrela sinensis.*

☀ ◐
❀ ❀ ❀

Z 6–8

HEIGHT
50ft (15m)

SPREAD
22ft (7m)

Rhamnaceae	JAPANESE RAISIN TREE

HOVENIA DULCIS

Habit Broadly conical, later spreading. **Flowers** Small, in clusters. Greenish-yellow with red, fleshy, edible leaf-stalks in summer. **Leaves** Deciduous, broadly oval, pointed at tip, heart-shaped at the base, coarsely toothed. Very glossy dark green.
• NATIVE HABITAT E. Asia; native range uncertain.
• CULTIVATION Grow in fertile soil, in a sheltered site. Young growth susceptible to frost damage.
• PROPAGATION By softwood cuttings in summer or by seed in autumn.

☀ ◐
❀ ❀ ❀

Z 5–7

HEIGHT
43ft (13m)

SPREAD
30ft (10m)

Salicaceae	WEEPING ASPEN

POPULUS TREMULA 'Pendula'

Habit Vigorous, weeping. **Flowers** Catkins. Male: long, pendent, purplish; female: greenish, on separate plants, in late winter to early spring. **Leaves** Deciduous, rounded to broadly oval, with rounded teeth. Bronze on emergence, later dark gray-green, yellow in autumn. The long, flat leaf-stalks "tremble" in a breeze.
• NATIVE HABITAT Garden origin.
• CULTIVATION Grow in deep, fertile soil. Plant at least 100ft (30m) away from drains and buildings.
• PROPAGATION By hardwood cuttings in winter.

☀ ◐
❀ ❀ ❀

Z 2–5

HEIGHT
50ft (15m)

SPREAD
22ft (7m)

Betulaceae	AMERICAN HORNBEAM, BLUE BEECH, WATER BEECH

CARPINUS CAROLINIANA

Habit Broadly spreading. **Flowers** Catkins. Male: pendent, yellowish; female: small, upright, on same plant in spring. **Fruits** Nuts, with 2–3 toothed bracts. Green. **Leaves** Deciduous, oval, taper-pointed, toothed. Blue-green, turning orange-red in autumn.
• NATIVE HABITAT Swamps and damp woods of E. North America and Mexico.
• CULTIVATION Tolerates semi-shade. Grow in any deep, fertile, moisture-retentive soil.
• PROPAGATION By seed in autumn.

☀ ◐
❀ ❀ ❀

Z 3–9

HEIGHT
30ft (10m)
or more

SPREAD
25ft (8m)

Fagaceae	BLACK JACK OAK

QUERCUS MARILANDICA

Habit Broadly spreading. **Fruits** Acorns, to ¾in (2cm) long, half enclosed in hairy-scaly cup. **Leaves** Deciduous, triangular, with 3 pointed lobes at the broad tip. Glossy dark green above, tawny beneath, turning yellow, red, and brown in autumn.
• NATIVE HABITAT Woods, often in poor, sandy soils, of E. United States.
• CULTIVATION Grow in deep, fertile soil. Unsuitable for alkaline soils. Tolerates semi-shade.
• PROPAGATION By seed in autumn.

Z 6–9

HEIGHT
40ft (12m)

SPREAD
30ft (10m)

Sabiaceae	

MELIOSMA VEITCHIORUM

Habit Rounded, with stout, upright branches. **Flowers** Small, fragrant, in large panicles in late spring. White. **Fruits** Rounded, berry-like. Rich violet. **Leaves** Deciduous, with 7–9 oval to oblong leaflets. Dark green, with red leaf-stalks.
• NATIVE HABITAT W. and C. China.
• CULTIVATION Grow in deep, fertile, freely draining soil, in a warm, sheltered site. Flowers reliably only in areas with long, hot summers. Makes an attractive architectural specimen.
• PROPAGATION By seed in autumn.

Z 8–9

HEIGHT
40ft (12m)

SPREAD
22ft (7m)

Araliaceae	CASTOR ARALIA

KALOPANAX PICTUS

Habit Broadly columnar. **Flowers** Tiny, in large, rounded clusters in late summer. White. **Fruits** Small, round, berry-like. Blue-black. **Leaves** Deciduous, with 5–7 toothed lobes. Glossy dark green. **Bark** Spiny, deeply fissured.
• NATIVE HABITAT Riversides and damp forests from China and E. Russia to Japan and Korea.
• CULTIVATION Grow in moist, well-drained soil.
• PROPAGATION By softwood cuttings in summer.
• OTHER NAMES *K. septemlobus.*

Z 4–8

HEIGHT
40ft (12m)

SPREAD
25ft (8m)

Oleaceae	ARIZONA ASH

FRAXINUS VELUTINA

Habit Open, rounded, spreading. **Leaves** Deciduous, with 3–5 paired, lance-shaped to elliptic leaflets. Dull green, usually clothed in velvety-gray down, turning yellow in autumn.
• NATIVE HABITAT In moist soils by riverbanks, in canyons, desert grasslands, and oak and pine forest of S.W. United States.
• CULTIVATION Tolerates dry and alkaline soils, but grows best in moisture-retentive but well-drained soil.
• PROPAGATION By seed in autumn.

Z 6–9

HEIGHT
40ft (12m)

SPREAD
25ft (8m)

Leguminosae	JAPANESE HONEY LOCUST

GLEDITSIA JAPONICA

Habit Pyramidal, very spiny. **Leaves** Deciduous, finely divided, fern-like, with tiny, oblong to lance-shaped leaflets. Bright green. **Bark** Shoots are purplish when young.
• NATIVE HABITAT Woodlands of Japan.
• CULTIVATION Grow in any fertile, well-drained soil in a warm, sunny site. A delicate and graceful tree, suitable for specimen plantings.
• PROPAGATION By seed in autumn.

Z 6–9

HEIGHT
50ft (15m)

SPREAD
50ft (15m)

Fagaceae	OREGON WHITE OAK

QUERCUS GARRYANA

Habit Slow-growing, dense, rounded, spreading. **Fruits** Edible acorns, to 1¼in (3cm) long, up to one-third enclosed in a thin, shallow cup. **Leaves** Deciduous, elliptic, rounded at both ends, with deep, rounded lobes. Glossy bright green.
• NATIVE HABITAT Deciduous woodlands, in valleys and on mountains of W. North America.
• CULTIVATION Tolerates semi-shade. Grow in any deep, fertile, well-drained soil.
• PROPAGATION By seed in autumn.

Z 7–9

HEIGHT
50ft (15m)

SPREAD
30ft (10m)

Fagaceae	BUR OAK, MOSSY-CUP OAK

QUERCUS MACROCARPA

Habit Slow-growing, broadly spreading. **Fruits** Acorns, to 2in (5cm) long, half or more enclosed in a cup fringed with long scales. **Leaves** Deciduous, oblong-oval, lobed. Glossy dark green, but paler, sometimes white-downy, beneath. Turns pale yellow and brown in autumn.
• NATIVE HABITAT Rich woodlands of E. North America.
• CULTIVATION Unsuitable for alkaline soils. Tolerates semi-shade. Grow in deep, fertile soil.
• PROPAGATION By seed in autumn.

Z 2–8

HEIGHT
50ft (15m)

SPREAD
30ft (10m)

Rubiaceae	

EMMENOPTERYS HENRYI

Habit Open, spreading. **Flowers** Small, with conspicuous white bracts, in large, pyramidal clusters in summer. White. **Leaves** Deciduous, elliptic-oval, pointed. Bronze-purple when young, lustrous dark green above, paler beneath.
• NATIVE HABITAT C. and W. China, Burma, and Thailand.
• CULTIVATION Tolerates alkaline soil. Grow in a warm, sunny, sheltered site, in deep, fertile, moisture-retentive soil. Flowers best in long, hot summers.
• PROPAGATION By softwood cuttings in summer.

Z 8–10

HEIGHT
50ft (15m)

SPREAD
40ft (12m)

Fagaceae	

QUERCUS MACROLEPIS

Habit Spreading, with a rounded crown.
Fruits Acorns, to 1¾in (4.5cm) long, two-thirds enclosed in a cup with woody scales. Ripens in second year. **Leaves** Deciduous or semi-evergreen, oblong, with sharp, bristly lobes. Olive gray-green.
• NATIVE HABITAT Dry foothills and mountain woods in the Balkans.
• CULTIVATION Tolerates semi-shade. Grow in any deep, fertile, well-drained soil.
• PROPAGATION By seed in autumn.
• OTHER NAMES *Q. ithaburensis* subsp. *macrolepis*.

Z 7–9

HEIGHT
43ft (13m)

SPREAD
43ft (13m)
or more

Tiliaceae	LITTLELEAF LINDEN

TILIA CORDATA 'Rancho'

Habit Dense, conical, spreading when young.
Flowers Fragrant, small, cup-shaped, in clusters in mid-summer. **Leaves** Deciduous, small, oval, taper-pointed, heart-shaped at the base. Glossy dark green.
• NATIVE HABITAT Garden origin.
• CULTIVATION Tolerates semi-shade. Grow in deep, fertile soil. May be infested by aphids, which drip sticky honeydew onto the ground beneath.
• PROPAGATION By grafting in late summer.

Z 3–7

HEIGHT
43ft (13m)

SPREAD
20ft (6m)

Flacourtiaceae	IIGIRI TREE

IDESIA POLYCARPA

Habit Broadly spreading. **Flowers** Fragrant, small, in drooping clusters in mid-summer. Yellow-green. **Fruits** Small berries, in pendent clusters. Red. **Leaves** Deciduous, heart-shaped. Bronze-purple when young, turning glossy dark green, with red veins and leaf-stalks.
• NATIVE HABITAT Mountains of China and Japan.
• CULTIVATION Prefers a fertile, neutral to acid soil. Grow in a sunny site.
• PROPAGATION By softwood cuttings in summer or by seed in autumn.

Z 6–9

HEIGHT
43ft (13m)

SPREAD
33ft (11m)

Fagaceae	GOLDEN RED OAK

QUERCUS RUBRA 'Aurea'

Habit Slow-growing, broadly columnar to spreading. **Fruits** Acorns, to 1¼in (3cm) long, one-quarter enclosed in a shallow cup.
Leaves Deciduous, long, elliptic-oval, sharply lobed, with slender teeth. Clear yellow when young, later mid-green, turning red in autumn.
• NATIVE HABITAT Garden origin.
• CULTIVATION Tolerant of urban pollution and almost any well-drained soils, including alkaline ones. Tolerates semi-shade, but colors best in sun.
• PROPAGATION By grafting in late winter.

Z 4–8

HEIGHT
50ft (15m)

SPREAD
30ft (10m)

Betulaceae	

ALNUS GLUTINOSA 'Imperialis'

Habit Open, with a conical crown.
Flowers Catkins. Male: drooping, reddish; female: small, upright, on same plant, red, on bare branches in early spring. *Fruits* Small, woody, cone-like. Dark brown. *Leaves* Deciduous, delicately cut into pointed lobes. Smooth above, with tufts of hairs in the vein axils beneath. Dark green.
Bark Fissured. Dark gray.
• NATIVE HABITAT Species occurs by rivers in N. Africa, W. Asia, and N. Europe.
• CULTIVATION Tolerates wet or even waterlogged soil. *Alnus glutinosa* 'Imperialis' makes an elegant and graceful specimen for waterside plantings. It is especially attractive in winter, when the woody 'cones' are clearly visible. It is one of the most lime-tolerant of alders.
• PROPAGATION By budding in late summer or by hardwood cuttings in early winter.

Z 3–7

HEIGHT
40ft (12m)

SPREAD
15ft (5m)

Rutaceae	CHINESE CORK TREE

PHELLODENDRON CHINENSE

Habit Spreading, with a rounded crown.
Flowers Small, in pendent racemes in early
summer. Greenish. **Fruits** Berry-like, in dense
clusters, on female trees. Black. **Leaves** Aromatic,
deciduous, divided into 7–13 oblong leaflets. Dark
green, turning yellow in autumn.
• NATIVE HABITAT Mountains of C. China.
• CULTIVATION Grow in a sunny, sheltered site in
any fertile, well-drained soil.
• PROPAGATION By softwood cuttings in summer,
by seed in autumn, or by root cuttings in winter.

☀ ◊
❀ ❀ ❀

Z 4–9

HEIGHT
30ft (10m)

SPREAD
30ft (10m)

Ulmaceae	DICKSON'S GOLDEN ELM

ULMUS CARPINIFOLIA 'Dicksonii'

Habit Slow-growing, dense, conical.
Leaves Deciduous, small, broadly oval. Bright
golden-yellow.
• NATIVE HABITAT Garden origin.
• CULTIVATION Grow in fertile, well-drained soil.
Susceptible to (usually fatal) Dutch elm disease,
but affected trees may re-sprout from the base.
• PROPAGATION By softwood cuttings in summer
or by suckers in autumn.
• OTHER NAMES *U. carpinifolia* 'Sarniensis Aurea',
U. 'Dicksonii', *U.* 'Wheatleyi Aurea'.

☀ ◊
❀ ❀ ❀

Z 5–9

HEIGHT
40ft (12m)

SPREAD
22ft (7m)

Leguminosae	

ROBINIA PSEUDOACACIA 'Frisia'

Habit Broadly columnar. **Flowers** Fragrant,
small, pea-like, in pendent clusters from early to
mid-summer. White. **Fruits** Smooth pod. Brown.
Leaves Deciduous, with 11–23 oval leaflets.
Golden-yellow on emergence, later yellow-green,
turning clear orange-yellow in autumn.
• NATIVE HABITAT Garden origin.
• CULTIVATION Grow in any but waterlogged soil.
Branches may suffer damage in strong winds.
• PROPAGATION By suckers in autumn or by root
cuttings in winter.

☀ ◊
❀ ❀ ❀

Z 3–9

HEIGHT
50ft (15m)

SPREAD
25ft (8m)

Bignoniaceae	

CATALPA BIGNONIOIDES 'Aurea'

Habit Broadly spreading. **Flowers** Trumpet-
shaped, 2-lipped, in large, upright panicles in mid-
to late summer. White, yellow- and purple-spotted.
Fruits Long, narrow, pendent pods.
Leaves Deciduous, heart-shaped, pointed at the
tip. Bright yellow, bronzed when young.
• NATIVE HABITAT Garden origin.
• CULTIVATION Grow in deep, fertile, well-
drained soil. Provide shelter from strong winds.
• PROPAGATION By softwood cuttings in summer
or by budding in late summer.

☀ ◐
❀ ❀ ❀

Z 5–9

HEIGHT
50ft (15m)

SPREAD
40ft (12m)

Eucryphiaceae	

EUCRYPHIA × *NYMANSENSIS*

Habit Upright, columnar. **Flowers** Large, fragrant, in clusters in late summer-early autumn. Glistening white, with yellow, pink-tipped stamens. **Leaves** Evergreen, elliptic, toothed, sometimes with 3 leaflets. Glossy dark green.
• NATIVE HABITAT Garden origin.
• CULTIVATION Tolerates semi-shade and some lime. Grow in fertile, moist, well-drained soil, with shade at the roots. Shelter from cold, dry winds. Does best in mild, damp climates.
• PROPAGATION By semi-ripe cuttings in summer.

Z 9–10

HEIGHT
50ft (15m)

SPREAD
22ft (7m)

Myrtaceae	BRUSH CHERRY

SYZYGIUM PANICULATUM

Habit Broadly conical, shrubby. **Flowers** Creamy-white, with reddish sepals, and a brush of long white anthers. **Fruits** Globose, fleshy. Shades of purple, red, pink, and white. **Leaves** Evergreen, lance-shaped. Coppery, turning glossy dark green.
• NATIVE HABITAT Australia.
• CULTIVATION Grow in fertile soil or soil mix. Water freely when in growth, otherwise moderately.
• PROPAGATION By seed in spring or by semi-ripe cuttings in summer.
• OTHER NAMES *Eugenia australis, E. paniculata.*

Z 10–11

HEIGHT
43ft (13m)

SPREAD
25ft (8m)

Aceraceae	

ACER DAVIDII 'Madeline Spitta'

Habit Upright, columnar. **Fruits** 2 seeds, fused together, each with a wing, in long, pendent clusters. Orange-brown in autumn.
Leaves Deciduous, oval, pointed, toothed. Glossy dark green, turning orange in autumn. **Bark** Striped vertically. Gray-green and white.
• NATIVE HABITAT Garden origin.
• CULTIVATION Grow in moisture-retentive soil, preferably with shelter from cold winds.
• PROPAGATION By grafting in late winter or early spring or by budding in summer.

Z 5–7

HEIGHT
46ft (14m)

SPREAD
22ft (7m)

Rosaceae	MOUNTAIN ASH

SORBUS HUPEHENSIS var. OBTUSA

Habit Open, spreading. **Flowers** Small, in open, rounded clusters in late spring. White.
Fruits Small, round, persistent berries. Pink.
Leaves Deciduous, up to 17 paired, sharply toothed, pointed leaflets. Blue-green; scarlet in autumn.
• NATIVE HABITAT Garden origin.
• CULTIVATION Tolerates dappled shade. Grow in any fertile, moisture-retentive soil.
• PROPAGATION By softwood cuttings or budding in summer or by grafting in winter.
• OTHER NAMES *S. hupehensis* 'Rosea',

Aceraceae	

ACER RUBRUM 'Columnare'

Habit Erect, columnar, slender. **Flowers** Small, in dense clusters, on bare branches in spring. Red.
Fruits 2 seeds, fused together, each with a wing. Red. **Leaves** Deciduous, 3–5 lobes. Dark green, turning brilliant red and yellow in autumn.
• NATIVE HABITAT Garden origin.
• CULTIVATION Tolerates some lime, but grow in fertile, moisture retentive, neutral to acid soil for best autumn color. Suitable for confined spaces.
• PROPAGATION By grafting in late winter or early spring or by budding in summer.

☀ ◊
❀ ❀ ❀

Z 5–7

HEIGHT
40ft (12m)

SPREAD
25ft (8m)

☀ ◊
❀ ❀ ❀

Z 3–9

HEIGHT
50ft (15m)

SPREAD
20ft (6m)

Rosaceae	MOUNTAIN ASH

SORBUS COMMIXTA

Habit Delicate, open, broadly conical.
Flowers Small, in broad clusters in late spring. White. **Fruits** Small, round, in long-persistent clusters. Bright orange-red. **Leaves** Deciduous, up to 15 paired, elliptic- to lance-shaped, taper-pointed leaflets. Deep green; orange and red in autumn.
• NATIVE HABITAT Mountain forest, Japan, Korea.
• CULTIVATION Tolerates dappled shade. Grow in any fertile, moisture-retentive soil.
• PROPAGATION By seed in autumn.
• OTHER NAMES *S. discolor* of gardens.

☀ ◊
❀ ❀ ❀

Z 5–6

HEIGHT
30ft (10m)

SPREAD
22ft (7m)

Rosaceae	MOUNTAIN ASH

SORBUS AUCUPARIA

Habit Broadly conical. **Flowers** Small, creamy-white, in large clusters in late spring.
Fruits Round berries in dense clusters. Orange-red. **Leaves** Deciduous, with up to 15 paired, toothed, lance-shaped leaflets. Dark green above, blue-green beneath, turning red in autumn.
• NATIVE HABITAT Woods, heaths, and moorland throughout Europe and Asia.
• CULTIVATION Tolerates dappled shade. Grow in any fertile, moisture-retentive soil.
• PROPAGATION By seed in autumn.

Z 3–7

HEIGHT
To 50ft
(15m)

SPREAD
22ft (7m)

Aceraceae	

ACER RUFINERVE

Habit Broadly columnar. **Flowers** Small, in upright clusters in spring. Yellow-green.
Fruits 2 seeds, fused together, each with a red wing. **Leaves** Deciduous, with 3 coarsely toothed lobes. Dark green; red in autumn. **Bark** Striped white and pale green, with diamond-shaped markings.
• NATIVE HABITAT Mountain woods of Japan.
• CULTIVATION Tolerates lime, but grow in moisture-retentive, neutral to acid soil for best autumn color. Excellent for confined spaces.
• PROPAGATION By seed in autumn.

Z 5–7

HEIGHT
30ft (10m)

SPREAD
22ft (7m)

Rosaceae	CRAB APPLE

MALUS TSCHONOSKII

Habit Broadly conical, dense, with upswept branches. **Flowers** 5-petaled, in small clusters in late spring. White flushed pink, with yellow anthers. **Fruits** Small, rounded crab apples. Yellow-green, flushed red. **Leaves** Deciduous, broadly oval, sharply and irregularly toothed, pointed. Glossy mid-green, turning golden-bronze to red and purple in autumn.
• NATIVE HABITAT Woodlands of Japan.
• CULTIVATION Grow in any but waterlogged soil.
• PROPAGATION By seed in autumn.

Z 5–8

HEIGHT
40ft (12m)
or more

SPREAD
22ft (7m)

Theaceae	

STEWARTIA MONADELPHA

Habit Broadly columnar. **Flowers** Shallowly cup-shaped, opening from silky buds in summer. Glistening white, with golden stamens.
Leaves Deciduous, elliptic, toothed. Dark green, turning deep red-purple in autumn. **Bark** Peeling. Red-brown, gray-fawn beneath.
• NATIVE HABITAT Woods in Japan and Korea.
• CULTIVATION Grow in humus-rich soil. Shelter from cold winds. Prefers shade at the roots.
• PROPAGATION By softwood cuttings in summer or by seed in autumn.

Z 6–9

HEIGHT
40ft (12m)

SPREAD
25ft (8m)

Aceraceae	

ACER SACCHARUM 'Temple's Upright'

Habit Upright, narrowly conical.
Leaves Deciduous, 5 lobes, heart-shaped at the base. Dark green; brilliant orange and red in autumn.
• NATIVE HABITAT Garden origin.
• CULTIVATION Tolerates lime, but grow in fertile, moisture-retentive, neutral to acid soil for best autumn color. Excellent for planting in confined spaces.
• PROPAGATION By grafting in late winter or early spring or by budding in summer.
• OTHER NAMES *A saccharum* 'Monumentale'.

Z 4–8

HEIGHT
50ft (15m)

SPREAD
10ft (3m)

Aceraceae	

ACER CISSIFOLIUM subsp. HENRYI

Habit Broadly spreading. **Flowers** Tiny, in long, slender racemes. Yellow. **Fruits** 2 seeds, fused together, each with a red wing. **Leaves** Deciduous, divided into 3 elliptic, taper-pointed leaflets. Dark green, turning bright orange and red in autumn.
• NATIVE HABITAT Mountain woods of C. China.
• CULTIVATION Tolerates lime, but grow in moisture-retentive, neutral to acid soil for best autumn color.
• PROPAGATION By seed in autumn.
• OTHER NAMES *A. henryi*.

Z 4–8

HEIGHT
25ft (8m)

SPREAD
30ft (10m)

Hippocastanaceae	SWEET BUCKEYE, YELLOW BUCKEYE

AESCULUS FLAVA

Habit Broadly conical. **Flowers** Appear in conical, upright panicles in late spring to early summer. Yellow, blotched pink. **Fruits** Smooth, rounded husks enclosing usually 2 small, shiny chestnuts. **Leaves** Deciduous, with 5 oval, sharply toothed, short-stalked leaflets. Dark green; red in autumn.
• NATIVE HABITAT Damp woods, E. United States.
• CULTIVATION Tolerates dappled shade. Grow in fertile, moisture-retentive but well-drained soil.
• PROPAGATION By seed in autumn.
• OTHER NAMES *A. octandra*.

Z 3–8

HEIGHT
50ft (15m)

SPREAD
30ft (10m)

Hamamelidaceae	PERSIAN IRONWOOD

PARROTIA PERSICA

Habit Short-trunked, broadly spreading.
Flowers Tiny, apetalous, on bare branches in spring. Crimson anthers. **Leaves** Deciduous, elliptic to oval, wavy-margined. Green, turning yellow, orange, and crimson in autumn.
Bark Flaking. Gray-fawn.
• NATIVE HABITAT Forests of Caucasus, Iran.
• CULTIVATION Grow in deep, fertile soil. Autumn color is best on neutral to acid soils.
• PROPAGATION By softwood cuttings in summer or by seed in autumn.

Z 4–8

HEIGHT
25ft (8m)

SPREAD
40ft (12m)

Nyssaceae	CHINESE TUPELO

NYSSA SINENSIS

Habit Broadly conical. **Leaves** Deciduous, oblong-lance-shaped to elliptic. Dark green, flushed red when young, turning yellow, orange, and rich scarlet in autumn.
• NATIVE HABITAT Stream sides and mountain woodland in C. China.
• CULTIVATION Tolerates semi-shade. Grow in fertile, neutral to acid soil. Resents transplanting and performs best in areas with long, hot summers.
• PROPAGATION By softwood cuttings in summer or by seed in autumn.

Z 7–9

HEIGHT
30ft (10m)

SPREAD
30ft (10m)

Aceraceae	SNAKE-BARK MAPLE

ACER CAPILLIPES

Habit Broadly conical, with ascending branches. **Leaves** Deciduous, with 3 slender-pointed, toothed lobes. Bright green, turning yellow, orange, and crimson in autumn. **Bark** Green and gray, with vertical white stripes.
• NATIVE HABITAT Mountain stream banks and woods in Japan.
• CULTIVATION Tolerates dappled shade but colors best in sun. Grow in fertile, humus-rich, well-drained soil.
• PROPAGATION By seed in autumn.

Z 5–7

HEIGHT
33ft (11m)

SPREAD
25ft (8m)

Rosaceae	HAWTHORN

CRATAEGUS × LAVALLEI 'Carrierei'

Habit Vigorous, broadly spreading. **Flowers** 5-petaled, to 1in (2.5cm) across, in flattened clusters in late spring-early summer. White. **Fruits** Rounded haws, to ¾in (2cm) across. Red. **Leaves** Deciduous, elliptic, tapered at base, leathery. Glossy dark green; red in late autumn.
• NATIVE HABITAT Garden origin.
• CULTIVATION Tolerant of urban pollution, coastal exposure, and any but waterlogged soil.
• PROPAGATION By budding in late summer.
• OTHER NAMES C. carrierei.

Z 4–7

HEIGHT
30ft (10m)

SPREAD
30ft (10m)

Fagaceae	BARTRAM'S OAK

QUERCUS × HETEROPHYLLA

Habit Spreading, with a broadly domed crown.
Fruits Acorns to 1¼in (3cm) long, one-quarter
enclosed in a shallow cup. **Leaves** Deciduous,
variable, oblong to lance-shaped or broadly oval and
deeply lobed. Glossy bright green, turning scarlet
and yellow in autumn.
• **NATIVE HABITAT** Damp woodlands in
E. United States.
• **CULTIVATION** Unsuitable for alkaline soils.
Grow in deep, fertile, moisture-retentive soil.
• **PROPAGATION** By grafting in late winter.

Z 5–9

HEIGHT
50ft (15m)

SPREAD
40ft (12m)

Leguminosae	YELLOWWOOD

CLADRASTIS LUTEA

Habit Broadly spreading, round-headed.
Flowers Fragrant, small, pea-like, in hanging
clusters in early summer. White, marked yellow.
Leaves Deciduous, with 7–9 rounded-oval leaflets.
Dark green, turning clear yellow in autumn.
• **NATIVE HABITAT** Woods and rocky bluffs in
S.E. United States.
• **CULTIVATION** Grow in any fertile soil. Older
specimens are prone to damage by strong winds.
• **PROPAGATION** By seed in autumn or by root
cuttings in late winter.

Z 4–8

HEIGHT
40ft (12m)

SPREAD
30ft (10m)

Rosaceae	MOUNTAIN ASH

SORBUS 'Joseph Rock'

Habit Upright, broadly columnar. **Flowers** Small,
in flattened heads in late spring and early summer.
White. **Fruits** Small, round. Creamy-yellow,
becoming orange-yellow. **Leaves** Deciduous, with
15–19 narrowly oblong, toothed leaflets. Bright
green, turning orange, red, and purple in autumn.
• **NATIVE HABITAT** Uncertain, probably China.
• **CULTIVATION** Grow in fertile, moisture-
retentive soil. Is very susceptible to fireblight.
• **PROPAGATION** By softwood cuttings or budding
in summer or by grafting in winter.

Z 6–7

HEIGHT
30ft (10m)

SPREAD
22ft (7m)

Moraceae	BLACK MULBERRY

MORUS NIGRA

Habit Broadly spreading, with a rounded crown.
Flowers Tiny. Male and female on separate
plants. **Fruits** Small, oval, fleshy, edible clusters.
Dark red to black. **Leaves** Deciduous, heart-
shaped, toothed. Glossy dark green, turning yellow
in autumn.
• **NATIVE HABITAT** Long cultivated, hence origin
obscure.
• **CULTIVATION** Grow in any fertile soil, in a
warm, sunny, sheltered site, for good cropping.
• **PROPAGATION** By seed in autumn.

Z 6–8

HEIGHT
40ft (12m)

SPREAD
50ft (15m)

Betulaceae	WEST HIMALAYAN BIRCH

BETULA UTILIS var. *JACQUEMONTII*

Habit Open, broadly conical. *Flowers* Catkins. Male: to 6in (15cm) long; female: shorter, upright, inconspicuous, on same plant. *Leaves* Deciduous, oval, with tapering point, toothed. Dark green, turning rich golden-yellow in autumn. *Bark* Smooth, peeling. Shining white, with pale brown markings.

• NATIVE HABITAT High mountain forests of the Himalayas.

• CULTIVATION Grow in any moist but well-drained soil, in an open, sunny position. It makes a beautiful tree for specimen plantings and is especially effective in group plantings against a dark backdrop, where the brilliant white bark may be seen to best advantage.

• PROPAGATION By softwood cuttings in early summer or by seed in autumn. Birches hybridize readily. Seed may not come true.

Z 5–7

HEIGHT
50ft (15m)

SPREAD
23ft (7.5m)

Magnoliaceae	

MICHELIA DOLTSOPA

Habit Broadly spreading. **Flowers** Fragrant, magnolia-like, in late winter-early spring. Many white to pale yellow petals. **Leaves** Evergreen or semi-evergreen, oval. Glossy dark green.
• NATIVE HABITAT Forests of E. Himalayas.
• CULTIVATION Tolerates partial shade. Grow in humus-rich soil. Suitable for mild, sheltered sites or cool conservatories. Water freely when in full growth, less in winter.
• PROPAGATION By semi-ripe cuttings in summer or by seed in autumn or spring.

Z 9–10

HEIGHT
40ft (12m)

SPREAD
40ft (12m)

Leguminosae	MIMOSA, SILVER WATTLE

ACACIA DEALBATA

Habit Fast-growing, broadly conical.
Flowers Fragrant, tiny, in globular clusters, carried in dense panicles in late winter to early spring. Yellow. **Leaves** Evergreen, feathery, with many tiny leaflets. Blue-green.
• NATIVE HABITAT Mountain gullies and stream sides in S.E. Australia and Tasmania.
• CULTIVATION Grow in any well-drained soil in a warm, sunny, sheltered site.
• PROPAGATION By seed in spring.

Z 8–10

HEIGHT
43ft (13m)

SPREAD
25ft (8m)

Myrtaceae	CHRISTMAS TREE, POHUTUKAWA

METROSIDEROS EXCELSA

Habit Robust, rounded, wide-spreading, often multi-stemmed. **Flowers** Carried in broad clusters in winter. Small petals with many long, showy, crimson stamens. **Leaves** Evergreen, elliptic to oblong, leathery. Gray-green above, densely white-downy beneath.
• NATIVE HABITAT Warm to temperate coastal forests in New Zealand.
• CULTIVATION Grow in fertile, free-draining soil or soil mix. Water freely when in growth, less in low temperatures. The tree may be pruned after

flowering, if necessary. It makes a handsome specimen when grown in large containers in the conservatory and may bear flowers, even on quite young plants.
• PROPAGATION By semi-ripe cuttings in summer or by seed in spring.
• OTHER NAMES *M. tomentosa.*

Z 10–11

HEIGHT
43ft (13m)

SPREAD
43ft (13m)

Ericaceae

ARBUTUS X *ANDRACHNOIDES*

Habit Dense, bushy when young, later broadly spreading. *Flowers* Small, urn-shaped, in pendent clusters at the branch tips, from autumn to spring. White. *Fruits* Small, strawberry-like, ripening with the previous year's flowers. Red.
Leaves Evergreen, oval to elliptic, toothed. Glossy dark green, paler beneath. *Bark* Peeling in strips. Red-brown.
• NATIVE HABITAT Thickets and woodland of Greece.
• CULTIVATION Tolerates alkaline soil, but prefers a deep, fertile, humus-rich soil. Provide shelter from cold, dry winds, especially when young. A fine specimen for open areas in the woodland garden, *A.* x *andrachnoides* is a naturally occurring hybrid between *A. andrachne* and *A. unedo*.
• PROPAGATION By semi-ripe cuttings in late summer.

Z 8–9

HEIGHT
28ft (9m)

SPREAD
25ft (8m)

Moraceae	

FICUS BENJAMINA 'Variegata'

Habit Dense, round-headed, weeping, often with aerial roots. **Leaves** Evergreen, slender, oval, pointed. Lustrous, rich green, with white variegation.
- NATIVE HABITAT Garden origin.
- CULTIVATION Grow in fertile, free-draining soil or soil mix. Water freely when in full growth, sparingly when temperatures are low. An elegant specimen for the home or the conservatory.
- PROPAGATION By leaf bud or stem-tip cuttings or by air-layering in summer.

☼ ◊

Z 10–11

HEIGHT
43ft (13m)

SPREAD
30ft (10m)

Myrtaceae	SNOW GUM

EUCALYPTUS PAUCIFLORA subsp. *NIPHOPHILA*

Habit Open, spreading. **Flowers** Small, in clusters in leaf axils in summer. White. **Leaves** Evergreen. Juvenile: oval to rounded, dull blue-green. Adult: broadly lance-shaped, glossy green to deep blue-green. **Bark** Peeling. White and gray.
- NATIVE HABITAT Mountains of S.E. Australia and Tasmania.
- CULTIVATION Grow in well-drained soil.
- PROPAGATION By seed in spring or autumn.
- OTHER NAMES *E. niphophila.*

☼ ◊
❄❄

Z 8–10

HEIGHT
40ft (12m)

SPREAD
20ft (6m)

Myrtaceae	GHOST GUM, WHITE SALLY

EUCALYPTUS PAUCIFLORA

Habit Open, broadly spreading. **Flowers** Small, in small clusters in the leaf axils in summer. White. **Leaves** Evergreen. Juvenile: oval to rounded. Gray. Adult: lance-shaped. Glossy gray to deep green. **Bark** Peeling. White and gray; young shoots red to cream.
- NATIVE HABITAT From sea level to mountains of S.E. Australia and Tasmania.
- CULTIVATION Grow in fertile, well-drained soil.
- PROPAGATION By seed in spring or autumn in a cold frame or greenhouse.

☼ ◊
❄❄

Z 9–10

HEIGHT
40ft (12m)

SPREAD
22ft (7m)

Palmae	CHUSAN PALM, CHINESE WINDMILL PALM

TRACHYCARPUS FORTUNEI

Habit Upright, with unbranched trunk. **Flowers** Tiny, fragrant, in large, drooping clusters in early summer; male and female in separate clusters. Yellow. **Fruits** Small, kidney-shaped, 3-lobed berries. Blue-black. **Leaves** Evergreen, fan-shaped, to 4ft (120cm) across. Dark green above, blue-green beneath.
- NATIVE HABITAT Mountains of C. and S. China.
- CULTIVATION Grow in any fertile, well-drained soil. Provide shelter from cold, dry winds.
- PROPAGATION By seed in spring.

☼ ◊
❄❄

Z 8–10

HEIGHT
30ft (10m)

SPREAD
8ft (2.5m)

Rosaceae	AMUR CHERRY, MANCHURIAN CHERRY

PRUNUS MAACKII

Habit Vigorous, broadly conical.
Flowers Small, fragrant, with prominent stamens, in dense clusters at the tips of old shoots, as the leaves emerge in mid-spring. White. **Fruits** Tiny, rounded, berry-like. Black when ripe.
Leaves Deciduous, oval, long-pointed at the tip, finely toothed. Dark green, turning yellow in autumn. **Bark** Peeling. Shining, golden orange-brown.
• NATIVE HABITAT Woodlands of N.E. Asia.
• CULTIVATION Grow in any but waterlogged soil.

A beautiful species for specimen plantings, especially in small gardens. It has a long season of interest and its attractive bark is seen to best advantage in winter. The shining bark is sometimes obscured by algal growth; remove with clean water and a soft brush in summer.
• PROPAGATION By seed in autumn.

☼ ◊
✹ ✹ ✹

Z 3–6

HEIGHT
30ft (10m)

SPREAD
25ft (8m)

Fagaceae	

QUERCUS MYRSINIFOLIA

Habit Open-branched, broadly spreading.
Fruits Acorns, to ¾in (2cm) long, rounded,
pointed at the tip, one-third enclosed in a ridged
cup. **Leaves** Evergreen, lance-shaped, short-
pointed. Glossy dark green above, blue-green
beneath; bronze-red when young,
• NATIVE HABITAT Forests of China and Japan.
• CULTIVATION Unsuitable for alkaline soils.
Grow in deep, fertile soils, with shelter from winds.
• PROPAGATION By seed in autumn.
• OTHER NAMES *Q. vibrayeana.*

☼ ◊
❀ ❀

Z 7–9

HEIGHT
43ft (13m)

SPREAD
23ft (7.5m)

Aceraceae	MOOSEWOOD

ACER PENSYLVANICUM

Habit Broadly columnar. **Leaves** Deciduous,
with 3 triangular, taper-pointed, toothed lobes.
Dark olive green, turning clear yellow in autumn.
Bark Boldly striped in rich jade green and white.
• NATIVE HABITAT Damp woodlands of E. North
America.
• CULTIVATION Does not thrive on alkaline soils.
Tolerates dappled shade, but colors best in sun.
Grow in deep, fertile, humus-rich soil.
• PROPAGATION By seed in autumn.
• OTHER NAMES *A. striatum.*

☼ ◊
❀ ❀ ❀

Z 3–7

HEIGHT
To 40ft
(12m)

SPREAD
25ft (8m)

Araliaceae	AUSTRALIAN UMBRELLA TREE

SCHEFFLERA ACTINOPHYLLA

Habit Upright, with a broadly spreading crown.
Flowers Small, in large sprays in summer or
autumn. Dull red. **Leaves** Evergreen, oblong, in
rosettes at branch tips. Glossy bright green.
• NATIVE HABITAT N. Australia and New Guinea.
• CULTIVATION Grow in fertile, moisture-
retentive soil or soil mix. Water freely in growth. An
elegant specimen for the home or conservatory.
• PROPAGATION By seed or air-layering in spring
or by semi-ripe cuttings in summer.
• OTHER NAMES *Brassaia actinophylla.*

☼ ◊

Z 9–11

HEIGHT
40ft (12m)

SPREAD
28ft (9m)

Palmae	CHILEAN WINE PALM, COQUITO PALM

JUBAEA CHILENSIS

Habit Slow-growing, with an unbranched trunk.
Flowers Small, in large clusters between the leaves
in spring. Maroon and yellow. **Fruits** Egg-shaped,
in woody, yellow capsules. **Leaves** Evergreen,
large, feather-shaped. Silvery-green.
• NATIVE HABITAT Coastal valleys of Chile.
• CULTIVATION Grow in fertile soil or soil mix.
Water moderately in growth, otherwise sparingly.
An elegant specimen for the home or conservatory.
• PROPAGATION By seed in spring.
• OTHER NAMES *J. spectabilis.*

☼ ◊

Z 10–11

HEIGHT
40ft (12m)

SPREAD
15ft (5m)

Palmae	CHINESE FAN PALM

LIVISTONA CHINENSIS

Habit Slow-growing, with a stout, unbranched trunk. **Leaves** Evergreen, fan-shaped, 3–10ft (1–3m) across. Dull yellow-green.
• NATIVE HABITAT Damp soils of S. Japan and S. Taiwan.
• CULTIVATION Tolerates partial shade. Grow in fertile, neutral to acid soil or soil mix. Water moderately when in growth, less in winter. Suitable for pots or tubs in the home or the conservatory.
• PROPAGATION By seed in spring.
• OTHER NAMES *L. oliviformis.*

Z 9–11

HEIGHT
40ft (12m)

SPREAD
15ft (5m)

Corynocarpaceae	

CORYNOCARPUS LAEVIGATA

Habit Upright, conical. **Flowers** Small, in panicles in spring to summer. Greenish-white. **Fruits** Plum-like. Orange. **Leaves** Evergreen, elliptic-oblong, leathery. Glossy dark green.
• NATIVE HABITAT New Zealand.
• CULTIVATION Tolerates partial shade. Grow in fertile, moisture-retentive but free-draining soil or soil mix. Water moderately when in full growth, less in winter. Prune after flowering if necessary.
• PROPAGATION By seed when ripe or by semi-ripe cuttings in summer.

Z 10–11

HEIGHT
46ft (14m)

SPREAD
25ft (8m)

Salicaceae	DRAGON'S CLAW WILLOW

SALIX BABYLONICA var. PEKINENSIS 'Tortuosa'

Habit Fast-growing, spreading, with ascending, twisted shoots. **Leaves** Deciduous, lance-shaped, very contorted. Bright green.
• NATIVE HABITAT Origin uncertain.
• CULTIVATION Grows in any but very dry soil, but does best in fertile, moisture-retentive soil. Plant well away from drains, since roots may invade.
• PROPAGATION By semi-ripe cuttings in summer or by hardwood cuttings in winter.
• OTHER NAMES *S. matsudana* 'Tortuosa'.

Z 5–8

HEIGHT
50ft (15m)

SPREAD
25ft (8m)

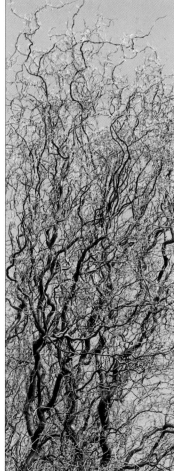

Rosaceae	MEDLAR

MESPILUS GERMANICA

Habit Broadly spreading, sometimes shrubby. **Flowers** Large, 5-petaled, on short stalks, in late spring to early summer. White. **Fruits** Flattened pear-shape, fleshy, edible when over-ripe. Brown-green. **Leaves** Deciduous, elliptic to oblong. Dark green, turning russet-brown in autumn.
• NATIVE HABITAT Forests, mountain thickets, and woodland edge, in S.W. Asia and S. Europe.
• CULTIVATION Tolerates semi-shade and almost any fertile, free-draining soil.
• PROPAGATION By seed in autumn.

Rosaceae	CUTLEAF HAWTHORN

CRATAEGUS LACINIATA

Habit Broadly spreading. **Flowers** Cup-shaped, in dense clusters in early summer. White. **Fruits** Rounded-oblong. Red, flushed yellow in autumn. **Leaves** Deciduous, diamond-shaped, deeply lobed. Glossy dark green above, gray-downy beneath. **Bark** Flaking. Gray.
• NATIVE HABITAT Thickets and woodland edge in S.E. Europe and S.W. Asia.
• CULTIVATION Grow in any but waterlogged soil.
• PROPAGATION By seed in autumn.
• OTHER NAMES C. orientalis.

Z 5–8

HEIGHT
23ft (7.5m)

SPREAD
25ft (8m)

Z 6–8

HEIGHT
25ft (8m)

SPREAD
25ft (8m)

Hippocastanaceae	CALIFORNIA BUCKEYE

AESCULUS CALIFORNICA

Habit Broadly spreading, often multi-stemmed. **Flowers** Small, fragrant, in dense, slender, upright panicles, to 8in (20cm) long, in summer. Creamy or pale pink. **Fruits** Rough-textured, pear-shaped husks enclosing a single, large seed. **Leaves** Deciduous, with 5–7 narrowly oblong, taper-pointed leaflets. Dark blue-green.
• NATIVE HABITAT Dry hillsides and canyons of California.
• CULTIVATION A. californica is an easily cultivated species, tolerant of a range of soil types, but preferring deep, fertile, well-drained soil. Provide it with a warm, sunny site, with shelter from cold winds. Avoid planting in frost pocket areas where young growth will be damaged by late frosts.
• PROPAGATION By seed in autumn.

Z 7–8

HEIGHT
25ft (8m)

SPREAD
30ft (10m)

Cornaceae	

CORNUS FLORIDA 'White Cloud'

Habit Broadly spreading. **Flowers** Tiny, in dense clusters, surrounded by 4 broad, white bracts, in late spring. Green. **Leaves** Deciduous, oval to elliptic, pointed. Dark green, often bronzed, turning red and purple in autumn.
• NATIVE HABITAT Garden origin.
• CULTIVATION Unsuitable for shallow, alkaline soils. Tolerates dappled shade. Grow in deep, fertile, moisture-retentive soil.
• PROPAGATION By softwood cuttings in summer.

Z 5–9

HEIGHT
25ft (8m)

SPREAD
29ft (9.5m)

Rosaceae	FUJI CHERRY

PRUNUS INCISA

Habit Vigorous, broadly spreading, often shrubby. **Flowers** Delicate, single, saucer-shaped, in clusters in mid-spring. White or pale pink. **Leaves** Deciduous, oval, sharply toothed, taper-pointed. Red-bronze when young, later dark green, hairy above and beneath; orange-red in autumn.
• NATIVE HABITAT Mountain woodlands in Japan.
• CULTIVATION Tolerates alkaline soils. Useful as hedging. Trim after flowering.
• PROPAGATION By seed in autumn.

Z 6–8

HEIGHT
25ft (8m)

SPREAD
25ft (8m)

Rosaceae	FLOWERING CHERRY

PRUNUS 'Shogetsu'

Habit Wide-spreading, with a broad, flattened crown. **Flowers** Large, double, with sharply toothed petal margins, opening from pink buds, carried in pendent clusters in late spring. White. **Leaves** Deciduous, oval. Bright green, later dark green, turning rich orange-red in autumn.
• NATIVE HABITAT Garden origin.
• CULTIVATION Grow in any well-drained soils, including alkaline ones.
• PROPAGATION By softwood cuttings in summer.
• OTHER NAMES *P*. 'Shimidsu'.

Z 5–7

HEIGHT
22ft (7m)

SPREAD
30ft (10m)

Rosaceae	GREAT WHITE CHERRY

PRUNUS 'Taihaku'

Habit Vigorous, broadly spreading. **Flowers** Fragrant, very large, single, saucer-shaped, with notched petal-tips, in clusters in mid-spring. Pure white, pink in bud. **Leaves** Deciduous, oval, finely toothed. Coppery-bronze when young, later dark green, turning red-gold in autumn.
• NATIVE HABITAT Garden origin.
• CULTIVATION Grow in any well-drained soils, including alkaline ones.
• PROPAGATION By softwood cuttings in summer.
• OTHER NAMES *P*. 'Tai Haku'.

Z 6–8

HEIGHT
25ft (8m)

SPREAD
30ft (10m)

Rosaceae	FLOWERING CHERRY

PRUNUS 'Ukon'

Habit Vigorous, funnel-shaped, horizontally spreading. *Flowers* Large, fragrant, double or semi-double, in clusters in mid-spring. Pale yellowish, tinted green. *Leaves* Deciduous, oval. Pale bronze on emergence, later dark green, turning rich rusty-red or purple in autumn.
• NATIVE HABITAT Garden origin.
• CULTIVATION Grow in any well-drained soils, including alkaline ones.
• PROPAGATION By softwood cuttings in summer.

Z 5–6

HEIGHT
25ft (8m)

SPREAD
30ft (10m)

Rosaceae	FLOWERING CHERRY

PRUNUS 'Amanogawa'

Habit Vigorous, narrowly upright, with strongly ascending branches. *Flowers* Large, double, opening with or before the leaves, in mid-spring. Pale pink, with yellow anthers. *Leaves* Deciduous, oval, finely toothed. Coppery-bronze when young, later dark green, turning red-gold in autumn.
• NATIVE HABITAT Garden origin.
• CULTIVATION Grow in any well-drained soils, including alkaline ones. An attractive specimen for small gardens, but branches tend to splay with age.
• PROPAGATION By softwood cuttings in summer.

Z 5–7

HEIGHT
25ft (8m)

SPREAD
10ft (3m)

Rosaceae	MOUNT FUJI CHERRY

PRUNUS 'Shirotae'

Habit Broadly spreading, with slightly arching branches. *Flowers* Large, fragrant, single or semi-double, bowl-shaped, in clusters in mid-spring. Pure white. *Leaves* Deciduous, oval, fringed. Bright green on emergence, later dark green, turning red-gold in autumn.
• NATIVE HABITAT Garden origin.
• CULTIVATION Grow in any well-drained soils, including alkaline ones.
• PROPAGATION By softwood cuttings in summer.
• OTHER NAMES *P.* 'Mount Fuji'.

Z 6–8

HEIGHT
25ft (8m)

SPREAD
30ft (10m)

Rosaceae	YOSHINO CHERRY

PRUNUS × *YEDOENSIS*

Habit Wide-spreading, with a broad, rounded crown. *Flowers* Almond-scented, petals notched at the tip, in delicate clusters in early to mid-spring. Pale pink, fading to white. *Leaves* Deciduous, elliptic, taper-pointed, sharply toothed. Pale green on emergence, later dark green, turning rich red-purple in autumn.
• NATIVE HABITAT Hilly woodlands of Japan.
• CULTIVATION Grow in any well-drained soils, including alkaline ones.
• PROPAGATION By softwood cuttings in summer.

Z 5–8

HEIGHT
26ft (8.5m)

SPREAD
30ft (10m)

Rosaceae	FLOWERING CHERRY

PRUNUS 'Pandora'

Habit Broadly upright, with nodding branch tips, sometimes shrubby. **Flowers** Large, single, in profuse clusters in early spring, before the leaves. Pale shell-pink, darker at petal margins, opening from pink buds. **Leaves** Deciduous, oval-elliptic. Bronze-red on emergence, later dark green, and coloring well in autumn in shades of orange and red.
• NATIVE HABITAT Garden origin.
• CULTIVATION Grow in any well-drained soils, including alkaline ones. A vigorous hybrid between

P. subhirtella 'Ascendens Rosea' and *P.* x *yedoensis*. This, and the other flowering cherries described in this volume, make exceptionally beautiful specimen trees. Many ornamental cherries are ideal for small gardens, as they are small in stature and most are of interest in spring and again when the foliage colors in autumn.
• PROPAGATION By softwood cuttings in summer.

Z 6–8

HEIGHT
30ft (10m)

SPREAD
25ft (8m)

Rosaceae	FLOWERING CHERRY

PRUNUS 'Spire'

Habit Vase-shaped, conical when young.
Flowers Large, single, in profusion in early to mid-spring, with the emerging leaves. Soft almond-pink. **Leaves** Deciduous, broadly oval, coarsely toothed, short-pointed at tip. Bronze on emergence, later matte dark green, turning orange-red in autumn.
• NATIVE HABITAT Garden origin.
• CULTIVATION Grow in any well-drained soils, including alkaline ones.
• PROPAGATION By softwood cuttings in summer.
• OTHER NAMES *P. x hillieri* 'Spire'.

Z 5–7

HEIGHT
30ft (10m)

SPREAD
22ft (7m)

Rosaceae	SARGENT CHERRY

PRUNUS SARGENTII

Habit Broadly spreading, round-headed.
Flowers Single, with notched petal-tips, in clusters in mid-spring with, or just before, the leaves. Pink.
Fruits Shiny, rounded to egg-shaped berries. Purple-black. **Leaves** Deciduous, elliptic to broadly oval, long-pointed. Bronze-red when young, later dark green. Brilliant yellow, red, and maroon in autumn.
• NATIVE HABITAT Mountain woods of Japan.
• CULTIVATION Grow in any well-drained soil.
• PROPAGATION By seed in autumn.
• OTHER NAMES *P. serrulata* var. *sachalinensis*.

Z 4–7

HEIGHT
30ft (10m)

SPREAD
50ft (15m)

Rosaceae	FLOWERING CHERRY

PRUNUS 'Hokusai'

Habit Vigorous, wide-spreading. **Flowers** Large, semi-double, opening from pink buds, carried in pendent, long-stalked clusters in mid-spring. Soft pale pink, darkening at the center with age.
Leaves Deciduous, oval. Bronze on emergence, later dark green, turning rich orange-red in autumn.
• NATIVE HABITAT Garden origin.
• CULTIVATION Grow in any well-drained soils, including alkaline ones.
• PROPAGATION By softwood cuttings in summer.
• OTHER NAMES *P.* 'Uzu-zakura'.

Z 5–7

HEIGHT
25ft (8m)

SPREAD
40ft (12m)

Rosaceae	SPRING CHERRY

PRUNUS X SUBHIRTELLA 'Stellata'

Habit Upright, slightly spreading, forming a rounded crown. **Flowers** Single, with long, narrow, pointed petals, in large clusters at the branch tips in early to mid-spring. Clear shell-pink.
Leaves Deciduous, narrowly elliptic, toothed. Dark green, turning yellow in autumn.
• NATIVE HABITAT Garden origin.
• CULTIVATION Grow in any well-drained soils, including alkaline ones.
• PROPAGATION By softwood cuttings in summer.
• OTHER NAMES *P. x subhirtella* 'Pink Star'.

Z 4–8

HEIGHT
25ft (8m)

SPREAD
25ft (8m)

Rosaceae	FLOWERING CHERRY

PRUNUS 'Shirofugen'

Habit Vigorous, wide-spreading, with a flattened crown. **Flowers** Large, fragrant, double, carried in long-stalked clusters in late spring. White, becoming pale pink with age, opening from pink buds. **Leaves** Deciduous, oval. Bronze-crimson when young, then dark green, orange-red in autumn.
• NATIVE HABITAT Garden origin.
• CULTIVATION Grow in any well-drained soils, including alkaline ones. One of the latest, and longest, in bloom.
• PROPAGATION By softwood cuttings in summer.

Rosaceae	DOUBLE FLOWERING ALMOND

PRUNUS DULCIS 'Roseoplena'

Habit Broadly spreading. **Flowers** Large, double, opening from deep pink buds, with the leaves in early spring. Pink, fading to pale pink or white. **Leaves** Deciduous, lance-shaped to narrowly elliptic, taper-pointed, finely toothed. Dark green.
• NATIVE HABITAT Species occurs in scrub, woodlands, and on dry hillsides in N. Africa and S.W. Asia. Garden origin.
• CULTIVATION Grow in any but waterlogged soil
• PROPAGATION By softwood cuttings in summer.

Z 5–7

HEIGHT 25ft (8m)

SPREAD 30ft (10m)

Z 7–9

HEIGHT 25ft (8m)

SPREAD 25ft (8m)

Rosaceae	FLOWERING CHERRY

PRUNUS 'Pink Perfection'

Habit Vase-shaped. **Flowers** Large, double, carried in long-stalked, pendulous clusters in mid- to late spring. Pale rose-pink, opening from deep pink buds. **Leaves** Deciduous, oval. Bronze when young, then dark green, turning orange-red in autumn.
• NATIVE HABITAT Garden origin.
• CULTIVATION Grow in any well-drained soil, including alkaline soil.
• PROPAGATION By softwood cuttings in summer.

Z 6–8

HEIGHT 25ft (8m)

SPREAD 25ft (8m)

Rosaceae	FLOWERING CHERRY

PRUNUS 'Accolade'

Habit Broadly spreading, round-headed.
Flowers Semi-double, in a profusion of pendulous clusters in early spring, with or just before the leaves. Rich pink, deep pink in bud.
Leaves Deciduous, elliptic-oblong, sharply toothed, pointed. Dark green, turning orange-red in autumn.
• NATIVE HABITAT Garden origin.
• CULTIVATION Grow in any well-drained soils, including alkaline ones.
• PROPAGATION By softwood cuttings in summer.

Z 4–7

HEIGHT
25ft (8m) or more

SPREAD
25ft (8m)

Rosaceae	

PRUNUS 'Kiku-shidare-zakura'

Habit Weeping, with strongly pendulous branches. *Flowers* Large, very double, with pointed petals, densely clustered along pendent branches from mid- to late spring. Deep, clear pink.
Leaves Deciduous, lance-shaped. Pale green and slightly bronzed on emergence, later dark green.
• NATIVE HABITAT Garden origin.
• CULTIVATION Grow in any well-drained soils, including alkaline ones.
• PROPAGATION By softwood cuttings in summer.
• OTHER NAMES *P*. 'Cheal's Weeping'.

Z 6–8

HEIGHT
To 25ft (8m) usually less

SPREAD
22ft (7m)

Leguminosae	JUDAS TREE

CERCIS SILIQUASTRUM

Habit Broadly spreading, with a rounded crown.
Flowers Small, pea-like, in clusters in mid-spring, with or before the leaves. Bright pink. *Fruits* Long, purplish-red pods. *Leaves* Deciduous, heart-shaped. Bronze when young, then dark blue-green.
• NATIVE HABITAT Dry, rocky hills of S.E. Europe and W. Asia.
• CULTIVATION Grow in deep, fertile soil, which must be well drained. Flowers best in areas with long, hot summers. An attractive foliage specimen.
• PROPAGATION By seed in autumn.

Z 7–9

HEIGHT
30ft (10m)

SPREAD
30ft (10m)

Rosaceae	WEEPING HIGAN CHERRY

PRUNUS × *SUBHIRTELLA* 'Pendula Rubra'

Habit Weeping, dome-shaped, with slender branches. *Flowers* Single, in spring, before the leaves. Deep pink, ruby-red in bud.
Leaves Deciduous, lance-shaped, finely toothed. Pale green on emergence, later dark green.
• NATIVE HABITAT Garden origin.
• CULTIVATION Grow in any well-drained soils, including alkaline ones.
• PROPAGATION By softwood cuttings in summer.
• OTHER NAMES *P*. × *subhirtella* 'Ibara Ito Sakura'.

Z 4–8

HEIGHT
25ft (8m)

SPREAD
25ft (8m)

Rosaceae	CRAB APPLE

MALUS × MAGDEBURGENSIS

Habit Rounded when young, later spreading; sometimes shrubby. *Flowers* Large, semi-double, in dense clusters in late spring. Deep pink, deep red in bud. *Fruits* Small crab apples. Yellow. *Leaves* Deciduous, elliptic, pointed. Dark green, downy beneath.
• NATIVE HABITAT Garden origin.
• CULTIVATION Tolerates dappled shade, but flowers and fruits best in sun. Grow in any but waterlogged soil. This, and other crab apples (*Malus*), makes a beautiful specimen tree for smaller gardens. They have a long season of interest, with flowers in spring and fruits in autumn that are also useful for making jellies and preserves. Many also color well in autumn.
• PROPAGATION By budding in summer or by grafting in winter.
• OTHER NAMES *M.* 'Magdeburgensis'.

☀ ◊
❀ ❀ ❀

Z 4–7

HEIGHT
22ft (7m)

SPREAD
25ft (8m)

Rosaceae	FLOWERING PEACH ·

PRUNUS PERSICA 'Prince Charming'

Habit Upright, bushy-headed. *Flowers* Double, carried singly or in pairs, along bare branches in mid-spring. Deep rose-pink. *Leaves* Deciduous, narrowly elliptic to lance-shaped. Bright green.
• NATIVE HABITAT Garden origin.
• CULTIVATION Grow in any well-drained soils, including alkaline ones. Susceptible to peach leaf curl.
• PROPAGATION By softwood cuttings in summer.

Z 5–9

HEIGHT
22ft (7m)

SPREAD
15ft (5m)

Rosaceae	FLOWERING CHERRY

PRUNUS 'Yae-murasaki'

Habit Slow-growing, wide-spreading. *Flowers* Semi-double, in profusion in mid-spring. Pink-purple, opening from red buds. *Leaves* Deciduous, oval, toothed. Coppery-red when young, later dark green, turning brilliant orange-red in autumn.
• NATIVE HABITAT Garden origin.
• CULTIVATION Grow in any well-drained soils, including alkaline ones.
• PROPAGATION By softwood cuttings in summer.
• OTHER NAMES *P.* 'Yae-marasakizakura'.

Z 6–8

HEIGHT
15ft (5m)

SPREAD
25ft (8m)

Sterculiaceae	

DOMBEYA X *CAYEUXII*

Habit Bushy, rounded. *Flowers* Small, in dense, round, pendent clusters in winter or spring. Pink. *Leaves* Evergreen, rounded, toothed, heart-shaped at base, hairy. Dark green.
• NATIVE HABITAT Garden origin.
• CULTIVATION Tolerates partial shade. Grow in fertile, free-draining soil or soil mix. Water freely when in full growth, less in low temperatures. Prune, if necessary, after flowering.
• PROPAGATION By semi-ripe cuttings in summer.

Z 10–11

HEIGHT
20ft (6m)

SPREAD
22ft (7m)

Rosaceae	CRAB APPLE

MALUS 'Royalty'

Habit Broadly pyramidal, spreading. *Flowers* Large, in clusters from mid- to late spring. Crimson-purple, opening from dark red buds. *Fruits* Small crab apples. Glossy dark red, black when ripe. *Leaves* Deciduous, oval, taper-pointed. Glossy red-purple, turning red in late autumn.
• NATIVE HABITAT Garden origin.
• CULTIVATION Tolerates dappled shade but flowers and fruits best in sun.
• PROPAGATION By budding in summer or by grafting in winter.

Z 4–7

HEIGHT
25ft (8m)

SPREAD
25ft (8m)

Rosaceae	CRAB APPLE

MALUS 'Lemoinei'

Habit Round-headed, spreading. **Flowers** Large, single, in profusion in late spring. Wine-red, dark red in bud. **Fruits** Small, glossy, cherry-like crab apples. Red-purple. **Leaves** Deciduous, oval. Deep red-purple when young, later bronze-red, turning red in late autumn.
• NATIVE HABITAT Garden origin.
• CULTIVATION Tolerates dappled shade. Flowers and fruits best in sun. Avoid waterlogged soil.
• PROPAGATION By budding in summer or by grafting in winter.

☀ ◊
❀ ❀ ❀

Z 4–7

HEIGHT
25ft (8m)

SPREAD
25ft (8m)

Hippocastanaceae	

AESCULUS × *NEGLECTA* 'Erythroblastos'

Habit Slow-growing, broadly columnar.
Flowers Small, narrow, in open, upright panicles in summer. Creamy-white, flushed peach-pink.
Leaves Deciduous, with 5 elliptic, taper-pointed, finely toothed leaflets. Bright pink, later yellow, then dark green, turning orange and red in autumn.
• NATIVE HABITAT Garden origin. Species occurs on the coastal plains of S.E. United States.
• CULTIVATION Grow in any deep, fertile soil.
• PROPAGATION By budding in late summer or by grafting in winter.

☀ ◊
❀ ❀ ❀

Z 5–8

HEIGHT
30ft (10m)

SPREAD
25ft (8m)

Aceraceae	SYCAMORE MAPLE

ACER PSEUDOPLATANUS 'Brilliantissimum'

Habit Slow-growing, spreading, with a domed crown. **Leaves** Deciduous, with 5 coarsely toothed lobes. Brilliant shrimp-pink on emergence, later pale with green veins, becoming yellow-green.
• NATIVE HABITAT Garden origin.
• CULTIVATION Tolerates exposure and almost any soil. Smaller and slower-growing than the species. An attractive specimen for smaller gardens.
• PROPAGATION By grafting in late winter or early spring or by budding in summer.

☀ ◊
❀ ❀

Z 4–7

HEIGHT
20ft (6m) or
more

SPREAD
25ft (8m)

Leguminosae	KOWHAI

SOPHORA TETRAPTERA

Habit Open, spreading, with slender branches.
Flowers Small, tubular, in pendulous racemes in late spring. Golden-yellow. **Leaves** Semi-evergreen or deciduous, with up to 20 pairs of tiny, elliptic leaflets. Dark green.
• NATIVE HABITAT Forest margins and open woods in New Zealand and Chile.
• CULTIVATION Grow in any well-drained soil, in a warm, sunny, sheltered site.
• PROPAGATION By seed in autumn or by semi-ripe cuttings in summer.

☀ ◊
❀ ❀ ❀

Z 8–10

HEIGHT
30ft (10m)

SPREAD
15ft (5m)

Cornaceae	WEDDING CAKE TREE

CORNUS CONTROVERSA 'Variegata'

Habit Slow-growing, tiered, horizontally branching. **Flowers** Tiny, in large, flattened heads in summer. White. **Leaves** Deciduous, alternate, broadly oval to elliptic, taper-pointed. Bright green, broadly margined with creamy-white.
• NATIVE HABITAT Species occurs in thickets and woodland in E. Asia. Garden origin.
• CULTIVATION Tolerates dappled shade. Grow in deep, fertile, moisture-retentive soil. The tree requires no regular pruning, which would spoil the gracefully tiered habit; the branches and foliage are held in distinctive, well-separated horizontal layers. It is an excellent specimen for open areas in the woodland garden, and because it is very slow-growing, it is also suitable for medium-sized gardens as a lawn specimen. *C. alternifolia* 'Argentea' is similar, but smaller.
• PROPAGATION By grafting in winter.

Z 4–8

HEIGHT
25ft (8m) or more

SPREAD
25ft (8m)

Cornaceae	

CORNUS ALTERNIFOLIA 'Argentea'

Habit Dense, with tiered, horizontally spreading branches. *Flowers* Tiny, in small heads in spring. Creamy. *Leaves* Deciduous, alternate, narrowly oval. Bright green, margins variegated creamy-white.
• NATIVE HABITAT Species occurs in damp woods of E. North America. Garden origin.
• CULTIVATION Tolerates dappled shade. Grow in deep, fertile, moisture-retentive soil.
• PROPAGATION By grafting in winter.
• OTHER NAMES *C. alternifolia* 'Variegata'.

☼ ◊
❀ ❀ ❀

Z 3–7

HEIGHT
25ft (8m)

SPREAD
25ft (8m)

Aceraceae	HAWTHORN MAPLE

ACER CRATAEGIFOLIUM 'Veitchii'

Habit Bushy, round-headed to conical. *Flowers* Small, in slender racemes in spring. Yellow-green. *Fruits* 2 seeds, fused together, each with a red-tinged wing. *Leaves* Deciduous, with 3 toothed lobes, the middle lobe long and taper-pointed. Dark green, blotched white and pale green, turning pink and red-purple in autumn.
• NATIVE HABITAT Garden origin.
• CULTIVATION Grow in any fertile soil.
• PROPAGATION By grafting in late winter or early spring or by budding in summer.

☼ ◊
❀ ❀ ❀

Z 6–8

HEIGHT
28ft (9m)

SPREAD
25ft (8m)

Rosaceae	YELLOW HAWTHORN

CRATAEGUS FLAVA

Habit Spreading, with a broadly rounded crown. *Flowers* Small, in neat, rounded clusters in late spring and early summer. Creamy-white, with pink anthers. *Fruits* Rounded to pear-shaped, edible. Yellow. *Leaves* Deciduous, small, broadly oval to oblong, leathery. Bright green.
• NATIVE HABITAT E. North America.
• CULTIVATION Tolerates coastal conditions and exposed sites. Grow in any but waterlogged soil.
• PROPAGATION By seed in autumn.

☼ ◊
❀ ❀ ❀

Z 6–9

HEIGHT
25ft (8m) or more

SPREAD
30ft (10m)

Myrtaceae	WILLOW MYRTLE, WILLOW PEPPERMINT

AGONIS FLEXUOSA

Habit Graceful, weeping. *Flowers* Small, in profuse clusters on mature trees, in spring and summer. White. *Leaves* Aromatic, evergreen, narrowly lance-shaped, leathery. Bronze-red and silky when young, later dark green.
• NATIVE HABITAT Coastal areas of W. Australia.
• CULTIVATION Best grown as a conservatory plant in cooler climates. Grow in moisture-retentive, well-drained soil or soil mix.
• PROPAGATION By seed in spring or by semi-ripe cuttings in summer.

☼ ◊

Z 10–11

HEIGHT
22ft (7m)

SPREAD
10ft (3m)

Malvaceae

HOHERIA ANGUSTIFOLIA

Habit Narrowly columnar. **Flowers** Shallowly cup-shaped, with narrow petals, from mid- to late summer. White. **Leaves** Evergreen, narrowly oblong to lance-shaped, toothed or serrated. Dark green.
• NATIVE HABITAT Damp forests of New Zealand.
• CULTIVATION Tolerates semi-shade. Grow in fertile, humus-rich soil. Shelter from cold, dry winds. In cold areas, provide the shelter of a south- or southwest-facing wall. It makes a very attractive

small tree and is suitable for growing in the shrub border or as a free-standing specimen. The honey-scented flowers of this and other species of *Hoheria* are attractive to honey bees and butterflies.
• PROPAGATION By seed in autumn or by semi-ripe cuttings in summer.
• OTHER NAMES *H. populnea* var. *angustifolia*.

Z 9–10

HEIGHT
To 30ft
(10m)

SPREAD
12ft (4m)

Cornaceae

CORNUS 'Porlock'

Habit Graceful, open, broadly spreading.
Flowers Tiny, in rounded clusters in summer.
Green, surrounded by large, creamy-white bracts,
flushed pink with age. *Fruits* Pendent, strawberry-
like, in profusion in autumn. Red.
Leaves Deciduous, oval, taper-pointed. Dark
green, turning red in autumn. *Bark* Smooth,
flaking at the base. Gray, with shallow orange
fissures.
• NATIVE HABITAT Garden origin.
• CULTIVATION Tolerates dappled shade.

Grow in deep, fertile, moisture-retentive soil. This,
and the very similar *C.* 'Norman Hadden', makes
an elegant and graceful specimen for the smaller
garden, of interest in summer and again in autumn,
with fruit and foliage color. It is also suitable for
woodland gardens.
• PROPAGATION By softwood cuttings in summer.

Z 6–8

HEIGHT
25ft (8m)

SPREAD
25ft (8m)

Eucryphiaceae	NIRRHE

EUCRYPHIA GLUTINOSA

Habit Narrowly columnar. **Flowers** Fragrant, large, 4-petaled, in late summer. Glistening white, with a prominent boss of stamens, **Fruits** Woody capsules. **Leaves** Semi-evergreen or deciduous, with 3–5 elliptic-oblong, toothed leaflets. Glossy dark green, often turning orange-red in autumn.
• NATIVE HABITAT Forests and riversides, Chile.
• CULTIVATION Grow in humus-rich, moisture-retentive, neutral to acid soil.
• PROPAGATION By semi-ripe cuttings in late summer or by seed in autumn (may not come true).

Z 9–10

HEIGHT
30ft (10m)

SPREAD
20ft (6m)

Eucryphiaceae	LEATHERWOOD, PINKWOOD

EUCRYPHIA LUCIDA

Habit Dense, narrowly columnar. **Flowers** Fragrant, large, with 4 rounded petals, cup-shaped at first, opening flat in late summer. Glistening white with pink anthers. **Leaves** Evergreen, narrowly oblong, leathery. Dark green, blue-white beneath.
• NATIVE HABITAT Mountain woods, Tasmania.
• CULTIVATION Grow in humus-rich, moisture-retentive, neutral to acid soil. Provide shelter from cold, dry winds.
• PROPAGATION By semi-ripe cuttings in late summer.

Z 9–10

HEIGHT
25ft (8m)

SPREAD
12ft (4m)

Malvaceae	LACEBARK

HOHERIA LYALLII

Habit Broadly conical. **Flowers** Shallowly cup-shaped, in a profusion of rounded clusters in mid-summer. White. **Leaves** Deciduous, oval, pointed, heart-shaped at the base, with neat, rounded teeth. Gray-green, downy-white above and beneath.
• NATIVE HABITAT Forest margins and damp mountain woodlands of New Zealand.
• CULTIVATION Grow in fertile, humus-rich soil with shelter from cold, dry winds.
• PROPAGATION By seed in autumn or by semi-ripe cuttings in summer.

Z 9–10

HEIGHT
20ft (6m)

SPREAD
12ft (4m)

Leguminosae	

MAACKIA AMURENSIS

Habit Spreading, with an irregularly rounded crown. **Flowers** Small, pea-like, in dense, upright spikes from mid- to late summer. Creamy-white. **Leaves** Deciduous, with 7–11 broadly oval to elliptic leaflets. Dark green.
• NATIVE HABITAT Mountain scrub and woodlands in E. Asia.
• CULTIVATION Grow in any fertile soil. Blooms best in a warm, sunny, sheltered site.
• PROPAGATION By seed in autumn.

Z 3–8

HEIGHT
22ft (7m)

SPREAD
28ft (9m)

Leguminosae	MIMOSA, SILK TREE

ALBIZIA JULIBRISSIN

Habit Broadly spreading, with a domed or flat-topped crown. **Flowers** Dense, round clusters of fine, clear pink stamens, carried in racemes from late summer to early autumn. **Fruits** Pods, to 6in (15cm) long. **Leaves** Deciduous, feathery, finely divided, with many small leaflets. Dark green.
• NATIVE HABITAT Woodlands and riverbanks of S.W. Asia.
• CULTIVATION Grow in a warm, sheltered site, such as a south- or west-facing wall.
• PROPAGATION By seed in autumn.

Z 6–9

HEIGHT
30ft (10m)

SPREAD
30ft (10m)

Rosaceae	PAUL'S SCARLET HAWTHORN

CRATAEGUS LAEVIGATA 'Paul's Scarlet'

Habit Spreading, with a rounded crown. **Flowers** Double, in dense clusters from late spring to summer. Pinkish-scarlet. **Fruits** Small haws. Red. **Leaves** Deciduous, lobed, toothed. Dark green.
• NATIVE HABITAT Garden origin.
• CULTIVATION Tolerant of urban pollution, coastal conditions, and exposed sites, and almost any but waterlogged soil.
• PROPAGATION By budding in late summer.
• OTHER NAMES *C. laevigata* 'Coccinea Plena', *C. oxyacantha* 'Paul's Scarlet'.

Z 4–7

HEIGHT
22ft (7m)

SPREAD
25ft (8m)

Cornaceae	FLOWERING DOGWOOD

CORNUS FLORIDA 'Spring Song'

Habit Broadly spreading. **Flowers** Tiny, in dense clusters in late spring or early summer. Green, surrounded by 4 broad, pink bracts.
Leaves Deciduous, oval to elliptic, pointed. Dark green, often bronzed, turning red and purple in autumn.
• NATIVE HABITAT Garden origin.
• CULTIVATION Unsuitable for shallow, alkaline soils. Tolerates dappled shade. Grow in deep, fertile, moisture-retentive soil.
• PROPAGATION By softwood cuttings in summer.

Z 5–9

HEIGHT
20ft (6m)

SPREAD
25ft (8m)

Leguminosae	*Red Bud*

CERCIS CANADENSIS 'Forest Pansy'

Habit Broadly spreading, with a rounded crown. **Flowers** Small, pea-like, in clusters in mid-spring, before the leaves. Pale pink, magenta in bud.
Leaves Deciduous, heart-shaped. Bronze-purple when young, dark red-purple when mature.
• NATIVE HABITAT Species occurs in damp woodland in North America. Garden origin.
• CULTIVATION Tolerates dappled shade. Grow in deep, fertile, moisture-retentive soil. A very attractive foliage specimen for small gardens.
• PROPAGATION By budding in late summer.

Z 6–9

HEIGHT
30ft (10m)

SPREAD
30ft (10m)

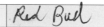

Rosaceae	PURPLELEAF PLUM

PRUNUS CERASIFERA 'Nigra'

Habit Broadly spreading, round-headed.
Flowers Small, single, 5-petaled, in a profusion of dense clusters in early to mid-spring, with or before the leaves. Rich pink, fading to blush-pink.
Fruits Rounded, plum-like, 1¼in (3cm) across, edible. Dark red.
Leaves Deciduous, oval, toothed, pointed. Dark red-purple.
• NATIVE HABITAT Garden origin.
• CULTIVATION Grow in any but waterlogged soil. May be used for hedging. Trim after flowering.

These trees, and other dark-leaved cherry plums such as *P. cerasifera* 'Pissardii' and *P. cerasifera* 'Rosea', are invaluable in small gardens because of their early spring blooming. They also make a handsome contrast to gray-leaved trees such as *Sorbus aria* 'Lutescens' and *Pyrus salicifolia* 'Pendula'.
• PROPAGATION By softwood cuttings in summer.

Z 4–8

HEIGHT
30ft (10m)

SPREAD
30ft (10m)

Boraginaceae (Ehretiaceae)	

EHRETIA DICKSONII

Habit Fast-growing, open, spreading.
Flowers Small, fragrant, star-shaped, in large, flattened heads in mid-summer. White.
Leaves Deciduous, large, oblong-elliptic. Lustrous dark green, roughly hairy above, velvety beneath.
• NATIVE HABITAT China, Japan, and Taiwan.
• CULTIVATION Grow in any fertile soil, in a warm, sunny, sheltered site. Young growth susceptible to frost damage.
• PROPAGATION By softwood cuttings in summer.
• OTHER NAMES *E. macrophylla* of gardens.

☼ ◊
❀ ❀

Z 7–10

HEIGHT
30ft (10m)

SPREAD
30ft (10m)

Araliaceae	TOOTHED LANCEWOOD

PSEUDOPANAX FEROX

Habit Narrowly upright, unbranched when young, becoming rounded with maturity.
Leaves Evergreen, long, narrow, rigid, with hooked marginal teeth, downward-pointing. Deep bronze-green, bloomed white, with an orange midrib.
• NATIVE HABITAT Scrub and lowland forests of New Zealand.
• CULTIVATION Tolerates partial shade. Grow in any fertile soil in a sunny, sheltered site.
• PROPAGATION By semi-ripe cuttings in summer or by seed in autumn or spring.

☼ ◊
❀ ❀

Z 9–11

HEIGHT
15ft (5m)

SPREAD
6ft (2m)

Rosaceae	WEEPING WILLOW-LEAVED PEAR

PYRUS SALICIFOLIA 'Pendula'

Habit Broadly weeping. **Flowers** 5-petaled, in clusters, opening with the leaves in spring. Creamy-white. **Fruits** Small, hard, pear-shaped.
Leaves Deciduous, narrowly elliptic to lance-shaped. Gray, downy when young.
• NATIVE HABITAT Species occurs in thickets in the Caucasus and N.E. Turkey.
• CULTIVATION Tolerant of urban pollution. Grow in any moderately fertile soil.
• PROPAGATION By budding in summer or by grafting in winter.

☼ ◊
❀ ❀ ❀

Z 5–9

HEIGHT
25ft (8m)

SPREAD
20ft (6m)

Ulmaceae	CAMPERDOWN ELM

ULMUS 'Camperdownii'

Habit Slow-growing, dense, with a dome-shaped head and pendulous branches. **Leaves** Deciduous, large, broadly oval, pointed, unequal at the base, rough-textured. Dull green.
• NATIVE HABITAT Garden origin.
• CULTIVATION Grow in any fertile, well-drained soil. Susceptible to Dutch elm disease.
• PROPAGATION By softwood cuttings in summer or by suckers in autumn.
• OTHER NAMES *U. glabra* 'Camperdownii', *U. pendula* 'Camperdownii'.

Z 4–6

HEIGHT
25ft (8m) or more

SPREAD
25ft (8m)

Rosaceae	

CYDONIA OBLONGA 'Vranja'

Habit Low-branching, broadly spreading. **Flowers** Large, 5-petaled, in late spring. Pink or white. **Fruits** Very fragrant, large, pear-shaped. Yellow when ripe. **Leaves** Deciduous, broadly elliptic-oval. Gray-downy when young, becoming dark green, but remaining downy beneath.
• NATIVE HABITAT Garden origin.
• CULTIVATION Grow in any fertile soil, with the shelter of a south- or west-facing wall to ensure good cropping.
• PROPAGATION By softwood cuttings in summer.

Z 5–8

HEIGHT
15ft (5m)

SPREAD
15ft (5m)

Juglandaceae	LITTLE WALNUT, TEXAN WALNUT

JUGLANS MICROCARPA

Habit Shrubby, round-headed. **Flowers** Catkins, male and female on same plant, in late spring. Yellow-green. **Leaves** Deciduous, aromatic, with 15–23 slender-pointed, narrowly lance-shaped leaflets. Glossy green, turning yellow in autumn.
• NATIVE HABITAT By stream sides on the plains and in the mountain foothills of Texas and New Mexico.
• CULTIVATION Grow in deep, fertile soil.
• PROPAGATION By seed in autumn.
• OTHER NAMES *J. rupestris.*

Z 6–9

HEIGHT
22ft (7m)

SPREAD
22ft (7m)

Aceraceae	HORNBEAM MAPLE

ACER CARPINIFOLIUM

Habit Broadly conical. **Leaves** Deciduous, oblong, unlobed, taper-pointed, with deeply impressed, parallel veins. Dark green, turning golden-yellow in autumn.
• NATIVE HABITAT Stream banks in deciduous woodlands of Japan.
• CULTIVATION Tolerates dappled shade, but colors best in sun. Grow in deep, fertile, humus-rich soil.
• PROPAGATION By seed in autumn.

Z 4–7

HEIGHT
30ft (10m)

SPREAD
22ft (7m)

Betulaceae	YOUNG'S WEEPING BIRCH

BETULA PENDULA 'Youngii'

Habit Weeping, dome-shaped, with slender, elegant branchlets. **Flowers** Catkins. Male, to 2½in (6cm) long; female shorter, on same plant. **Leaves** Deciduous, triangular, serrated. Glossy green, turning golden-yellow in autumn. **Bark** White. Rough, black fissures with age.
• NATIVE HABITAT Garden origin.
• CULTIVATION Grow in any moist but well-drained soil in an open, sunny site.
• PROPAGATION By grafting in late winter or softwood cuttings in early summer.

Z 2–6

HEIGHT
25ft (8m)

SPREAD
30ft (10m)

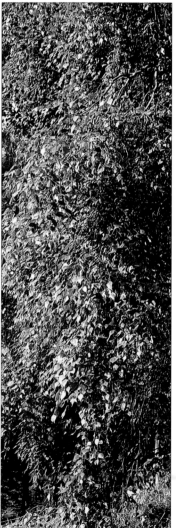

Aceraceae	GOLDEN FULLMOON MAPLE

ACER SHIRASAWANUM f. *AUREUM*

Habit Round-headed, bushy. **Leaves** Deciduous, with 11 pointed, sharply toothed lobes. Soft, pale yellow, turning orange and red in autumn.
• NATIVE HABITAT Species occurs on mountain slopes and in valleys in Japan.
• CULTIVATION Grow in fertile, moisture-retentive, well-drained soil in semi-shade or dappled shade. Leaves may scorch in full sun.
• PROPAGATION By grafting in late winter or early spring or by budding in summer.
• OTHER NAMES *A. japonicum* 'Aureum'.

Z 6–7

HEIGHT
To 25ft
(8m)

SPREAD
25ft (8m)

Moraceae	CUT-LEAVED WHITE MULBERRY

MORUS ALBA 'Laciniata'

Habit Broadly spreading, with a rounded crown. **Flowers** Tiny, male and female on separate plants. **Fruits** Small, edible, oval, fleshy clusters. Pink, red, or purple. **Leaves** Deciduous, rounded, deeply lobed. Glossy dark green, turning yellow in autumn.
• NATIVE HABITAT Species occurs on hillsides in N. China. Garden origin.
• CULTIVATION Grow in any fertile soil, in a warm, sunny, sheltered site for good cropping.
• PROPAGATION By softwood cuttings in summer.

Z 4–9

HEIGHT
30ft (10m)

SPREAD
30ft (10m)

Leguminosae	GOLDEN CHAIN TREE

LABURNUM × *WATERERI* 'Vossii'

Habit Broadly spreading. *Flowers* Small, pea-like, in pendent clusters, to 20in (50cm) long, in late spring to early summer. Yellow. *Fruits* Small, brown pods, enclosing few seeds.
Leaves Deciduous, divided into 3 elliptic leaflets. Dark green, turning yellow in autumn.
• NATIVE HABITAT Garden origin.
• CULTIVATION Grow in any but waterlogged soil. All parts, especially the seeds, are poisonous and potentially very dangerous to children.
• PROPAGATION By budding in summer.

Z 5–7

HEIGHT
30ft (10m)

SPREAD
30ft (10m)

Sapindaceae	GOLDEN RAIN TREE, VARNISH TREE

KOELREUTERIA PANICULATA

Habit Broadly spreading. *Flowers* Small, 4-petaled, in upright panicles in mid- to late summer. Yellow. *Fruits* Papery, bladder-like capsules. Bronze-pink or red, *Leaves* Deciduous, divided, deeply toothed or lobed. Dark green.
• NATIVE HABITAT Hot, dry river valleys in China and Korea.
• CULTIVATION A warm, sunny, sheltered site. Flowers best in hot summers.
• PROPAGATION By seed in autumn or by root cuttings in winter.

Z 4–9

HEIGHT
30ft (10m)

SPREAD
30ft (10m)

Leguminosae	PLUME ALBIZIA

ALBIZIA LOPHANTHA

Habit Broadly spreading, with a rounded crown.
Flowers Dense clusters carried in slender spikes in spring and summer. Fine, creamy-yellow stamens. *Leaves* Deciduous, feathery, finely divided, with many small leaflets. Bright green.
• NATIVE HABITAT W. Australia.
• CULTIVATION In mild areas grow on a south- or west-facing wall; otherwise, grow in a cool conservatory.
• PROPAGATION By seed in autumn.
• OTHER NAMES *A. distachya.*

Z 8–10

HEIGHT
25ft (8m)

SPREAD
25ft (8m)

Leguminosae	ALPINE GOLDEN CHAIN

LABURNUM ALPINUM

Habit Open, broadly spreading.
Flowers Fragrant, small, pea-like, in long, slender racemes, to 18in (45cm) long, in early summer. Bright golden-yellow. **Fruits** Brown pods, enclosing shiny, brown seeds. **Leaves** Deciduous, with 3 elliptic, slightly pointed, smooth leaflets. Dark green.
• NATIVE HABITAT Mountains, C. and S. Europe.
• CULTIVATION Grow in any but waterlogged soil. All parts are very poisonous.
• PROPAGATION By seed in autumn.

Rosaceae	

SORBUS CASHMIRIANA

Habit Delicate, open, spreading. **Flowers** Small, in broad clusters in late spring. White, pink-flushed. **Fruits** Large, round, in clusters. White, tinted pink at the top at first. **Leaves** Deciduous, with up to 17 sharply toothed leaflets. Deep green above, gray-green beneath. Orange and yellow in autumn.
• NATIVE HABITAT Forests of the W. Himalayas.
• CULTIVATION Tolerates dappled shade. Grow in any fertile, moisture-retentive soil.
• PROPAGATION By softwood cuttings in summer or by seed in autumn.

Z 4–7

HEIGHT
25ft (8m)

SPREAD
25ft (8m)

Z 4–6

HEIGHT
25ft (8m)

SPREAD
25ft (8m)

Apocynaceae	YELLOW OLEANDER

THEVETIA PERUVIANA

Habit Upright, with a rounded crown.
Flowers Large, funnel-shaped. Yellow or orange, winter to summer. **Leaves** Evergreen, lance-shaped. Rich, glossy green.
• NATIVE HABITAT Tropical America.
• CULTIVATION Water moderately when in growth, otherwise sparingly. Best grown in a conservatory in cooler climates. Sap is poisonous.
• PROPAGATION By seed in spring or by semi-ripe cuttings in summer.
• OTHER NAMES *T. neriifolia.*

Ericaceae	STRAWBERRY TREE

ARBUTUS UNEDO

Habit Dense, broadly spreading. **Flowers** Small, urn-shaped, in pendent clusters in autumn. White. **Fruits** Small, strawberry-like. Red. **Leaves** Evergreen, elliptic to oblong, toothed. Glossy dark green.
• NATIVE HABITAT Thickets and rocky places in S.W. Ireland and the Mediterranean.
• CULTIVATION Tolerates lime, but prefers a deep, fertile, humus-rich soil. Shelter from wind.
• PROPAGATION By seed in autumn or by semi-ripe cuttings in late summer.

Z 10–11

HEIGHT
30ft (10m)

SPREAD
20ft (6m)

Z 7–9

HEIGHT
25ft (8m)

SPREAD
25ft (8m)

Cornaceae	FLOWERING DOGWOOD

CORNUS FLORIDA 'Welchii'

Habit Broadly spreading. *Flowers* Tiny, in dense clusters in late spring. Green, surrounded by 4 broad, white bracts. *Leaves* Deciduous, oval to elliptic, pointed. Dark green, edged white and pink, turning red and purple in autumn.
• NATIVE HABITAT Garden origin.
• CULTIVATION Unsuitable for shallow, alkaline soils. Tolerates dappled shade. Grow in deep, fertile, moisture-retentive soil.
• PROPAGATION By softwood cuttings in summer.

Rosaceae	CRAB APPLE

MALUS 'Veitch's Scarlet'

Habit Spreading, with a rounded crown.
Flowers Large, cup-shaped, in late spring. White.
Fruits Large crab apples. Scarlet, flushed crimson.
Leaves Deciduous, oval. Dark green.
• NATIVE HABITAT Garden origin.
• CULTIVATION Tolerates dappled shade, but flowers and fruits best in sun. Grow in any but waterlogged soil.
• PROPAGATION By budding in summer or by grafting in winter.

☀ ◊
❀ ❀ ❀

Z 5–9

HEIGHT
22ft (7m)

SPREAD
25ft (8m)

☀ ◊
❀ ❀ ❀

Z 5–7

HEIGHT
28ft (9m)

SPREAD
28ft (9m)

Rosaceae	MOUNTAIN ASH

SORBUS VILMORINII

Habit Delicate, open, broadly spreading.
Flowers Small, in broad clusters, from late spring to early summer. White. *Fruits* Round. Pink, white flushed with rose when ripe. *Leaves* Deciduous, up to 25 oblong leaflets. Deep green, grayish beneath, turning red-purple in autumn.
• NATIVE HABITAT Mountain woods, S.W. China.
• CULTIVATION Tolerates dappled shade. Grow in any fertile, moisture-retentive soil.
• PROPAGATION By softwood cuttings in summer or by seed in autumn.

☀ ◊
❀ ❀ ❀

Z 6–8

HEIGHT
15ft (5m)

SPREAD
15ft (5m)

Rosaceae	HAWTHORN

CRATAEGUS MACROSPERMA 'Acutiloba'

Habit Spreading, with a domed crown.
Flowers Small, in clusters in late spring. White, with red anthers. **Fruits** Small, rounded haws. Bright red. **Leaves** Deciduous, broad, jaggedly toothed. Dark green.
• NATIVE HABITAT North America.
• CULTIVATION Tolerant of urban pollution, coastal conditions, and exposed sites, and almost any but waterlogged soil.
• PROPAGATION By budding in late summer.

Z 3–7

HEIGHT
20ft (6m)

SPREAD
25ft (8m)

Rosaceae	CRAB APPLE

MALUS 'Cowichan'

Habit Vigorous, spreading, round-headed.
Flowers Large, cup-shaped, in mid-spring. Red-pink. **Fruits** Large crab apples. Reddish-purple. **Leaves** Deciduous, oval. Dark green, red-purple when young.
• NATIVE HABITAT Garden origin.
• CULTIVATION Tolerates dappled shade, but flowers and fruits best in sun. Grow in any but waterlogged soil.
• PROPAGATION By budding in summer or by grafting in winter.

Z 5–7

HEIGHT
25ft (8m)

SPREAD
25ft (8m)

Rosaceae	

PHOTINIA DAVIDIANA

Habit Open, spreading. **Flowers** Tiny, in broad clusters in mid-summer. White, with pink anthers.
Fruits Round berries. Bright red.
Leaves Evergreen, elliptic to oblong, taper-pointed at tip. Dark green, then red.
• NATIVE HABITAT Woodlands and thickets in China and Vietnam.
• CULTIVATION Grow in any fertile soil.
• PROPAGATION By seed in autumn or by semi-ripe cuttings in summer.
• OTHER NAMES *Stranvaesia davidiana.*

Z 7–9

HEIGHT
25ft (8m)

SPREAD
20ft (6m)

Aceraceae	JAPANESE MAPLE

ACER PALMATUM 'Koreanum'

Habit Bushy-headed or shrubby. **Flowers** Small, in pendent clusters in spring. Red-purple.
Fruits 2 seeds, fused together, each with a red-tinted wing. **Leaves** Deciduous, with deeply cut lobes. Green, turning brilliant crimson in autumn.
• NATIVE HABITAT Mountain woods of Korea.
• CULTIVATION Grow in fertile, moist but well-drained soil, with shelter from cold winds.
• PROPAGATION By seed in autumn.
• OTHER NAMES *A. palmatum* var. *coreanum.*

Z 5–8

HEIGHT
22ft (7m)

SPREAD
22ft (7m)

Aceraceae	FULLMOON MAPLE

ACER JAPONICUM 'Vitifolium'

Habit Vigorous, bushy, open, with a rounded crown. **Flowers** Small, in delicate, drooping clusters in spring. Red-purple. **Fruits** 2 seeds, fused together, each with a green wing. **Leaves** Deciduous, with 10–12 sharply toothed lobes. Green, turning rich crimson, orange, and purple in autumn.

• NATIVE HABITAT The species occurs in mountain woodlands, usually in dry, sunny areas, of Japan. Garden origin.

• CULTIVATION *A. japonicum* 'Vitifolium' will thrive in dappled shade. Grow in fertile, moist but well-drained soil. Strong winds and hot sun may scorch the foliage. This tree makes a beautiful specimen for sheltered sites in small or medium-sized gardens.

• PROPAGATION By grafting in late winter or early spring or by budding in summer.

Z 5–7

HEIGHT
30ft (10m)

SPREAD
30ft (10m)

Aceraceae	CUTLEAF FULLMOON MAPLE

ACER JAPONICUM 'Aconitifolium'

Habit Bushy, with a rounded crown.
Flowers Small, in drooping clusters in spring. Red.
Fruits 2 seeds, fused together, each with a wing.
Leaves Deciduous, with 7–11 deeply cut, deeply toothed lobes. Green, turning rich crimson in autumn.
• NATIVE HABITAT Garden origin.
• CULTIVATION Grow in fertile, moist but well-drained soil. Strong winds may scorch the foliage.
• PROPAGATION By grafting in late winter or early spring or by budding in summer.

☼ ◊
✿ ✿ ✿

Z 5–7

HEIGHT
20ft (6m)

SPREAD
22ft (7m)

Rosaceae	SCARLET HAWTHORN

CRATAEGUS PEDICELLATA

Habit Wide-spreading, very thorny.
Flowers Small, in clusters in late spring. White, with red anthers. *Fruits* Bright haws in broad clusters. Scarlet. *Leaves* Deciduous, lobed, sharply toothed. Dark green, then red and orange in autumn.
• NATIVE HABITAT N.E. North America.
• CULTIVATION Tolerant of urban pollution, coastal conditions, exposed sites, and almost any but waterlogged soil.
• PROPAGATION By seed in autumn.
• OTHER NAMES *C. coccinea.*

☼ ◊
✿ ✿ ✿

Z 5–7

HEIGHT
15ft (5m)

SPREAD
15ft (5m)

Rosaceae	CRAB APPLE

MALUS 'John Downie'

Habit Vigorous, narrowly upright when young, conical with age. *Flowers* Large, cup-shaped, in late spring. White, opening from pink buds.
Fruits Large, egg-shaped crab apples. Yellow-orange, flushed red. *Leaves* Deciduous, elliptic-oval. Bright green when young, then dark green.
• NATIVE HABITAT Garden origin.
• CULTIVATION Tolerates dappled shade, but flowers and fruits best in sun.
• PROPAGATION By budding in summer or by grafting in winter.

☼ ◊
✿ ✿ ✿

Z 5–7

HEIGHT
30ft (10m)

SPREAD
22ft (7m)

Anacardiaceae	SUMAC

RHUS TRICHOCARPA

Habit Open, broadly spreading. *Flowers* Tiny, in conical panicles in summer. Yellowish.
Fruits Small, pendent, bristly, in clusters on female plants. Yellow-brown. *Leaves* Deciduous, long, up to 17 pointed, downy leaflets. Reddish, later matte green, then orange-red in autumn.
• NATIVE HABITAT China, Japan, and Korea.
• CULTIVATION Grow in any fertile soil.
• PROPAGATION By semi-ripe cuttings in summer, by seed in autumn or by root cuttings in winter.
• OTHER NAMES *Toxicodendron succedaneum.*

☼ ◊
✿ ✿ ✿

Z 8–10

HEIGHT
22ft (7m)

SPREAD
22ft (7m)

Rosaceae	

MALUS PRUNIFOLIA

Habit Broadly spreading, with a neatly domed head. **Flowers** Fragrant, large, in large clusters in mid-spring. White, opening from soft pink buds. **Fruits** Small, rounded to egg-shaped crab apples, in large, long-persistent clusters. Bright red. **Leaves** Deciduous, elliptic, toothed. Dark green.
• NATIVE HABITAT Probably of garden origin.
• CULTIVATION Tolerates dappled shade, but flowers and fruits best in sun.
• PROPAGATION By budding in summer or by grafting in winter.

Z 4–7

HEIGHT
28ft (9m)

SPREAD
25ft (8m)

Aceraceae	AMUR MAPLE

ACER GINNALA

Habit Broadly spreading. **Flowers** Small, creamy-white, in erect clusters in late spring. **Fruits** 2 seeds, fused together, each with a wing. **Leaves** Deciduous, small, 3-lobed, toothed. Glossy dark green above, then red in early autumn.
• NATIVE HABITAT Thickets in mountain valleys of China and Japan.
• CULTIVATION Tolerates semi-shade, but colors best in sun. Grow in any fertile soil.
• PROPAGATION By seed in autumn.
• OTHER NAMES A. tataricum subsp. ginnala.

Z 2–8

HEIGHT
28ft (9m)

SPREAD
28ft (9m)

Rosaceae	

MALUS × ZUMI 'Calocarpa'

Habit Spreading, rounded to pyramidal. **Flowers** Small, cup-shaped, in late spring. White, pink in bud. **Fruits** Small, cherry-like, long-lasting and in profusion. Red. **Leaves** Deciduous, long-tapered, sometimes deeply lobed. Dark green.
• NATIVE HABITAT Garden origin.
• CULTIVATION Tolerates dappled shade, but flowers and fruits best in sun. Grow in any but waterlogged soil.
• PROPAGATION By budding in summer or by grafting in winter.

Z 4–8

HEIGHT
28ft (9m)

SPREAD
22ft (7m)

Aceraceae	THREE-FLOWERED MAPLE

ACER TRIFLORUM

Habit Slow-growing, broadly spreading, with an irregularly rounded crown. *Flowers* Tiny, in pendent clusters of 3, in spring, with the new leaves. Yellow. *Fruits* 2 seeds, fused together, enclosed in small, downward-pointing wings. Yellow-green. *Leaves* Deciduous, with 3 leaflets. Pale green, turning brilliant orange and crimson in autumn. *Bark* Peeling, in vertical strips. Pale brown to gray-brown.
• NATIVE HABITAT Mountain woods of N.E. China and Korea.

• CULTIVATION Tolerates semi-shade, but colors best in sun. This is one of the most reliable of species for good autumn color. Grow in any fertile, moisture-retentive soil. It makes an attractive and elegant specimen tree for medium-sized gardens.
• PROPAGATION By seed in autumn.

Z 5–7

HEIGHT
28ft (9m)

SPREAD
28ft (9m)

Cornaceae	DOGWOOD

CORNUS 'Eddie's White Wonder'

Habit Dense, upright, broadly conical.
Flowers Tiny, in dense clusters in late spring, with the young leaves. Green, surrounded by 4 large, white, pink-tinted bracts, **Leaves** Deciduous, broadly elliptic, pointed, slightly glossy. Dark green, turning brilliant orange, red, and purple in autumn.
• NATIVE HABITAT Garden origin.
• CULTIVATION Unsuitable for shallow, alkaline soils. Tolerates dappled shade. Grow in deep, fertile, moisture-retentive soil.
• PROPAGATION By softwood cuttings in summer.

Z 6–9

HEIGHT
20ft (6m)

SPREAD
15ft (5m)

Rosaceae	CRAB APPLE

MALUS 'Marshall Oyama'

Habit Upright, broadly conical. **Flowers** Large, cup-shaped, in late spring. White, flushed pink.
Fruits Large, rounded crab apples, in profusion. Crimson and yellow. **Leaves** Deciduous, broadly oval, pointed at the tip. Dark green.
• NATIVE HABITAT Garden origin.
• CULTIVATION Tolerates dappled shade, but flowers and fruits best in sun. Grow in any but waterlogged soil.
• PROPAGATION By budding in summer or by grafting in winter.

Z 5–7

HEIGHT
28ft (9m)

SPREAD
15ft (5m)

Rosaceae	HAWTHORN

CRATAEGUS PERSIMILIS 'Prunifolia'

Habit Broadly spreading, thorny. **Flowers** 5 petals, to ⅝in (1.5cm) across, in rounded clusters in early summer. White. **Fruits** Rounded haws. Bright red.
Leaves Deciduous, broadly elliptic, sharply toothed. Glossy dark green, turning gold, red, and orange in autumn.
• NATIVE HABITAT Garden origin.
• CULTIVATION Tolerant of urban pollution, coastal exposure, and any but waterlogged soil.
• PROPAGATION By budding in late summer.
• OTHER NAMES *C.* x *prunifolia.*

Z 5–7

HEIGHT
20ft (6m)

SPREAD
20ft (6m)

Rosaceae	CRAB APPLE

MALUS YUNNANENSIS var. VEITCHII

Habit Broadly columnar. **Flowers** Small, in flattened heads in late spring. White. **Fruits** Small, hard, round, in clusters in autumn. Red. **Leaves** Deciduous, lobed, heart-shaped at the base. Matte green above, gray-downy beneath, turning crimson and orange in autumn.
• NATIVE HABITAT Mountain woods of C. China.
• CULTIVATION Tolerates dappled shade. Grow in any but waterlogged soil.
• PROPAGATION By budding in late summer or by grafting in winter. Seed may not come true.

Z 4–7
HEIGHT 25ft (8m)
SPREAD 20ft (6m)

Apocynaceae	FRANGIPANI

PLUMERIA RUBRA

Habit Wide-spreading, sparingly branched. **Flowers** Intensely fragrant, large, salver-shaped in summer to autumn. Shades of yellow, orange, pink, red, or white. **Leaves** Deciduous, broadly elliptic or oblong to lance-shaped. Mid-green.
• NATIVE HABITAT Mexico to Panama.
• CULTIVATION Best grown in a conservatory in cooler climates. Grow in very free-draining soil or soil mix. Keep dry in winter when leafless.
• PROPAGATION By seed or leafless stem-tip cuttings in late spring.

Z 10–11
HEIGHT 15ft (5m)
SPREAD 22ft (7m)

Rosaceae	CRAB APPLE

MALUS 'Professor Sprenger'

Habit Dense, round-headed. **Flowers** Small, cup-shaped, in great profusion from mid- to late spring. White, pink in bud. **Fruits** Small, rounded crab apples. Amber-gold. **Leaves** Deciduous, broadly oval. Dark green, turning yellow in autumn.
• NATIVE HABITAT Garden origin.
• CULTIVATION Tolerates dappled shade, but flowers and fruits best in sun. Grow in any but waterlogged soil.
• PROPAGATION By budding in summer or by grafting in winter.

Z 5–7
HEIGHT 22ft (7m)
SPREAD 22ft (7m)

Bignoniaceae	YELLOW BELLS

TECOMA STANS

Habit Upright, rounded, sometimes shrubby. **Flowers** Funnel-shaped, in clusters, from spring to autumn. Bright yellow. **Leaves** Evergreen, with 5–13 lance-shaped leaflets. Dark green.
• NATIVE HABITAT Mexico, N. Venezuela, and Argentina.
• CULTIVATION Best grown in a conservatory in cooler climates. Grow in soil or soil mix.
• PROPAGATION By seed in spring or by semi-ripe cuttings in summer.
• OTHER NAMES *Bignonia stans, Stenolobium stans.*

Z 10–11
HEIGHT 20ft (6m)
SPREAD 10ft (3m)

Simaroubaceae	QUASSIA

PICRASMA AILANTHOIDES

Habit Spreading. *Flowers* Insignificant.
Fruits Small, pea-like, in early summer. Red.
Leaves Deciduous, with 9–13 sharply toothed
leaflets. Glossy bright green, turning brilliant
yellow, orange, and red in autumn.
• NATIVE HABITAT Japan, N. China, and Korea.
• CULTIVATION Tolerates semi-shade and lime-
rich soil, but grows best in fertile, moisture-
retentive, neutral to acid, loamy soils.
• PROPAGATION By seed in autumn.
• OTHER NAMES *P. quassioides.*

Leguminosae	

BAUHINIA VARIEGATA 'Candida'

Habit Dense, rounded, spreading with age.
Flowers Fragrant, large, in short, few-flowered
racemes from winter to early summer. Pure white.
Leaves Deciduous, broadly oval, deeply notched.
Dark green.
• NATIVE HABITAT Garden origin.
• CULTIVATION Best grown in a conservatory in
cooler climates. Grow in fertile soil or soil mix.
Water freely in growth, then moderately.
• PROPAGATION By leafless cuttings of semi-ripe
wood in summer.

☀ ◊
❄ ❄ ❄

Z 5–8

HEIGHT
30ft (10m)

SPREAD
22ft (7m)

☀ ◊

Z 10–11

HEIGHT
25ft (8m)

SPREAD
30ft (10m)

Rosaceae	CRAB APPLE

MALUS 'Golden Hornet'

Habit Broadly pyramidal. *Flowers* Large, cup-
shaped, in profusion in late spring. White, flushed
pink, deep pink in bud. *Fruits* Small, rounded
crab apples. Golden-yellow. *Leaves* Deciduous,
broadly oval. Dark green, then yellow in autumn.
• NATIVE HABITAT Garden origin.
• CULTIVATION Tolerates dappled shade, but
flowers and fruits best in sun. Grow in any but
waterlogged soil.
• PROPAGATION By budding in summer or by
grafting in winter.

Leguminosae	ORCHID TREE, MOUNTAIN EBONY

BAUHINIA VARIEGATA

Habit Dense, rounded, spreading with age.
Flowers Fragrant, large, in short, few-flowered
racemes from winter to early summer. Magenta to
lavender. *Leaves* Deciduous, broadly oval, deeply
notched. Dark green.
• NATIVE HABITAT Tropical mountain forests of
E. Asia.
• CULTIVATION Best grown in a conservatory in
cooler climates. Water freely when in growth.
• PROPAGATION By seed in spring.
• OTHER NAMES *B. purpurea* of gardens.

☀ ◊
❄ ❄ ❄

Z 4–8

HEIGHT
30ft (10m)

SPREAD
25ft (8m)

☀ ◊

Z 10–11

HEIGHT
25ft (8m)

SPREAD
30ft (10m)

Bignoniaceae	GOLDEN TRUMPET TREE

TABEBUIA CHRYSOTRICHA

Habit Round-headed. **Flowers** Large, trumpet-shaped, in late winter or early spring. Rich yellow. **Leaves** Deciduous, divided into 3–5 oblong-elliptic leaflets. Dark green.
• NATIVE HABITAT Colombia and Brazil.
• CULTIVATION Grow in fertile, free-draining soil or soil mix. Water moderately when in growth, but very sparingly in winter. Prune when young, but only to shape. Does best grown in the conservatory.
• PROPAGATION By seed or air-layering in spring or by semi-ripe cuttings in summer.

Z 10–11

HEIGHT
30ft (10m)

SPREAD
25ft (8m)

Pittosporaceae	VARIEGATED KARO

PITTOSPORUM CRASSIFOLIUM
'Variegatum'

Habit Bushy-headed, dense. **Flowers** Tiny, fragrant, in clusters in spring. Deep red-purple. **Leaves** Evergreen, oval-elliptic. Gray-green, irregularly edged creamy-white.
• NATIVE HABITAT Species occurs in lowland and coastal forest of New Zealand. Garden origin.
• CULTIVATION Thrives in mild, coastal areas. In cold areas, site against a south- or west-facing wall. Protect from cold winds. Will not survive long frosts.
• PROPAGATION By semi-ripe cuttings in summer.

Z 9–11

HEIGHT
25ft (8m)

SPREAD
15ft (5m)

Pittosporaceae	

PITTOSPORUM EUGENIOIDES
'Variegatum'

Habit Bushy, columnar, dense. **Flowers** Honey-scented, tiny, star-shaped, in clusters in spring. Pale yellow. **Leaves** Evergreen, narrowly oval, wavy-edged. Glossy dark green, with creamy-white edges.
• NATIVE HABITAT Species occurs in lowland and coastal forests of New Zealand. Garden origin.
• CULTIVATION Thrives in mild areas, especially on the coast. In cold areas, site against a south- or west-facing wall. Protect from cold winds.
• PROPAGATION By semi-ripe cuttings in summer.

Z 9–11

HEIGHT
15ft (5m)

SPREAD
10ft (3m)

Aceraceae	LOOSEFLOWER MAPLE

ACER LAXIFLORUM

Habit Spreading. **Flowers** Small, in clusters in spring. Yellow-green. **Fruits** 2 seeds, fused together, each with a pale red wing.
Leaves Deciduous, pointed, shallowly lobed, red-stalked. Dark green, turning orange in autumn.
Bark Streaked white and pale green.
• NATIVE HABITAT Mountain woods in W. China.
• CULTIVATION Dislikes lime-rich soils. Grow in fertile, moisture-retentive, neutral to acid soil.
• PROPAGATION By seed in autumn.
• OTHER NAMES *A. pectinatum* subsp. *laxiflorum*.

☼ ◊
❀ ❀ ❀

Z 6–7

HEIGHT
30ft (10m)

SPREAD
30ft (10m)

Proteaceae	

GREVILLEA BANKSII

Habit Rounded, loosely branched.
Flowers Tubular, with protruding, recurved styles, in dense racemes, at intervals from early spring to late summer. Crimson. **Leaves** Evergreen, divided into 5–11 slender leaflets. Dark green, silky beneath.
• NATIVE HABITAT E. Australia.
• CULTIVATION Suitable for growing in a conservatory. Grow in neutral to acid soil or soil mix. Needs protection in hard winters or exposed areas.
• PROPAGATION By seed in spring or by semi-ripe cuttings in summer.

☼ ◊

Z 9–11

HEIGHT
15ft (5m)

SPREAD
10ft (3m)

Agavaceae (Dracaenaceae)	

DRACAENA CINCTA 'Tricolor'

Habit Slow-growing, upright. **Leaves** Evergreen, narrow, strap-shaped. Rich green, striped cream and prominently margined with red.
• NATIVE HABITAT Garden origin.
• CULTIVATION Tolerates partial shade. Grow in well-drained soil or soil mix. Water moderately when in growth, otherwise sparingly. A beautiful specimen for the home or conservatory.
• PROPAGATION By air-layering in spring or by stem-tip cuttings in summer.
• OTHER NAMES *D. marginata* 'Tricolor'.

☼ ◊

Z 10–11

HEIGHT
To 10ft
(3m)

SPREAD
3–6ft
(1–2m)

Agavaceae	

CORDYLINE AUSTRALIS 'Atropurpurea'

Habit Slow-growing, upright, sparsely branched.
Flowers Scented, small, in sprays in summer. White. **Fruits** Small, round berries in autumn. White. **Leaves** Evergreen, long, linear, arching, in rosettes at stem tips. Purplish-green.
• NATIVE HABITAT Garden origin.
• CULTIVATION Suitable for growing in a conservatory. Grow in well-drained soil or soil mix. Needs protection in hard winters or exposed areas.
• PROPAGATION By suckers in spring or by stem cuttings in summer.

☼ ◊

Z 10–11

HEIGHT
To 30ft
(10m)

SPREAD
25ft (8m)

HOLLIES

Hollies belong to the genus *Ilex* and are evergreen or deciduous trees and shrubs that naturally occur in a variety of habitats in both temperate and tropical regions of the world.

Much valued for its glossy, light-reflecting qualities, holly foliage varies considerably, from smooth and undulating to densely spiny, and from shiny and glossy to a flat, matte texture. Leaf colors range from rich, deep greens to creamy, golden, or silvery-gray variegation.

Hollies are also grown for their mainly spherical berries, which range in color from red to yellow to orange and black in autumn and follow the insignificant flowers of spring. Most hollies are unisexual (bear flowers of only one sex), so to ensure a good crop of fruits on female plants, males must also be grown. Many hollies make handsome specimen plants, and their stems may be used for floral arrangements.

Most are tolerant of urban pollution and coastal conditions, while the tallest and most vigorous cultivars of *Ilex aquifolium* and *I.* x *altaclerensis* make fine, wind-resistant hedging. Hollies are usually easy to grow in any moderately fertile, well-drained soil, in sun or shade; however, they resent transplanting. Deciduous species and variegated cultivars will do best in sun or semi-shade. Some deciduous varieties of holly shed large numbers of hard, spiny leaves that may present a threat to playing children, so care should be taken when siting a holly tree. Hollies respond well to hard pruning; prune in late spring. Propagate holly species by seed in spring or by taking semi-ripe cuttings in late summer or early autumn. Hollies can also be propagated by grafting, although cultivars are more usually grown by cuttings. Watch out for holly leaf miner and holly fruitworm, and treat as necessary.

I. MACROCARPA
Habit Upright, spreading, with spur-like branches. *Fruits* Very large, rounded, cherry-like berries. Black. *Leaves* Deciduous, oval-elliptic, saw-toothed, to 4in (11cm) long. Mid-green.
• CULTIVATION Needs a warm, sheltered site.
• HEIGHT 30ft (10m).
• SPREAD 20ft (6m).

I. macrocarpa

☀ ◊ ❀❀   Z 8–9

I. OPACA
Habit Upright. *Fruits* Rounded berries. Crimson, orange, or yellow. *Leaves* Oblong to elliptic, spiny or spineless, leathery. Matte green above, yellow-green beneath.
• CULTIVATION Does not thrive in alkaline soils. Prefers a warmer climate.
• HEIGHT 46ft (14m).
• SPREAD 30ft (10m).

I. opaca
American holly

☀ ◊ ❀❀❀   Z 5–8

I. x *ALTACLERENSIS*
'Belgica'
Habit Dense, upright, free-fruiting. *Fruits* Large, rounded, berries. Orange-red. *Leaves* Lance-shaped to oblong, spiny or spineless. Glossy mid-green. *Stems* Young growth green to yellow-green.
• HEIGHT 40ft (12m).
• SPREAD 15ft (5m).

I. x *altaclerensis*
'Belgica'
FEMALE

☀ ◊ ❀❀   Z 7–9

I. x *ALTACLERENSIS*
'N. N. Barnes'
Habit Dense, shrubby. *Fruits* Berries. Red. *Leaves* Oval, mainly spineless but spine-tipped. Glossy dark green. *Stems* Young stems purple.
• HEIGHT 18ft (5.5m).
• SPREAD 12ft (4m).

I. x *altaclerensis*
'N. N. Barnes'
FEMALE

☀ ◊ ❀❀   Z 7–9

I. × *ALTACLERENSIS* 'Balearica'

Habit Vigorous, upright, conical when young. Free-fruiting. **Fruits** Large, round, berries. Bright red. **Leaves** Large, broadly oval, spiny or spineless. Glossy dark green.
• HEIGHT 40ft (12m).
• SPREAD 15ft (5m).

I. × *altaclerensis* 'Balearica'
FEMALE

☼ ◊ ❀❀   Z 7–9

I. × *ALTACLERENSIS* 'Camelliifolia'

Habit Pyramidal. Free-fruiting. An excellent specimen tree. **Fruits** Large berries. Scarlet. **Leaves** Large, oblong, mainly spineless. Glossy dark green. Red-purple when young. **Stems** Young stems purple.
• HEIGHT 46ft (14m).
• SPREAD 10ft (3m).

I. × *altaclerensis* 'Camelliifolia'
FEMALE

☼ ◊ ❀❀   Z 7–9

I. AQUIFOLIUM 'Pyramidalis'

Habit Conical, dense, broadening with age. Free-fruiting. **Fruits** Round, self-fertile berries. Scarlet. **Leaves** Narrowly elliptic, slightly spiny. Glossy mid-green. **Stems** Young stems green.
• HEIGHT 20ft (6m).
• SPREAD 15ft (5m).

I. aquifolium 'Pyramidalis'
FEMALE

☼ ◊ ❀❀❀   Z 6–9

I. AQUIFOLIUM 'Scotica'

Habit Compact, stiffly upright. **Fruits** Round berries. Red. **Leaves** Oval, thick, leathery, usually spineless, slightly undulated. Very dark green.
• HEIGHT 15ft (5m).
• SPREAD 10ft (3m).

I. aquifolium 'Scotica'
FEMALE

☼ ◊ ❀❀❀   Z 6–9

I. AQUIFOLIUM

Habit Upright, much-branched. Often shrubby and multi-stemmed. **Fruits** Globose berries. Red. **Leaves** Variable, elliptic or oval, wavy-margined or spiny. Glossy dark green.
• CULTIVATION Tolerates industrial pollution and coastal conditions. Excellent for hedging.
• HEIGHT Up to 60ft (18m).
• SPREAD 20ft (6m).

I. aquifolium
English holly

☼ ◊ ❀❀❀   Z 6–9

I. AQUIFOLIUM 'Silver Milkmaid'

Habit Dense, shrubby. Free-fruiting. **Fruits** Round berries. Scarlet. **Leaves** Elliptic, wavy-edged, very spiny. Bright green, centrally blotched creamy-white. Shrimp-pink when young.
• CULTIVATION Tends to revert. Cut out shoots that are green only.
• HEIGHT 18ft (5.5m).
• SPREAD 12ft (4m).

I. aquifolium 'Silver Milkmaid'
FEMALE

☼ ◊ ❀❀❀   Z 6–9

I. AQUIFOLIUM 'Argentea Marginata Pendula'

Habit Compact, domed, weeping. **Fruits** Round berries. Red. **Leaves** Elliptic, spiny. Mottled gray-green, broadly margined creamy-white. Pink when young. **Stems** Young stems purple.
• HEIGHT 20ft (6m).
• SPREAD 15ft (5m).

I. aquifolium 'Argentea Marginata Pendula'
Perry's weeping silver
FEMALE

☼ ◊ ❀❀❀   Z 6–9

I. AQUIFOLIUM 'Elegantissima'

Habit Compact, dense, shrubby. **Leaves** Small, oval, wavy-margined, spiny. Bright green, margined, and faintly marbled creamy-white. Pink when young. **Stems** Young stems green, streaked yellow.
• HEIGHT To 20ft (6m).
• SPREAD 15ft (5m).

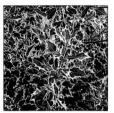

I. aquifolium 'Elegantissima'
MALE

☼ ◊ ❀❀❀   Z 6–9

I. AQUIFOLIUM 'Argentea Marginata'

Habit Columnar. Free-fruiting. **Fruits** Round berries. Red. **Leaves** Broadly oval, spiny. Green, broadly margined creamy-white. Shrimp-pink when young. **Stems** Young stems green, streaked cream.
• HEIGHT 46ft (14m).
• SPREAD 15ft (5m).

I. aquifolium 'Argentea Marginata'
Silver-margined holly
FEMALE

☼ ◊ ❀❀❀   Z 6–9

I. × ALTACLERENSIS 'Belgica Aurea'

Habit Dense, upright. **Fruits** Berries. Red. **Leaves** Large, lance-shaped, slightly spiny or spineless. Dark green, mottled gray-green, and irregularly margined yellow.
• OTHER NAMES *I. × altaclerensis* 'Silver Sentinel', *I. perado* 'Aurea'.
• HEIGHT 25ft (8m).
• SPREAD 10ft (3m).

I. × altaclerensis 'Belgica Aurea'
FEMALE

☼ ◊ ❀❀   Z 7–9

I. × ALTACLERENSIS 'Lawsoniana'

Habit Dense, bushy. **Fruits** Not freely produced. **Leaves** Large, oblong to oval, usually spineless. Bright green, irregularly splashed with gold; paler green in the center.
• CULTIVATION Tends to revert. Cut out shoots that are green only.
• HEIGHT 20ft (6m).
• SPREAD 15ft (5m).

I. × altaclerensis 'Lawsoniana'
FEMALE

☼ ◊ ❀❀   Z 7–9

I. AQUIFOLIUM 'Madame Briot'

Habit Vigorous, bushy. **Fruits** Round berries. Bright scarlet. **Leaves** Large, broadly oval, spiny. Dark green, mottled and margined golden-yellow. **Stems** Young stems purplish.
• HEIGHT 30ft (10m).
• SPREAD 20ft (6m).

I. AQUIFOLIUM 'Silver Queen'

Habit Dense, shrubby. **Leaves** Elliptic, spiny. Very dark green, broadly margined cream. Shrimp-pink when young. **Stems** Young shoots very dark purple.
• OTHER NAMES *I. aquifolium* 'Argentea Regina'.
• HEIGHT 15ft (5m).
• SPREAD 12ft (4m).

I. aquifolium 'Silver Queen'
MALE

☼ ◊ ❀❀❀   Z 6–9

I. aquifolium 'Madame Briot'
FEMALE

☼ ◊ ❀❀❀   Z 6–9

I. AQUIFOLIUM 'Aurifodina'
Habit Erect, dense, shrubby. Free-fruiting. *Fruits* Round berries. Deep scarlet. *Leaves* Elliptic, spiny. Olive green, golden margins tawny-yellow in winter. *Stems* Young stems purplish.
• OTHER NAMES *I. aquifolium* 'Muricata'.
• HEIGHT 20ft (6m).
• SPREAD 10ft (3m).

I. aquifolium 'Aurifodina' FEMALE

☼ ◊ ❀❀❀ Z 6–9

I. x *ALTACLERENSIS* 'Camelliifolia Variegata'
Habit Slow-growing, pyramidal. *Fruits* Rarely produced. *Leaves* Large, oblong. Glossy dark green, marbled pale green, broadly margined golden-yellow.
• HEIGHT 15ft (5m).
• SPREAD 10ft (3m).

I. x *altaclerensis* 'Camelliifolia Variegata' FEMALE

☼ ◊ ❀❀ Z 7–9

I. AQUIFOLIUM 'Pyramidalis Aurea Marginata'
Habit Vigorous, upright, pyramidal. Free-fruiting. *Fruits* Round berries. Red. *Leaves* Narrowly elliptic, spiny on upper half. Glossy mid-green, irregularly margined golden-yellow. *Stems* Young stems green.
• HEIGHT 20ft (6m).
• SPREAD 15ft (5m).

I. aquifolium 'Pyramidalis Aurea Marginata' FEMALE

☼ ◊ ❀❀❀ Z 6–9

I. AQUIFOLIUM 'Ovata Aurea'
Habit Dense, shrubby. One of the most brightly variegated cultivars. *Leaves* Oval, thick, regularly short-spined. Dark green, margined bright golden yellow. *Stems* Young stems deep purple.
• HEIGHT 15ft (5m).
• SPREAD 12ft (4m).

I. aquifolium 'Ovata Aurea' MALE

☼ ◊ ❀❀❀ Z 6–9

I. AQUIFOLIUM 'Crispa Aurea Picta'
Habit Upright, open. *Leaves* Narrowly oval, twisted, sparsely spiny. Very dark green, with central splash of pale green and yellow.
• CULTIVATION Tends to revert.
• HEIGHT 30ft (10m).
• SPREAD 20ft (6m).

I. aquifolium 'Crispa Aurea Picta' MALE

☼ ◊ ❀❀❀ Z 6–9

I. PURPUREA
Habit Upright. *Flowers* Small. Red or lavender. *Fruits* Oval. Scarlet. *Leaves* Oblong-elliptic, tapered, rounded teeth. Dark green. Bright pink when young.
• CULTIVATION Tender. Needs protection; will defoliate in harsh winters.
• OTHER NAMES *I. chinensis*.
• HEIGHT 10–15ft (3–5m).
• SPREAD 10–15ft (3–5m).

I. purpurea

☼ ◊ ❀ Z 7–9

I. AQUIFOLIUM 'Watereriana'
Habit Slow-growing, dense, compact. An excellent specimen plant. *Leaves* Oval, spiny or almost spineless. Gray-green, mottled, and irregularly and broadly margined golden-yellow. *Stems* Young stems green, streaked yellow.
• HEIGHT 15ft (5m).
• SPREAD 15ft (5m).

I. aquifolium 'Watereriana' Waterer's gold holly MALE

☼ ◊ ❀❀❀ Z 6–9

I. PEDUNCULOSA
Habit Upright, often shrubby. *Fruits* Rounded, on very long stalks. Bright red. *Leaves* Oval, pointed, spineless, wavy-edged. Glossy dark green.
• CULTIVATION Unsuitable for alkaline soils.
• HEIGHT 30ft (10m).
• SPREAD 20ft (6m).

I. pedunculosa

☼ ◊ ❀❀❀ Z 5–8

Proteaceae	SILVER TREE

LEUCADENDRON ARGENTEUM

Habit Conical to columnar, spreading with age.
Flowers Individually tiny, in spherical heads,
surrounded by broadly ovate, silvery, shining bracts,
from autumn to winter. *Leaves* Evergreen, lance-
shaped, clothed in long, silky, white hairs.
• NATIVE HABITAT The Cape, South Africa.
• CULTIVATION Grow in a mix of peat and sand
that is low in phosphates and nitrogen. Water
moderately when in growth, otherwise sparingly.
Makes a handsome plant for home or conservatory.
• PROPAGATION By seed in spring.

Z 10–11

HEIGHT
28ft (9m)

SPREAD
6ft (2m)

Myrtaceae	SILVER DOLLAR GUM, SPINNING GUM

EUCALYPTUS PERRINIANA

Habit Open, broadly spreading. *Flowers* Small,
in clusters in the leaf axils in late summer. White.
Leaves Evergreen. Juvenile: semi-circular, clasping
each other across the stem, blue-gray. Adult: lance-
shaped, purple, turning deep blue-green.
Bark Peeling. Gray and brown.
• NATIVE HABITAT In moist soils in the
mountains of S.E. Australia and Tasmania.
• CULTIVATION Grow in fertile, well-drained soil
and provide shelter from cold winds.
• PROPAGATION By seed in spring or autumn.

Z 9–10

HEIGHT
22ft (7m)

SPREAD
15ft (5m)

Agavaceae (Dracaenaceae)	DRAGON TREE

DRACAENA DRACO

Habit Slow-growing, upright, with a wide-branching
head when mature. *Leaves* Evergreen, narrowly
lance-shaped, stiff. Gray-green or blue-green.
• NATIVE HABITAT Canary Islands.
• CULTIVATION Tolerates partial shade. Grow in
well-drained soil or soil mix. Water moderately
when in growth, otherwise sparingly. Leggy plants
may be cut back almost to soil level in spring.
Makes a handsome plant for home or conservatory.
• PROPAGATION By air-layering in spring or by
stem-tip cuttings in summer.

Z 10–11

HEIGHT
To 25ft
(8m)

SPREAD
25ft (8m)

Palmae	JELLY PALM, YATAY PALM

BUTIA CAPITATA

Habit Slow-growing, unbranched, with a
spreading crown. *Leaves* Evergreen, feather-
shaped, to 6ft (2m) or more in length, strongly
arching, with many leathery leaflets. Blue-green.
• NATIVE HABITAT Woodlands and grasslands of
Argentina.
• CULTIVATION Tolerates partial shade. Grow in
any fertile, well-drained soil or soil mix. Water
moderately when in growth, less in winter.
• PROPAGATION By seed in spring.
• OTHER NAMES *Cocos capitata*.

Z 8–11

HEIGHT
To 20ft
(6m)

SPREAD
10ft (3m)

Araliaceae	PUKA

MERYTA SINCLAIRII

Habit Round-headed, multi-stemmed.
Flowers Small, in dense umbels, sporadically from spring to autumn. Greenish-white. **Fruits** Small, rounded, berry-like. Black. **Leaves** Evergreen, oblong to broadly oval, leathery. Glossy dark green.
• NATIVE HABITAT New Zealand.
• CULTIVATION Grow in the home or conservatory in cooler climates. Grow in humus-rich soil or soil mix. Water freely in growth, then moderately.
• PROPAGATION By semi-ripe cuttings in summer, or by seed as soon as ripe in autumn.

Z 10–11

HEIGHT
To 25ft
(8m)

SPREAD
20ft (6m)

Betulaceae	

CARPINUS BETULUS 'Fastigiata'

Habit Very distinctive, pyramidal – narrowly so when young, later spreading. **Leaves** Deciduous, narrowly oval, pointed at the tip, rounded at the base. Neatly and prominently veined. Bright green on emergence, later dark green, turning orange and gold in autumn.
• NATIVE HABITAT Garden origin.
• CULTIVATION Grow in any fertile soils, including clay and alkaline ones. An elegant specimen tree, also well suited to avenue plantings.
• PROPAGATION By budding in late summer.

Z 4–8

HEIGHT
30ft (10m)

SPREAD
40ft (12m)

Fagaceae	

LITHOCARPUS HENRYI

Habit Broadly conical. **Flowers** Catkins: slender, upright, in late summer. Creamy-white.
Fruits Acorns, rounded, to ¾in (2cm) long, enclosed in a shallow cup. **Leaves** Evergreen, elliptic to lance-shaped, slender-pointed. Glossy pale green, becoming darker with age.
• NATIVE HABITAT Mountain woodland in China.
• CULTIVATION Tolerates semi-shade. Grow in deep, fertile, neutral to acid soil. Provide shelter from strong, cold winds.
• PROPAGATION By seed in autumn.

Z 7–9

HEIGHT
30ft (10m)

SPREAD
30ft (10m)

Pittosporaceae	

PITTOSPORUM DALLII

Habit Round-headed, dense, sometimes shrubby.
Flowers Small, honey-scented, cup-shaped, in clusters in summer. White. **Leaves** Evergreen, oblong-elliptic, sharply toothed, leathery, carried in clusters at stem tips. Dark green.
• NATIVE HABITAT Mountain forests of the South Island of New Zealand.
• CULTIVATION Thrives in sheltered places, especially near the coast. In cold, frosty areas, site against a south- or west-facing wall.
• PROPAGATION By budding in summer.

Z 9–11

HEIGHT
15ft (5m)

SPREAD
20ft (6m)

Palmae	GOLDEN-YELLOW PALM, YELLOW PALM

CHRYSALIDOCARPUS LUTESCENS

Habit Upright, suckering, with thick, cane-like stems. **Leaves** Evergreen, arching, feather-shaped, to 6ft (2m) long, with slender leaflets. Yellow-green.
• NATIVE HABITAT Moist, tropical forests of Madagascar.
• CULTIVATION Best grown in a conservatory in cooler climates. Tolerates partial shade. Water moderately when in growth, otherwise very sparingly.
• PROPAGATION By seed or suckers in spring.
• OTHER NAMES *Areca lutescens.*

☼ ◊

Z 9–11

HEIGHT
To 30ft
(10m)

SPREAD
3ft (1m)

Cyatheaceae	ROUGH TREE FERN

CYATHEA AUSTRALIS

Habit Upright, with a light, open crown.
Leaves Evergreen fronds, 6–12ft (2–4m) long, in finely divided leaflets. Light green, bluish beneath.
Bark Trunk almost black.
• NATIVE HABITAT Forests of Australia, Tasmania.
• CULTIVATION Best grown in a conservatory in cooler climates. Grow in humus-rich, moisture-retentive but well-drained soil or soil mix. Water freely when in growth, otherwise moderately.
• PROPAGATION By spores in spring.
• OTHER NAMES *Alsophila australis.*

☼ ◊

Z 8–10

HEIGHT
25ft (8m) or
more

SPREAD
12ft (4m) or
more

Agavaceae	ELEPHANT'S FOOT, PONY-TAIL

BEAUCARNEA RECURVATA

Habit Slow-growing, with sparsely branched stems and a flask-shaped trunk.
Leaves Evergreen, to 3ft (1m) long, linear, recurved. Persisting after turning brown.
• NATIVE HABITAT Arid areas of S.E. Mexico.
• CULTIVATION Best grown as a house plant in cooler climates. Tolerates drought. Grow in sharply drained soil or soil mix.
• PROPAGATION By seed or suckers in spring or by stem-tip cuttings in summer.
• OTHER NAMES *Nolina recurvata, N. tuberculata.*

☼ ◊

Z 10–11

HEIGHT
To 25ft
(8m)

SPREAD
15ft (5m)

Aceraceae	PAPERBARK MAPLE

ACER GRISEUM

Habit Broadly columnar, later spreading.
Flowers Small, pendent clusters in late spring. Greenish. **Fruits** 2 seeds, fused together, each with a wing. **Leaves** Deciduous, with 3 elliptic leaflets. Dark green, paler beneath, turning orange and red.
Bark Peeling. Chestnut to cinnamon-brown.
• NATIVE HABITAT Mountain woods in C. China.
• CULTIVATION Tolerates dappled shade but colors best in sun. Grow in any fertile, moisture-retentive soil.
• PROPAGATION By seed in autumn.

☼ ◊
❀ ❀ ❀

Z 4–8

HEIGHT
30ft (10m)
or more

SPREAD
30ft (10m)

Pinaceae	BLUE ATLAS CEDAR

CEDRUS LIBANI subsp. *ATLANTICA*
Glauca Group

Habit Broadly conical, flat-topped with age, branches ascending or horizontal. *Fruits* Barrel-shaped cones, upright, to 3in (8cm) long, smooth. Green-purple, turning brown when ripe. *Leaves* Needle-like, slender, sharp-pointed, to ¾in (2cm) long, in dense whorls. Silver-blue, especially bright in early summer. *Bark* Fissured into scaly plates. Dark gray.
• NATIVE HABITAT Atlas Mountains, N. Africa.
• CULTIVATION Tolerates dry soils, both acid and alkaline, and cool summers. This conifer thrives in well-drained soil in warm, sunny, sheltered sites. It is widely planted as a specimen, but since it eventually reaches a considerable size, it is best suited to larger gardens.
• PROPAGATION By seed in autumn or spring.
• OTHER NAMES *C. atlantica* f. *glauca*.

Z 5–7

HEIGHT
80ft (25m)
or more

SPREAD
30ft (10m)
or more

Pinaceae	

ABIES CONCOLOR 'Argentea'

Habit Upright, conical, with branches in whorls. **Fruits** Upright, oblong to ovoid cones. Pale blue-green. **Leaves** Linear, blunt-tipped, uppermost needles upswept. Silver-white above and below.
• NATIVE HABITAT Mountains, W. United States.
• CULTIVATION Grow in moist but freely draining soil. Shelter from drying winds.
• PROPAGATION By grafting in late summer, winter or early spring. Seed sown in autumn; may not come true.
• OTHER NAMES *A. concolor* 'Candicans'.

Z 3–7

HEIGHT
65ft (20m)
or more

SPREAD
25ft (8m) or
more

Cupressaceae	KASHMIR CYPRESS

CUPRESSUS CASHMERIANA

Habit Broadly conical, branch tips weeping, spreading with age. **Fruits** Small, rounded cones, scales with hooked point. Blue-gray, ripening to brown. **Leaves** Aromatic, small, scale-like, carried in flattened, pendent sprays. Blue-green.
• NATIVE HABITAT Probably from the Himalayas.
• CULTIVATION Grow in moist but well-drained soil. Susceptible to wind scorch.
• PROPAGATION By seed in autumn or spring or by cuttings of current year's growth from autumn to spring.

Z 9–10

HEIGHT
60ft (16m)

SPREAD
30ft (10m)

Pinaceae	

PINUS × HOLFORDIANA

Habit Open, broadly conical. **Fruits** Large, pendent, slightly curved, resinous cones, to 12in (30cm) long. Brown. **Leaves** Needle-like, slender, to 7in (18cm) long, pendent and flexible, in clusters of 5. Glaucous blue-gray to silver-green.
• NATIVE HABITAT Garden origin.
• CULTIVATION Tolerant of dry soils, wind, and coastal conditions. Grow in any well-drained soil.
• PROPAGATION By grafting in late summer, winter or early spring.

Z 7–9

HEIGHT
To 80ft
(25m)

SPREAD
15ft (5m)

Cupressaceae	LEYLAND CYPRESS

× CUPRESSOCYPARIS LEYLANDII

Habit Vigorous, fast-growing, upright, columnar. **Leaves** Small, scale-like, in flattened sprays. Dark green or gray-green, paler beneath.
• NATIVE HABITAT Garden origin.
• CULTIVATION Tolerant of a wide range of soils and conditions, including alkaline soils and coastal exposure. Good for screens and hedges. Clip in summer. Do not cut back into old growth.
• PROPAGATION By cuttings of the current year's growth from autumn to spring.
• OTHER NAMES *Cupressus × leylandii*.

Z 6–10

HEIGHT
To 100ft
(30m)

SPREAD
10ft (3m) or
more

Pinaceae	MACEDONIAN PINE

PINUS PEUCE

Habit Upright, slender-pyramidal. *Flowers* Male and female on same plant in separate clusters on the young shoots. Males: yellow; females: red. *Fruits* Cylindrical to conical, drooping cones. Green, turning brown when ripe. Covered in white resin. *Leaves* Stiff, needle-like, to 4in (10cm) long, forward-pointing, in dense clusters of 5. Dark blue-green. *Bark* Fissured and cracked into plates. Purple-brown; young shoots bloomed, green.
• NATIVE HABITAT Mountains of S.E. Europe.
• CULTIVATION Tolerant of a wide range of soils and conditions including coastal exposure. The Macedonian pine maintains its dense, pyramidal outline, with branches reaching to ground level, making it an attractive and reliable species for specimen plantings. It grows consistently well in all sites.
• PROPAGATION By seed in autumn or spring.

Z 4–7

HEIGHT
To 100ft
(30m)

SPREAD
30ft (10m)

Cupressaceae	

CHAMAECYPARIS LAWSONIANA
'Intertexta'

Habit Elegant, weeping, columnar with age.
Fruits Round cones, to ¼in (8mm) across, at branch tips, carried in lax, flattened, pendulous sprays.
Leaves Aromatic, very small, scale-like. Gray-green.
• NATIVE HABITAT Garden origin.
• CULTIVATION Tolerant of shade, exposure, urban pollution, and dry, alkaline soils. Grow in moist but well-drained, neutral to acid soils.
• PROPAGATION By heeled greenwood cuttings in late summer or by softwood cuttings in summer.

Z 5–8

HEIGHT
80ft (25m)

SPREAD
25ft (8m)

Pinaceae	EASTERN WHITE PINE

PINUS STROBUS

Habit Narrowly conical when young, later open, rounded. **Fruits** Curved, cylindrical, pendent cones, to 6in (15cm) or more in length. **Leaves** Slender, needle-like, to 6in (15cm) long, in clusters of 5. Gray-green. **Bark** Smooth, fissured with age. Gray.
• NATIVE HABITAT Low altitude woodlands of E. North America.
• CULTIVATION Tolerant of a wide range of soils and conditions including coastal exposure, but intolerant of urban pollution.
• PROPAGATION By seed in autumn or spring.

Z 3–8

HEIGHT
To 160ft
(50m)

SPREAD
30ft (10m)

Pinaceae	BIG-CONE PINE

PINUS COULTERI

Habit Fast-growing, broadly spreading.
Fruits Large cones, broadly ovoid, to 14in (35cm) long, resinous, with hook-spined scales.
Leaves Stiff, needle-like, to 12in (30cm) long. Gray-green, in dense clusters of 3, sparsely set on branches. **Bark** Fissured, plated. Red-brown
• NATIVE HABITAT Rocky Mountains of California.
• CULTIVATION Tolerates most soils including heavy clay and very wet soils.
• PROPAGATION By seed in autumn or spring.

Z 7–9

HEIGHT
To 80ft
(25m)

SPREAD
50ft (15m)

Pinaceae	EUROPEAN LARCH

LARIX DECIDUA

Habit Narrowly conical. **Flowers** Male: pendent, red; female: upright, yellow, on same plant in spring. **Fruits** Upright, ovoid cones, to 1½in (4cm) long. Brown. **Leaves** Deciduous, soft, needle-like, to 1½in (4cm) long. Emerald green when young, later bright green, turning clear, russet-gold in autumn. **Bark** Fissured, scaly. Red-brown.
• NATIVE HABITAT Mountains of Europe.
• CULTIVATION Tolerates both alkaline and poor, acid soils.
• PROPAGATION By seed in autumn or spring.

This, and other species of larch, are best planted in their final location when young and left undisturbed. *L. decidua* is especially suitable for specimen plantings. It is exceptionally beautiful in spring when its new leaves emerge, and again in autumn, when they turn gold before falling.
• OTHER NAMES *L. europaea.*

Z 2–7

HEIGHT
130ft (40m)

SPREAD
15–50ft
(5–15m)

Pinaceae	VEITCH FIR

ABIES VEITCHII

Habit Fast-growing, narrowly conical.
Fruits Upright, cylindrical cones, to 3in (7.5cm)
long. Violet-blue, brown when ripe. **Leaves** Linear,
notched at the tip, to 1¼in (3cm) long, forward-
pointing on top of shoot, spreading beneath. Glossy
dark green above, with 2 silver-blue bands below.
Bark Smooth, becoming scaly with age. Gray.
• NATIVE HABITAT Forests and mountains, Japan.
• CULTIVATION Quite tolerant of urban pollution
but does not thrive in shallow alkaline soils.
• PROPAGATION By seed in autumn or spring.

Z 3–6

HEIGHT
To 80ft
(25m)

SPREAD
15ft (5m) or
more

Cupressaceae (Taxodiaceae)	DAWN REDWOOD

METASEQUOIA GLYPTOSTROBOIDES

Habit Fast-growing, narrowly conical. **Fruits** Small,
rounded cones. Green, turning brown when ripe.
Leaves Deciduous, opposite, linear, soft, flattened.
Bright green, then dark green, turning yellow and
red in autumn. **Bark** Fibrous. Red-brown.
• NATIVE HABITAT Riversides and damp soils in
S.W. China.
• CULTIVATION Tolerant of urban pollution and
alkaline and waterlogged soils. Best in moist, well-
drained soils.
• PROPAGATION By seed in autumn or spring.

Z 4–8

HEIGHT
To 120ft
(35m)

SPREAD
30ft (10m)

Cupressaceae	INCENSE CEDAR

CALOCEDRUS DECURRENS

Habit Narrowly columnar, but very variable.
Fruits Oblong cones, with overlapping scales.
Leaves Aromatic, scale-like, sharp-pointed in
flattened sprays. Dark green. **Bark** Scaly. Gray,
red-brown beneath.
• NATIVE HABITAT Mountain forests of W. North
America.
• CULTIVATION Grow in moist, well-drained,
preferably neutral to acid soils.
• PROPAGATION By seed in autumn or spring.
• OTHER NAMES *Libocedrus decurrens.*

Z 5–8

HEIGHT
100ft (30m)
or more

SPREAD
12ft (4m) or
more

Cupressaceae (Taxodiaceae)	BIG TREE, SIERRA REDWOOD

SEQUOIADENDRON GIGANTEUM

Habit Fast-growing, conical. **Fruits** Barrel-
shaped cones, to 3in (7.5cm) long. Green, turning
brown when ripe. **Leaves** Tiny, spirally arranged,
scale-like, pointed. Blue-green, with a musty scent
when crushed. **Bark** Spongy, fibrous. Red-brown.
• NATIVE HABITAT Rocky Mountains, California.
• CULTIVATION Tolerant of exposure and almost
any soil, except shallow, alkaline soil.
• PROPAGATION By seed in autumn or spring.
• OTHER NAMES *Sequoia wellingtonia, S. gigantea.*

Z 6–8

HEIGHT
To 260ft
(80m)

SPREAD
65ft (20m)

Pinaceae	BLUE DOUGLAS FIR

PSEUDOTSUGA MENZIESII var. *GLAUCA*

Habit Fast-growing, conical. **Fruits** Pendent cones to 4in (10cm) long. Red-brown, with distinctive, 3-pronged bracts protruding from between the scales. **Leaves** Aromatic – smelling of turpentine when crushed – linear, blunt-tipped, to 1¼in (3cm) long. Glaucous, blue-green. **Bark** Thick, grooved, corky. Gray-brown.
• NATIVE HABITAT Evergreen forests in the Rocky Mountains, from Montana to New Mexico.
• CULTIVATION Unsuitable for shallow, alkaline soils but more lime-tolerant than the species. It is a large, stately tree for large or medium-sized gardens, although it may only reach 80ft (25m) in cultivation. Grow in moist, well-drained soils. The tree's common name commemorates David Douglas, the 19th-century Scottish plant hunter.
• PROPAGATION By seed in autumn or spring.
• OTHER NAMES *P. glauca.*

Z 4–7

HEIGHT
To 200ft
(60m) less
in cult.

SPREAD
50ft (15m)

Pinaceae	CEDAR OF LEBANON

CEDRUS LIBANI

Habit Broadly conical, irregular with age, tiered branches horizontal or slightly ascending. **Fruits** Barrel-shaped cones, upright, to 5in (12cm) long, smooth. Purple-green, then brown. **Leaves** Needle-like, slender, sharp-pointed, to 1¼in (3cm) long, in dense whorls. Dark gray-green.
• NATIVE HABITAT Mountain forests of Lebanon and S.E. Turkey.
• CULTIVATION Tolerates dry soils, both acid and alkaline, and cool summers.
• PROPAGATION By seed in autumn or spring.

Z 5–7

HEIGHT
To 130ft
(40m)

SPREAD
65ft (20m)
or more

Pinaceae	HIMALAYAN PINE, BLUE PINE, BHUTAN PINE

PINUS WALLICHIANA

Habit Broadly conical. **Fruits** Curved, cylindrical cones, to 12in (30cm) long. Green, turning pale brown when ripe. **Leaves** Slender, needle-like, flexible, and drooping, to 8in (20cm) long, in clusters of 5. Blue-green. **Bark** Smooth, fissured with age. Gray.
• NATIVE HABITAT Mountain forests, Himalayas.
• CULTIVATION Tolerant of a range of soils and exposure, but dislikes shallow alkaline soils.
• PROPAGATION By seed in autumn or spring.
• OTHER NAMES *P. chylla, P. excelsa, P. griffithii*.

Z 5–8

HEIGHT
To 130ft
(40m)

SPREAD
50ft (15m)

Pinaceae	PONDEROSA PINE, WESTERN YELLOW PINE

PINUS PONDEROSA

Habit Upright, or broadly conical. **Fruits** Ovoid cones, with spine-tipped scales. Purple, turning glossy red-brown when ripe. **Leaves** Stiff, needle-like, to 10in (25cm) long, in clusters of 3, forward-pointing. Dark gray-green. **Bark** Thick, scaly, deeply fissured. Yellow-brown to red.
• NATIVE HABITAT Rocky Mountains, W. North America.
• CULTIVATION Tolerates coastal exposure and most soils, including heavy clay.
• PROPAGATION By seed in autumn or spring.

Z 4–8

HEIGHT
To 160ft
(50m)

SPREAD
65ft (20m)

Pinaceae	BISHOP PINE

PINUS MURICATA

Habit Fast-growing, broadly columnar, flat-topped with age. **Fruits** Ovoid cones, to 3in (8cm) long, persisting on branches. Red-brown. **Leaves** Stiff, needle-like, to 6in (15cm) long, in pairs. Blue- to gray-green. **Bark** Deeply ridged. Purple-brown.
• NATIVE HABITAT Low, coastal hills of California.
• CULTIVATION Tolerant of coastal exposure and poor, sandy soil. Dislikes shallow alkaline soils. Grow in well-drained soil.
• PROPAGATION By seed in autumn or spring.

Z 8–10

HEIGHT
To 80ft
(25m)

SPREAD
23ft (8m)

Pinaceae	JEFFREY PINE

PINUS JEFFREYI

Habit Upright, conical or spire-shaped.
Fruits Conical cones, to 12in (30cm) long, scales with a curved spine. **Leaves** Stiff, needle-like, to 10in (25cm) long, in clusters of 3. Blue-green.
Bark Finely fissured. Black; shoots gray-bloomed.
• NATIVE HABITAT Dry mountain slopes in S.W. United States.
• CULTIVATION Dislikes shallow, alkaline soils.
• PROPAGATION By seed in autumn or spring.
• OTHER NAMES *P. ponderosa* var. *jeffreyi*.

Z 5–8

HEIGHT
To 130ft
(40m)

SPREAD
30ft (10m)

Pinaceae	MARITIME PINE

PINUS PINASTER

Habit Vigorous, with a domed crown.
Fruits Cones, conical, to 8in (20cm) long, in whorls. Glossy brown. **Leaves** Stiff, needle-like, to 8in (20cm) long, sharply pointed, in pairs. Dark gray-green. **Bark** Deeply fissured. Purple-brown.
• NATIVE HABITAT Sandy soils of N. Africa and S.W. Europe.
• CULTIVATION Thrives on dry, sandy soils and tolerates coastal exposure in mild areas.
• PROPAGATION By seed in autumn or spring.
• OTHER NAMES *P. maritima*.

Z 8–9

HEIGHT
To 120ft
(35m)

SPREAD
40ft (12m)

Pinaceae	SERBIAN SPRUCE

PICEA OMORIKA

Habit Graceful, narrowly conical, spire-shaped, with pendulous branches that arch slightly outward at the tips. **Fruits** Narrowly ovoid cones. Violet-purple; brown when ripe. **Leaves** Slender, needle-like, to ¾in (2cm) long. Dark green, with blue-white bands beneath. **Bark** Plated. Purple-brown.
• NATIVE HABITAT On limestone rocks alongside the River Drina, Bosnia-Herzegovina.
• CULTIVATION Tolerates urban pollution and almost any soil, including alkaline or wet soils.
• PROPAGATION By seed in autumn or spring.

Z 4–7

HEIGHT
To 100ft
(30m)

SPREAD
12–15ft
(4–5m)

Araucariaceae	MONKEY PUZZLE, CHILE PINE

ARAUCARIA ARAUCANA

Habit Open, usually symmetrically domed.
Fruits Large, globose. Green, with golden spines, enclosing shining, brown seeds.
Leaves Triangular, rigid, spine-tipped. Dark green scales overlap around the shoot. **Bark** Wrinkled, with persistent branch scars. Dark gray.
• NATIVE HABITAT Mountains of Argentina and Chile.
• CULTIVATION Tolerates coastal exposure. Grow in any fertile, moisture-retentive soil.
• PROPAGATION By seed in autumn or spring.

Z 10

HEIGHT
80ft (25m)

SPREAD
To 50ft
(15m)

Pinaceae	WESTERN HEMLOCK

TSUGA HETEROPHYLLA

Habit Narrowly conical. **Fruits** Ovoid, pendent cones, to ¾in (2cm) long. **Leaves** Linear, of mixed sizes, to ¾in (2cm) long. Dark green above, with 2 broad, white bands beneath. **Bark** Ridged, flaking. Purple-brown.
• NATIVE HABITAT Mountain forests of W. North America.
• CULTIVATION Tolerates light, sandy soil and clay soil. Withstands clipping. Avoid exposed sites.
• PROPAGATION By seed in autumn or spring.
• OTHER NAMES *T. albertiana.*

Z 5–6

HEIGHT
130ft (40m)
or more

SPREAD
40ft (12m)

Cupressaceae (Taxodiaceae)	CALIFORNIA REDWOOD, COAST REDWOOD

SEQUOIA SEMPERVIRENS

Habit Narrowly conical. **Fruits** Barrel-shaped cones, to 1¼in (3cm) long. Red-brown. **Leaves** Linear, to ¾in (2cm) long. Dark green above, with 2 white bands beneath. **Bark** Thick, soft, fibrous. Red-brown.
• NATIVE HABITAT Foothills of coastal mountains in S. Oregon and California.
• CULTIVATION Intolerant of urban pollution. Grow in any fertile soil. Performs best in cool, humid areas.
• PROPAGATION By seed in autumn or spring.

Z 7–9

HEIGHT
130ft (40m)
or more

SPREAD
25ft (8m) or more

Pinaceae	JAPANESE LARCH

LARIX KAEMPFERI

Habit Broadly conical. **Flowers** Male: yellow, drooping; female: upright, creamy-pink, on same plant in spring. **Fruits** Upright, ovoid cones, to 1¼in (3cm) long. **Leaves** Deciduous, soft, needle-like, to 1½in (4cm) long, in dense whorls. Gray- to blue-green, turning gold in autumn. **Bark** Scaly. Red-brown.
• NATIVE HABITAT Mountains of C. Japan.
• CULTIVATION Tolerates poor and acid soils.
• PROPAGATION By seed in autumn or spring.
• OTHER NAMES *L. leptolepis.*

Z 4–7

HEIGHT
100ft (30m)
or more

SPREAD
15–25ft (5–8m) or more

Cupressaceae	EASTERN WHITE CEDAR, AMERICAN ARBORVITAE

THUJA OCCIDENTALIS

Habit Narrowly conical. **Fruits** Oblong, upright cones, to ½in (1cm) long. Yellow-green, brown when ripe. **Leaves** Aromatic, very small, scale-like, on flattened shoots, in flat sprays. Dark green above, paler beneath. **Bark** Peeling in strips. Orange-brown.
• NATIVE HABITAT Mountain slopes and swamps of E. North America.
• CULTIVATION Grow in any but waterlogged soil. Tolerates clipping and may be used for hedging. Plant several for hedging at 20in (60cm) apart.

Clip in spring and early autumn. *T. occidentalis* is slower growing as a hedge than some conifers and deciduous plants but is beautifully scented, with a fresh, apple-like smell.
• PROPAGATION By softwood cuttings in summer or by heeled greenwood cuttings in late summer.

Z 2–7

HEIGHT
65ft (20m)

SPREAD
15ft (5m)

Ginkgoaceae	GINKGO, MAIDENHAIR TREE

GINKGO BILOBA

Habit Variable: conical when young, later broadly columnar or spreading; often multi-stemmed.
Flowers Female flowers resemble small acorns; males on separate plants.
Fruits Rounded, smooth, plum-like; flesh smells putrid when ripe. **Leaves** Deciduous, fan-shaped, to 5in (12cm) across, deeply notched at the tip. Bright green, turning yellow in autumn. **Bark** Ridged and fissured. Dull gray.
• NATIVE HABITAT Once thought extinct in the wild, but occurs in Guizhou and Zheijiang, S. China.

Fossil evidence indicates that the tree has remained unchanged for some 200 million years.
• CULTIVATION Grow in any well-drained soil with shelter from cold, dry winds.
• PROPAGATION By seed in autumn, by softwood cuttings in summer, or by hardwood cuttings in winter.

Z 3–9

HEIGHT
100ft (30m)

SPREAD
40ft (12m)
or more

Pinaceae	AUSTRIAN PINE

PINUS NIGRA subsp. *NIGRA*

Habit Broadly columnar, sometimes multi-stemmed. *Fruits* Ovoid cones, to 3in (8cm) long. Brown. *Leaves* Stiff, needle-like, to 6in (15cm) long, in pairs. Very dark green, in dense tufts. *Bark* Ridged, scaly. Almost black.
• NATIVE HABITAT Foothills and mountains, often on limestone, in C. and S.E. Europe.
• CULTIVATION Very tolerant of exposure and alkaline soils.
• PROPAGATION By seed in autumn or spring.
• OTHER NAMES *P. nigra* var. *austriaca*.

Z 4–8

HEIGHT
120ft (35m)

SPREAD
40ft (12m)

Pinaceae	MONTEREY PINE

PINUS RADIATA

Habit Fast-growing, broadly conical, domed when mature. *Fruits* Ovoid cones, asymmetrical at base, persistent, remaining tightly closed for many years. Green; brown when ripe. *Leaves* Slender, needle-like, to 6in (15cm) long, in clusters of 3. Bright green. *Bark* Deeply fissured. Dark gray.
• NATIVE HABITAT Dry, coastal hills of California.
• CULTIVATION Tolerant of dry, sandy soils and exposure.
• PROPAGATION By seed in autumn or spring.
• OTHER NAMES *P. insignis*.

Z 7–9

HEIGHT
100ft (30m)
or more

SPREAD
30ft (10m)

Pinaceae	GIANT FIR, GRAND FIR

ABIES GRANDIS

Habit Vigorous, narrowly conical. *Fruits* Upright, cylindrical cones, to 4in (10cm) long. Green, turning brown when ripe. *Leaves* Very aromatic, linear, slender, flattened, to 2in (5cm) long, with a notched tip. Bright green, with 2 silver-white bands beneath. *Bark* Smooth, cracking with age. Gray-brown.
• NATIVE HABITAT Evergreen forests in mountain foothills of W. North America.
• CULTIVATION Dislikes alkaline soils. Very shade-tolerant once established.
• PROPAGATION By seed in autumn or spring.

Z 5–6

HEIGHT
160ft (50m)

SPREAD
20ft (6m)

Pinaceae	NORWAY SPRUCE

PICEA ABIES

Habit Fast-growing, narrowly conical. *Fruits* Curved, cylindrical, pendent cones to 6in (15cm) long. *Leaves* Rigid, slender, needle-like, to ¾in (2cm) long, 4-sided. Dark green. *Bark* Peeling. Red-brown to gray.
• NATIVE HABITAT Damp mountain forests in Europe.
• CULTIVATION Commonly grown as a windbreak tree. Prefers well-drained, acid soils.
• PROPAGATION By seed in autumn or spring.
• OTHER NAMES *P. excelsa*.

Z 2–8

HEIGHT
160ft (50m)

SPREAD
15ft (5m)

Pinaceae	BOSNIAN PINE

PINUS HELDREICHII var. *LEUCODERMIS*

Habit Narrowly conical, or ovoid, with ascending branches. **Fruits** Ovoid cones, to 4in (10cm) long. Deep cobalt-blue, turning yellow-brown when ripe. **Leaves** Rigid, needle-like, to 3½in (9cm) long, densely clustered, forward-pointing. Dark green. **Bark** Cracking into shallow plates with maturity. Gray.
• NATIVE HABITAT Limestone mountains in Bosnia-Herzegovina, Albania, and N. Greece.
• CULTIVATION Tolerates alkaline soils and dry or acid soils. The Bosnian pine is a distinctive tree,

notable for its dark foliage and slender outline, and is easily identified by its cobalt-blue young cones. As a dense, shapely, and attractive conifer, it is well suited to specimen planting.
• PROPAGATION By seed in autumn or spring.
• OTHER NAMES *P. leucodermis*.

Z 6–7

HEIGHT
65ft (20m)

SPREAD
10ft (3m)

Cupressaceae	

x *CUPRESSOCYPARIS LEYLANDII* 'Harlequin'

Habit Vigorous, fast-growing, upright, columnar.
Leaves Small, scale-like, in flattened, plume-like sprays. Dark green or gray-green, paler beneath, with ivory-white patches.
• NATIVE HABITAT Garden origin.
• CULTIVATION Tolerant of a wide range of soils and conditions, including alkaline soils and coastal exposure. Good for screens and hedges.
• PROPAGATION By cuttings of the current year's growth from autumn to spring.

☼ ◊
❀❀❀

Z 6–10

HEIGHT
65ft (20m)
or more

SPREAD
10ft (3m) or
more

Cupressaceae	

x *CUPRESSOCYPARIS LEYLANDII* 'Castlewellan'

Habit Vigorous, upright, columnar, slower-growing than the type. *Leaves* Small, scale-like, in flattened sprays. Bright green, tinted bronze-yellow.
• NATIVE HABITAT Garden origin.
• CULTIVATION Tolerant of a wide range of soils and conditions, including alkaline soils and coastal exposure. Good for screens and hedges. Clip in summer; do not cut back into old growth. ·
• PROPAGATION By cuttings of the current year's growth from autumn to spring.

☼ ◊
❀❀❀

Z 6–10

HEIGHT
80ft (25m)
or more

SPREAD
10ft (3m) or
more

Pinaceae	

PICEA ORIENTALIS 'Skylands'

Habit Slow-growing, dense, conical.
Fruits Cylindrical, slightly curved, pendent cone, to 4in (10cm) long, resinous. Purple, turning brown when ripe. *Flowers* Male flowers brick-red.
Leaves Needle-like, to ⅓in (8mm) long. Golden-yellow throughout the year.
• NATIVE HABITAT Garden origin.
• CULTIVATION Grow in moist but well-drained neutral to acid soil.
• PROPAGATION By grafting in late summer, winter or early spring.

☼ ◊
❀❀❀

Z 5–7

HEIGHT
80ft (25m)

SPREAD
6–10ft
(2–3m)

Cupressaceae (Taxodiaceae)	BALD CYPRESS, SWAMP CYPRESS

TAXODIUM DISTICHUM

Habit Broadly conical. *Fruits* Small, globose to ovoid cones. Green, turning brown when ripe.
Leaves Deciduous, alternate, linear, soft, flattened. Fresh green, turning gold in late autumn.
Bark Stringy. Pale red-brown.
• NATIVE HABITAT Swamps and stream sides in S.E. United States.
• CULTIVATION Thrives in waterlogged conditions and in deep, moisture-retentive soils.
• PROPAGATION By seed in autumn or spring or by cuttings of current year's growth in late summer.

☼ ◉
❀❀❀

Z 4–9

HEIGHT
120ft (35m)

SPREAD
15ft (5m)

Pinaceae	

ABIES PROCERA 'Glauca'

Habit Narrowly conical. *Fruits* Upright, cylindrical cones, to 10in (25cm) long, with protruding, down-curved bracts. Purple-brown. *Leaves* Linear. Bright silver-blue when young, turning blue-gray. *Bark* Smooth. Silvery.
• NATIVE HABITAT Mountains, W. United States.
• CULTIVATION Unsuitable for shallow, alkaline soils. Grow in moist but well-drained, neutral to slightly acid soil.
• PROPAGATION By seed in autumn or spring.
• OTHER NAMES *A. nobilis* 'Glauca'.

Pinaceae	

PICEA PUNGENS 'Koster'

Habit Upright, conical. *Fruits* Narrowly ovoid, slightly curved, pendent cones, to 4in (10cm) long. Pale brown. *Leaves* Rigid, needle-like, spine-tipped, to 1¼in (3cm) long. Bright silvery-blue, fading to green with age. *Bark* Scaly. Gray.
• NATIVE HABITAT Species occurs in high mountains of W. United States. Garden origin.
• CULTIVATION Grows best in fertile, well-drained, neutral to acid soil.
• PROPAGATION By grafting in late summer, winter or early spring.

Z 5–6

HEIGHT
To 130ft
(40m) or
more

SPREAD
15ft (5m)

Z 3–7

HEIGHT
50ft (15m)
or more

SPREAD
15ft (5m)

Pinaceae	ENGELMANN PINE

PICEA ENGELMANNII

Habit Broadly conical. *Fruits* Cylindrical, slightly curved cones, to 2in (5cm) long. Brown-purple. *Leaves* Aromatic, soft, flexible, needle-like, 4-angled. Blue-green. *Bark* Flaking. Orange.
• NATIVE HABITAT Mountains of W. North America.
• CULTIVATION Tolerates most poor soils, except shallow, alkaline soils.
• PROPAGATION By seed in autumn or spring.

Pinaceae	

PICEA GLAUCA 'Coerulea'

Habit Narrowly conical, dense, becoming rounded with age. *Fruits* Narrowly cylindrical, pendent cones, to 2½in (6cm) long. Coppery-brown. *Leaves* Slender, rigid, needle-like, 4-sided, to ⅝in (1.5cm) long. Blue-green to silver. *Bark* Scaly. Gray-brown.
• NATIVE HABITAT Species occurs in forests of Canada and N.E. United States. Garden origin.
• CULTIVATION Tolerates cold, exposed sites.
• PROPAGATION By grafting in late summer, winter or early spring.

Z 2–5

HEIGHT
80ft (25m)
or more

SPREAD
15ft (5m)

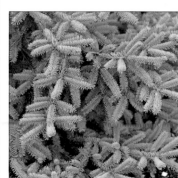

Z 4–7

HEIGHT
50ft (15m)
or more

SPREAD
15ft (5m)

Cupressaceae	

CHAMAECYPARIS LAWSONIANA 'Pembury Blue'

Habit Upright, conical. *Fruits* Round cones, to ¼in (8mm) across, at branch tips. *Leaves* Aromatic, very small, scale-like, carried in lax, flattened, pendulous sprays. Bright silver-blue.
• NATIVE HABITAT Garden origin.
• CULTIVATION Tolerant of shade, exposure, urban pollution, and dry, alkaline soils. Grow in moist but well-drained, neutral to acid soils.
• PROPAGATION By softwood cuttings in summer or by heeled greenwood cuttings in late summer.

Z 5–8

HEIGHT
50ft (15m)

SPREAD
15ft (5m)

Cupressaceae	ITALIAN CYPRESS

CUPRESSUS SEMPERVIRENS

Habit Narrowly columnar. *Fruits* Ovoid to rounded cones, with overlapping scales. *Leaves* Tiny, scale-like, closely pressed to the shoots, in erect, irregular sprays. Very dark gray-green. *Bark* Shallow, spiral ridges. Brown-gray.
• NATIVE HABITAT Rocky areas in the mountains of S.W. Asia and E. Mediterranean.
• CULTIVATION Tolerates lime-rich soils, but best on neutral to slightly acid soils, in a warm, sunny site with shelter from cold, dry winds.
• PROPAGATION By seed in autumn or spring.

Z 7–9

HEIGHT
50ft (15m)
or more

SPREAD
10ft (3m)

Cupressaceae	

JUNIPERUS CHINENSIS 'Keteleeri'

Habit Slender, narrowly conical to columnar; free-fruiting. *Fruits* Small, berry-like cones, to ⅜₆in (8mm) long. Bloomed blue-green. *Leaves* Aromatic, tiny, scale-like, closely pressed to the shoot. Bright, shining gray-green. *Bark* Peeling. Brown.
• NATIVE HABITAT Species occurs in hills and mountains of China and Japan. Garden origin.
• CULTIVATION Grow in any well-drained soil.
• PROPAGATION By cuttings of the current year's growth from autumn to spring.

Z 3–9

HEIGHT
50ft (15m)

SPREAD
12ft (4m)

Pinaceae	BREWER'S SPRUCE

PICEA BREWERIANA

Habit Broadly conical, with spreading branches and pendulous branchlets. *Fruits* Cylindrical, pendent cones, to 5in (12cm) long. Purple; red-brown when ripe. *Leaves* Slender, often curved, flattened, needle-like. Very dark green above, with 2 narrow, white bands beneath. *Bark* Pink-gray, becoming gray-purple and scaly with age.
• NATIVE HABITAT Mountains of Oregon and California.
• CULTIVATION Best grown in slightly acid soil.
• PROPAGATION By seed in autumn or spring.

Z 5–6

HEIGHT
40ft (12m)
or more

SPREAD
15ft (5m)

Pinaceae	JAPANESE WHITE PINE

PINUS PARVIFLORA

Habit Slow-growing, broadly columnar to spreading, with level branches. **Flowers** Males and females in separate clusters on the young shoots in early summer. Males: purple-red; females: red. **Fruits** Ovoid cones, to 3in (7cm) long, with leathery scales. Green, turning red-brown when ripe. **Leaves** Slightly twisted, needle-like, to 2½in (6cm) long, in clusters of 5. Blue-green on outer surface, blue-white within. **Bark** Curling scales. Purple-brown.
• NATIVE HABITAT On stony ground in the mountains of Japan.
• CULTIVATION Tolerates coastal exposure and poor soils but dislikes shallow, alkaline soils. Makes a picturesque specimen tree, valued for its layered, twisted foliage and much planted in Japanese-style gardens. Suitable for growing as a bonsai.
• PROPAGATION By seed in autumn or spring.

Z 4–7

HEIGHT
40ft (12m)
or more

SPREAD
15ft (5m)

Cupressaceae	PATAGONIAN CYPRESS

FITZROYA CUPRESSOIDES

Habit Conical when young; vase-shaped to sprawling with age. **Fruits** Small, rounded cones. Brown. **Leaves** Thick, oblong, in whorls of 3, in pendulous sprays. Blue-green above, white banded beneath. **Bark** Peeling in vertical strips. Red-brown.
• NATIVE HABITAT Mountains of Argentina and Chile.
• CULTIVATION Grow in well-drained, slightly acid soil. Shelter from cold, dry winds.
• PROPAGATION By seed in autumn or spring.
• OTHER NAMES *F. patagonica.*

☼ ◐
❀ ❀ ❀

Z 8–9

HEIGHT
40ft (12m)
or more

SPREAD
20ft (6m)

Pinaceae	JAPANESE BLACK PINE

PINUS THUNBERGII

Habit Conical when young, rounded with age. **Fruits** Ovoid cone. Green or purple-tinted, brown when ripe. **Leaves** Rigid, thick, needle-like, to 4in (10cm) long, forward pointing, in pairs. Dark green, emerging from silky white buds.
Bark Deeply fissured. Dark gray to purplish-pink.
• NATIVE HABITAT Coastal areas of Japan, Korea, and N.E. China.
• CULTIVATION Tolerant of coastal exposure, including sea spray, and of poor, sandy soils.
• PROPAGATION By seed in autumn or spring.

☼ ◐
❀ ❀ ❀

Z 5–8

HEIGHT
50ft (15m)
or more

SPREAD
22ft (7m)

Podocarpaceae	WILLOW PODOCARPUS

PODOCARPUS SALIGNUS

Habit Upright, often multi-stemmed, irregular. **Fruits** Fleshy, plum-like. Dark red-violet. **Leaves** Slender, narrowly lance-shaped, soft, flexible, to 5in (12cm) long. Glossy, bright gray-green, with yellow-green beneath. **Bark** Fibrous, peeling in strips. Red-brown.
• NATIVE HABITAT Mountains of Chile.
• CULTIVATION Grow in any moist but well-drained soil. Shelter from wind.
• PROPAGATION By seed in autumn or spring.
• OTHER NAMES *P. chilinus.*

☼ ◐
❀ ❀

Z 10–11

HEIGHT
40ft (12m)
or more

SPREAD
15ft (5m)

Pinaceae	PITCH PINE, NORTHERN PITCH PINE

PINUS RIGIDA

Habit Conical when young, later irregularly and broadly domed. **Fruits** Cylindrical to barrel-shaped cones to 3in (7cm) long. Red-brown. **Leaves** Thick, stiff, twisted, needle-like, to 3½in (9cm) long, in clusters of 3. Gray-green. **Bark** Deeply fissured. Brown.
• NATIVE HABITAT E. North America.
• CULTIVATION Tolerant of coastal conditions, exposure and poor soils. Good for shelter belts in coastal areas.
• PROPAGATION By seed in autumn or spring.

☼ ◐
❀ ❀ ❀

Z 4–7

HEIGHT
50ft (15m)
or more

SPREAD
20ft (6m)

Cupressaceae	CHILEAN CEDAR

AUSTROCEDRUS CHILENSIS

Habit Slow-growing, narrowly conical to columnar. *Fruits* Oblong cones, with 4 overlapping scales. Green; brown when ripe. *Leaves* Small, flattened, scale-like, in sprays. Glossy dark green, banded white beneath. *Bark* Scaly. Gray-brown.
• NATIVE HABITAT Mountains of Argentina and Chile.
• CULTIVATION Grow in moisture-retentive, neutral to slightly acid soil. Shelter from winds.
• PROPAGATION By seed in autumn or spring.
• OTHER NAMES *Libocedrus chilensis.*

Z 8–10

HEIGHT
50ft (15m)
or more

SPREAD
15ft (5m)

Cupressaceae (Taxodiaceae)	CHINA FIR

CUNNINGHAMIA LANCEOLATA

Habit Open, broadly columnar. *Fruits* Rounded cones, to 1½in (4cm) across. Green; brown when ripe. *Leaves* Lance-shaped, sharply pointed, to 2½in (6cm) long, firm but flexible. Glossy dark green, banded silver-white beneath. *Bark* Finely stringy. Chestnut-brown.
• NATIVE HABITAT Evergreen forests in China.
• CULTIVATION Grow in moisture-retentive, lime-free soils with shelter from cold, dry winds.
• PROPAGATION By seed in autumn or spring.
• OTHER NAMES *C. sinensis.*

Z 6–9

HEIGHT
50ft (15m)
or more

SPREAD
20ft (6m)

Phyllocladaceae	TANEKAHA

PHYLLOCLADUS TRICHOMANOIDES

Habit Slow-growing, conical when young, later rounded. *Fruits* Fleshy, berry-like. White. *Leaves* True leaves tiny, scale-like. Bears frond-like, modified, flattened stems, to 6in (15cm) long, with 5–10 lobed, deep green segments.
• NATIVE HABITAT New Zealand.
• CULTIVATION Grow in moisture-retentive, well-drained soil with shelter from cold, dry winds. Suitable for mild, damp climates.
• PROPAGATION By seed in spring.

Z 10–11

HEIGHT
30ft (10m)
or more

SPREAD
15ft (5m)

Sciadopityaceae	JAPANESE UMBRELLA PINE

SCIADOPITYS VERTICILLATA

Habit Narrowly conical. **Fruits** Ovoid cones. Green; red-brown when ripe. **Leaves** Slender, deeply grooved, needle-like, to 5in (12cm) long, in umbrella-like whorls at branch tips. Dark green, yellowish beneath. **Bark** Peeling. Red-brown.
• NATIVE HABITAT Mountains of Japan.
• CULTIVATION Tolerant of very wet and clay soils, but best in neutral to acid, moisture-retentive soils. Shelter from cold, dry winds. Prefers mild climates.
• PROPAGATION By seed in autumn or spring.

Z 5–8

HEIGHT
50ft (15m)
or more

SPREAD
15ft (5m)

Pinaceae	AROLLA PINE, SWISS STONE PINE

PINUS CEMBRA

Habit Narrowly columnar, dense, branching to ground level. **Fruits** Ovoid cones. Blue-purple, red-brown when ripe. Seed ½in (1cm). **Leaves** Needle-like, to 3½in (9cm) long, forward-pointing, in dense clusters of 5. Dark green on the outer surface, blue-white within.
• NATIVE HABITAT Mountains of N. Asia and Europe.
• CULTIVATION Tolerant of coastal conditions, exposure, and poor soils.
• PROPAGATION By seed in autumn or spring.

Z 4–7

HEIGHT
50ft (15m)
or more

SPREAD
15ft (5m)

Pinaceae	MONTEZUMA PINE

PINUS MONTEZUMAE

Habit Broadly spreading, with a rounded crown. **Fruits** Conical to egg-shaped cones, to 6in (15cm) long, with prickly scales. Blue-purple, turning red-brown when ripe. **Leaves** Upswept, needle-like, to 12in (30cm) long, in clusters of 5. Blue-gray to gray-green, in dense bunches at shoot tips.
• NATIVE HABITAT Mountains of Guatemala and Mexico.
• CULTIVATION Dislikes shallow, chalky soils and needs shelter from cold, dry winds.
• PROPAGATION By seed in autumn or spring.

Z 9–10

HEIGHT
To 60ft
(20m)

SPREAD
50ft (15m)

Pinaceae	LODGEPOLE PINE

PINUS CONTORTA var. LATIFOLIA

Habit Open, conical. **Fruits** Ovoid to conical cones, to 2in (5cm) long. Pink-brown. **Leaves** Twisted, needle-like, to 3in (8cm) long, in pairs. Dark green. **Bark** Thick, ridged. Dark red-brown.
• NATIVE HABITAT Mountains of W. North America.
• CULTIVATION Tolerant of poor and wet soils and exposure.
• PROPAGATION By seed in autumn or spring.

Z 6–8

HEIGHT
50ft (15m)
or more

SPREAD
20ft (6m)

Pinaceae	GOLDEN LARCH

PSEUDOLARIX AMABILIS

Habit Open, broadly conical. **Fruits** Ovoid cones, to 2in (5cm) long. Green; brown when ripe.
Leaves Deciduous, slender, linear, to 2in (5cm) long, soft, flexible, in dense whorls. Fresh bright green, turning orange-gold in autumn.
Bark Plated. Gray-brown.
• NATIVE HABITAT Mountain forests in E. China.
• CULTIVATION Grow in deep, fertile, lime-free soil. Shelter from cold, dry winds.
• PROPAGATION By seed in autumn or spring.
• OTHER NAMES *P. kaempferi.*

Z 6–8

HEIGHT
40ft (12m)
or more

SPREAD
15ft (5m)

Pinaceae	JACK PINE

PINUS BANKSIANA

Habit Slender, irregularly conical. **Fruits** Ovoid cones, curved and bumpy, to 2½in (6cm) long, pointing forwards along the shoots. **Leaves** Broad, twisted, needle-like, to 1½in (4cm) long, in pairs. Fresh yellow-green. **Bark** Shallowly fissured. Orange-gray.
• NATIVE HABITAT Forests of North America, almost as far north as the Arctic Circle.
• CULTIVATION Grow in any well-drained soil other than shallow, alkaline soil.
• PROPAGATION By seed in autumn or spring.

Z 2–6

HEIGHT
50ft (15m)
or more

SPREAD
15ft (5m)

Cupressaceae	

CHAMAECYPARIS LAWSONIANA
'Green Pillar'

Habit Conical, with upright branches.
Leaves Aromatic, very small, scale-like, carried in flattened sprays. Bright green; gold-tinted in spring.
• NATIVE HABITAT Garden origin.
• CULTIVATION Tolerant of shade, exposure, urban pollution, and dry, alkaline soils. Grow in moist but well-drained, preferably neutral to acid soils. Suitable for hedging; requires little clipping.
• PROPAGATION By softwood cuttings in summer or by heeled greenwood cuttings in late summer.

Z 5–8

HEIGHT
50ft (15m)

SPREAD
3–6ft
(1–2m)

Cupressaceae	EASTERN WHITE CEDAR

CHAMAECYPARIS THYOIDES

Habit Narrowly, often irregularly, columnar.
Fruits Small, rounded cones. Bloomed green;
brown when ripe. **Leaves** Aromatic, tiny, pointed,
scale-like, in flattened, fan-shaped sprays, on shoots.
Green or blue-gray. **Bark** Fibrous. Gray-brown.
• NATIVE HABITAT Swamps and damp soils of
E. United States.
• CULTIVATION Grow in neutral to acid soil.
• PROPAGATION By seed in autumn or spring, by
softwood cuttings in summer, or by heeled
greenwood cuttings in late summer.

Z 3–8

HEIGHT
40ft (12m)
or more

SPREAD
10ft (3m)

Pinaceae	BEACH PINE, SHORE PINE

PINUS CONTORTA

Habit Dense, conical or domed. **Fruits** Ovoid
cones, pointing backward along the shoot. Pale
brown. **Leaves** Twisted, needle-like, to 2in (5cm)
long, densely clustered, in pairs. Dark green or
yellow-green. **Bark** Fissured. Red-brown.
• NATIVE HABITAT Coastal dunes and bogs of
W. North America.
• CULTIVATION Tolerates coastal exposure, stony
or sandy soils, and very wet soils. Unsuitable for
shallow, alkaline soil.
• PROPAGATION By seed in autumn or spring.

Z 6–8

HEIGHT
To 50ft
(15m)

SPREAD
25ft (8m)

Pinaceae	TAIWAN SPRUCE

PICEA MORRISONICOLA

Habit Open, conical, columnar with age;
pendulous shoots. **Fruits** Oblong-cylindrical cones.
Leaves Slender, needle-like, sharply pointed,
closely pressed and forward-pointing, against the
shoots. Dark green. **Bark** Flaky. Red-brown.
• NATIVE HABITAT Mountains of Taiwan.
• CULTIVATION Grow in fertile, moisture-
retentive but well-drained, neutral to acid soil.
Shelter from cold, dry winds. A very elegant
specimen.
• PROPAGATION By seed in autumn or spring.

Z 7–8

HEIGHT
50ft (15m)
or more

SPREAD
20ft (6m)

Taxaceae	

TAXUS BACCATA 'Fastigiata'

Habit Dense, strongly upright, broadly columnar.
Fruits Fleshy, berry-like, to ¼in (8mm) across,
poisonous. Bright red. **Leaves** Evergreen, linear,
pointed at the tip, to 1¼in (3cm) long, standing out
all around the shoots. Very dark green.
• NATIVE HABITAT Originated in Ireland.
• CULTIVATION Tolerates very dry and shady
conditions, and a wide range of soil types and pH,
including alkaline ones.
• PROPAGATION By cuttings of the current year's
growth from autumn to spring.

Z 6–7

HEIGHT
30–50ft
(10–15m)

SPREAD
12–15ft
(4–5m)

Pinaceae	ALEPPO PINE

PINUS HALEPENSIS

Habit Conical, open-crowned. **Fruits** Ovoid cones, to 3in (7cm) long. Glossy brown.
Leaves In pairs, slender, sparse, needle-like, to 4¼in (11cm) long, on outer side of shoots, giving a very open appearance. Glossy bright green.
Bark Fissured. Deep purple-brown; terracotta-orange within the fissures.
• NATIVE HABITAT Mediterranean.
• CULTIVATION Tolerant of maritime exposure and shallow, alkaline soils.
• PROPAGATION By seed in autumn or spring.

☼ ◐
❀ ❀ ❀

Z 8–9

HEIGHT
50ft (15m)

SPREAD
20ft (6m)

Cupressaceae	

CHAMAECYPARIS LAWSONIANA 'Lane'

Habit Upright, conical when young, later columnar. **Fruits** Round cones at branch tips.
Leaves Aromatic, small, scale-like, carried in flattened sprays. Bright green, tipped golden-yellow.
• NATIVE HABITAT Garden origin.
• CULTIVATION Tolerant of shade. Grow in moist but well-drained, preferably neutral to acid soils.
• PROPAGATION By softwood cuttings in summer or by heeled greenwood cuttings in late summer.
• OTHER NAMES *C. lawsoniana* 'Lanei',
C. lawsoniana 'Lanei Aurea'.

☼ ◐
❀ ❀ ❀

Z 5–8

HEIGHT
40ft (12m)

SPREAD
12ft (4m)

Cephalotaxaceae	CALIFORNIA NUTMEG

TORREYA CALIFORNICA

Habit Open, broadly conical, with horizontal branches. **Fruits** Ovoid, fleshy, enclosing a large, single seed. Green, striped purple when ripe.
Leaves Aromatic, narrow, linear, sharp-pointed, to 1¼in (3cm) long. Glossy dark green above, with 2 white bands beneath. **Bark** Ridged. Red-brown.
• NATIVE HABITAT Slopes and canyons from the coast to mountains, in California.
• CULTIVATION Grow in fertile, moisture-retentive soil. Shelter from cold, dry winds.
• PROPAGATION By seed in autumn or spring.

☼ ◐
❀ ❀

Z 6–9

HEIGHT
50ft (15m)
or more

SPREAD
22ft (7m)

Pinaceae	SCRUB PINE, VIRGINIA PINE, JERSEY PINE

PINUS VIRGINIANA

Habit Round-headed, untidy. **Fruits** Oblong to conical cones, to 2½in (6cm) long. Red-brown.
Leaves Stiff, twisted, needle-like, to 2½in (6cm) long, in pairs. Gray- to yellow-green. **Bark** Red-brown; young shoots bloomed pinkish-white.
• NATIVE HABITAT E. North America.
• CULTIVATION Tolerates poor, sandy soils and exposure, but dislikes shallow, alkaline soils.
• PROPAGATION By seed in autumn or spring.

☼ ◐
❀ ❀ ❀

Z 5–8

HEIGHT
50ft (15m)

SPREAD
22ft (7m)

Pinaceae	BLACK SPRUCE

PICEA MARIANA 'Doumetii'

Habit Slow-growing, densely branched, shrubby and rounded. **Fruits** Ovoid cones, to 1½in (4cm) long, in pendulous clusters. Purplish; red-brown when ripe. **Leaves** Aromatic, slender, soft, needle-like, to ⅝in (1.5cm) long. Dark bluish-green, with 2 silver-blue bands beneath. **Bark** Flaking. Gray-pink, turning purple-gray with age.

• NATIVE HABITAT Species occurs in Canada and N. United States. Garden origin.

• CULTIVATION Grow in moist but well-drained, preferably neutral to acid soil, in an open position.

This very dense, irregularly rounded, shapely specimen is a very slow-growing conifer, taking 15–20 years to reach 10ft (3m) in height, and by as much across, and so is suitable for use as a specimen tree in a small or medium-sized garden.

• PROPAGATION By grafting in late summer, winter or early spring.

Z 2–6

HEIGHT
25ft (8m) or
more

SPREAD
15ft (5m)

Pinaceae	BRISTLECONE PINE

PINUS ARISTATA

Habit Slow-growing, bushy, rounded-conical.
Fruits Ovoid, spiny cones, to 4in (10cm) long.
Dark purple; brown when ripe. **Leaves** Retained
for 10–20 years, slender, needle-like, to 1½in (4cm)
long, in dense, forward-pointing clusters of 5. Dark
green, conspicuously flecked with resin.
• NATIVE HABITAT Rocky Mountains of
Colorado, Arizona, and New Mexico.
• CULTIVATION Tolerates poor, dry soils, lime-
rich soils, and exposure.
• PROPAGATION By seed in autumn or spring.

Z 4–7

HEIGHT
25ft (8m)

SPREAD
12ft (4m)

Cupressaceae	EASTERN RED CEDAR

JUNIPERUS VIRGINIANA 'Burkii'

Habit Slow-growing, dense, columnar.
Fruits Berry-like cones, to ¼in (6mm) long.
Bloomed, gray-green. **Leaves** Aromatic; juvenile:
needle-like; adult: tiny, scale-like; in pairs, both on
same shoots. Bluish gray-green. **Bark** Peeling.
Red-brown.
• NATIVE HABITAT Garden origin.
• CULTIVATION Grow in almost any well-drained
soil.
• PROPAGATION By cuttings of the current year's
growth from autumn to spring.

Z 2–9

HEIGHT
20ft (6m)

SPREAD
6ft (2m)

Cupressaceae	

CHAMAECYPARIS LAWSONIANA 'Columnaris'

Habit Upright, narrowly columnar. **Fruits** Round
cones at branch tips. **Leaves** Aromatic, small,
scale-like, in flattened sprays. Blue-gray.
• NATIVE HABITAT Garden origin.
• CULTIVATION Tolerant of shade, exposure,
urban pollution, and dry, alkaline soils. Grow in
moist, but well-drained soils, preferably neutral to
acid. Suitable for hedging and as a specimen.
• PROPAGATION By softwood cuttings in summer
or by heeled greenwood cuttings in late summer.

Z 5–7

HEIGHT
30ft (10m)

SPREAD
5ft (1.5m)

Cupressaceae	EASTERN RED CEDAR

JUNIPERUS VIRGINIANA 'Robusta Green'

Habit Slow-growing, dense, columnar, free-fruiting. **Fruits** Berry-like cones, to ¼in (6mm) long. Bloomed, gray-green. **Leaves** Aromatic, tiny, scale-like. Green. **Bark** Peeling. Red-brown.
• NATIVE HABITAT Garden origin.
• CULTIVATION Will grow in almost any well-drained soil.
• PROPAGATION By cuttings of the current year's growth from autumn to spring.
• OTHER NAMES *J. chinensis* 'Robusta Green'.

Cupressaceae	

JUNIPERUS CHINENSIS 'Obelisk'

Habit Slender, irregularly columnar, with ascending branches. **Leaves** Aromatic, long, prickly, awl-shaped, densely packed. Dark green.
• NATIVE HABITAT Garden origin.
• CULTIVATION Tolerates a wide range of soils and conditions but especially useful on hot, dry sites.
• PROPAGATION By cuttings of the current year's growth from autumn to spring.

☼ ◊
❀ ❀ ❀

Z 2–9

HEIGHT
12ft (4m)

SPREAD
3ft (1m)

☼ ◊
❀ ❀ ❀

Z 3–9

HEIGHT
15ft (5m)

SPREAD
3ft (1m)

Pinaceae	

PINUS SYLVESTRIS 'Fastigiata'

Habit Upright, narrowly columnar.
Fruits Conical cone, to 3in (7.5cm) long. Brown.
Leaves Twisted, needle-like, in pairs. Dark blue-green. **Bark** Flaky. Red-brown.
• NATIVE HABITAT Garden origin.
• CULTIVATION Grow in any well-drained soil. Ensure protection from cold wind, which may scorch the foliage.
• PROPAGATION By grafting in late summer, winter or early spring.
• OTHER NAMES *P. sylvestris* f. *fastigiata*.

☼ ◊
❀ ❀ ❀

Z 2–8

HEIGHT
25ft (8m)

SPREAD
3ft (1m)

Pinaceae	LACEBARK PINE

PINUS BUNGEANA

Habit Slow-growing, broadly conical, low-branching. *Fruits* Ovoid cones, to 3in (7cm) long. Yellow-brown. *Leaves* Rigid, slender, needle-like, to 3in (7.5cm) long, in clusters of 3. Yellow-green. *Bark* Smooth, flaking. Gray-green and olive green. Creamy-white patches beneath bark eventually darken to pale green and then purple-brown.
• NATIVE HABITAT On shale on the steep slopes of mountains in N. China.
• CULTIVATION Grow in any well-drained soil. It is drought-tolerant and needs full sun. It makes a beautiful specimen tree, especially if sited to give a clear view of its exquisite, flaking bark, which is uniquely attractive among the wide range of conifers. Since it is relatively small and slow-growing, it is one of the most suitable of the pines for smaller and medium-sized gardens.
• PROPAGATION By seed in autumn or spring.

Z 4–8

HEIGHT
30ft (10m)
or more

SPREAD
22ft (7m)

Pinaceae	MEXICAN NUT PINE, PINYON PINE

PINUS CEMBROIDES

Habit Slow-growing, bushy, domed.
Fruits Globose cones, to 1½in (4cm) across, opening to release edible seeds. Orange to buff-brown. **Leaves** Sparse, needle-like, in clusters of 2–3 at shoot tips. Olive green. **Bark** Scaly. Silver-gray or gray-brown.
• NATIVE HABITAT Mexico.
• CULTIVATION Tolerant of poor, dry soils. Needs a warm, sheltered site.
• PROPAGATION By seed in autumn or spring.

Cupressaceae (Taxodiaceae)	

CRYPTOMERIA JAPONICA 'Cristata'

Habit Conical, with twisted, curved, (cockscomb) shoots. **Leaves** Slender, flattened at the base, taper-pointed. Bright green, aging to brown. **Bark** Soft, fibrous. Orange-brown.
• NATIVE HABITAT Garden origin.
• CULTIVATION Grow in fertile, neutral to acid, moisture-retentive soil. Thrives in cool, humid, sheltered conditions.
• PROPAGATION By cuttings of the current year's growth from autumn to spring.

Z 7–9

HEIGHT
20–22ft
(6–7m)

SPREAD
15ft (5m)

Z 6–9

HEIGHT
To 30ft
(10m)

SPREAD
10ft (3m)

Pinaceae	KOREAN FIR

ABIES KOREANA

Habit Broadly conical. **Fruits** Cylindrical, upright cones, to 3in (7.5cm) long, carried even on young plants. Violet-blue. **Leaves** Linear, to ⅓in (2cm) long, rounded or notched at the tip. Dark green above, with 2 white bands, or all white, beneath. **Bark** Dark gray-brown.
• NATIVE HABITAT Mountains of S. Korea.
• CULTIVATION Grow in fertile, humus-rich, neutral to acid soils. Thrives in cool, humid, sheltered conditions.
• PROPAGATION By seed in autumn or spring.

Cupressaceae	FALSE ARBORVITAE

THUJOPSIS DOLABRATA 'Variegata'

Habit Slow-growing, broadly conical.
Leaves Scale-like, thick, broadly triangular, with pointed tips, to ¼in (6mm) long. Glossy bright green, splashed irregularly with cream, neatly and distinctively marked with silver-white beneath.
• NATIVE HABITAT Garden origin.
• CULTIVATION Grow in fertile, neutral to acid, moisture-retentive soil, preferably in a humid, sheltered site.
• PROPAGATION By cuttings of the current year's growth from autumn to spring.

Z 5–6

HEIGHT
30ft (10m)
or more

SPREAD
15ft (5m)

Z 5–7

HEIGHT
30ft (10m)
or more

SPREAD
15ft (5m)

Cupressaceae (Taxodiaceae)	

CRYPTOMERIA JAPONICA 'Pyramidata'

Habit Narrowly columnar. **Leaves** Slender, flattened at the base, taper-pointed. Blue-green when young, later dark green. **Bark** Soft, fibrous. Orange-brown.
• NATIVE HABITAT Garden origin.
• CULTIVATION Grow in fertile, neutral to acid, moisture-retentive soil. Thrives in cool, humid, sheltered conditions.
• PROPAGATION By cuttings of the current year's growth, from autumn to spring.

Z 6–9

HEIGHT
20ft (6m)

SPREAD
6ft (2m)

Taxaceae	JAPANESE YEW

TAXUS CUSPIDATA

Habit Broad, rounded, bushy. **Fruits** Poisonous. Fleshy, berry-like, to ¼in (8mm) across. Bright red. **Leaves** Hard, linear, short-pointed, to 1in (2.5cm) long, ascending from the shoots. Dark green above, yellow-green beneath.
• NATIVE HABITAT Japan.
• CULTIVATION Tolerates very dry and shady conditions and a wide range of soil types. Performs best in areas with hot, humid summers.
• PROPAGATION By seed in autumn or spring.

Z 4–7

HEIGHT
15ft (5m) or more

SPREAD
15ft (5m)

Pinaceae	STONE PINE

PINUS PINEA

Habit Short-trunked, with a rounded, umbrella-shaped crown. **Fruits** Broadly ovoid cones, to 5in (12cm) long. Glossy brown. **Leaves** Stout, needle-like, to 5in (12cm) long, in pairs. Gray-green; the blue-green juvenile foliage is retained on young trees. **Bark** Deeply fissured. Orange-brown.
• NATIVE HABITAT On sandy soils around the Mediterranean coast.
• CULTIVATION Tolerates poor, dry, sandy soils and coastal exposure. It is a useful tree for shelter belt plantings in seaside gardens. When grown as a specimen it becomes increasingly picturesque, especially when grown in exposed, windy sites. When given such growing conditions it frequently branches low and becomes wind-trained, leaning away from the prevailing winds.
• PROPAGATION By seed in autumn or spring.

Z 8–9

HEIGHT
30ft (10m) or more

SPREAD
30ft (10m)

Pinaceae	GOLDEN DEODAR

CEDRUS DEODARA 'Aurea'

Habit Slow-growing, upright, with pendent branch tips. **Leaves** Narrow, needle-like, to 1¼in (3cm) long, in dense whorls. Bright golden-yellow when young, maturing to yellow-green.
• NATIVE HABITAT Garden origin.
• CULTIVATION Grow in any moist but well-drained soils including alkaline or lime-rich soils. Excellent specimen for small gardens.
• PROPAGATION By grafting in late summer, winter or early spring.

Z 6–8

HEIGHT
15ft (5m)

SPREAD
12ft (4m)

Cupressaceae	

CHAMAECYPARIS OBTUSA 'Crippsii'

Habit Slow-growing, narrowly conical.
Fruits Small, rounded cones, to ½in (12mm) across. Green; brown when ripe. **Leaves** Aromatic, tiny, scale-like, in flattened sprays. Bright golden-yellow on outermost branchlets, dark green within.
Bark Stringy. Red-brown.
• NATIVE HABITAT Garden origin.
• CULTIVATION Tolerant of alkaline soils but best in moist, well-drained, neutral to acid soils.
• PROPAGATION By softwood cuttings in summer or by heeled greenwood cuttings in late summer.

Z 4–8

HEIGHT
30ft (10m)

SPREAD
15ft (5m)

Cupressaceae	MONTEREY CYPRESS

CUPRESSUS MACROCARPA 'Goldcrest'

Habit Fast-growing, conical. **Leaves** Aromatic, tiny, scale-like, with pointed tips, pressed closely to the shoot, in plume-like sprays. Brilliant golden-yellow.
• NATIVE HABITAT Garden origin.
• CULTIVATION Grow in any well-drained soil, except shallow alkaline soils. Does not respond well to clipping. Makes a beautiful specimen for small gardens. Foliage is useful in flower arrangements.
• PROPAGATION By softwood cuttings in summer or by heeled greenwood cuttings in late summer.

Z 7–9

HEIGHT
30ft (10m)

SPREAD
10ft (3m)

Pinaceae	PYRAMIDAL SCOTS PINE

PINUS SYLVESTRIS 'Aurea'

Habit Slow-growing, broadly conical, rounded with age. *Leaves* Slender, needle-like, in pairs, carried in twisted bundles. Blue-green, bright golden-yellow in winter and spring.
• NATIVE HABITAT Species occurs on sandy and gravelly soils in the mountains of Asia and Europe. Garden origin.
• CULTIVATION Grow in any well-drained soil. Ensure protection from cold wind which may scorch the foliage. This cultivar produces new growth with a grayish cast during summer that later assumes a characteristic bright golden coloration during winter. It is very slow-growing and makes an attractive companion plant for winter-flowering heaths and heathers. It may also be grown in collections of dwarf conifers.
• PROPAGATION By grafting in late summer, winter, or early spring.

Z 2–8

Height
30ft (10m)

Spread
12ft (4m)

DWARF CONIFERS

Slow-growing and dwarf conifers are invaluable in small gardens, offering year-round interest with an enormous range of color, form, and habit. The compact cultivars are ideal for rock gardens, while spreading and prostrate forms are invaluable when used as ground cover. Nearly all tolerate a range of growing conditions, thriving on acid to neutral soil, and yew and junipers tolerate lime. Some are not wind-tolerant and need a sheltered site. They may grow to exceed their stated height after 15–20 years but replacement plants can be propagated. *Cupressaceae* root easily with heeled, greenwood, or softwood cuttings, but *Cedrus, Picea, Pseudotsuga,* and *Tsuga* require hardwood cuttings. *Pinus* and *Arbies* are usually grafted.

PICEA PUNGENS
'Montgomery'
Habit Dense, rounded-conical. *Leaves* Rigid, stout, needle-like, sharply spine-tipped, ¾in (2cm) long. Bright gray-blue.
• HEIGHT 3ft (1m).
• SPREAD 3ft (1m).

Picea pungens
'Montgomery'

☼ ◊ ❀❀❀   Z 3–7

PINUS SYLVESTRIS
'Doone Valley'
Habit Irregularly conical, compact, upright. *Leaves* In pairs, straight, or slightly twisted, needle-like, 1½–2in (4–5cm) long. Dark blue-green.
• HEIGHT 3ft (1m).
• SPREAD 3ft (1m).

Pinus sylvestris
'Doone Valley'

☼ ◊ ❀❀❀   Z 2–8

ABIES LASIOCARPA
'Arizonica Compacta'
Habit Slow-growing, dense, regular, broadly conical. *Leaves* Linear, forward-pointing on top of the shoots, spreading below. Silvery-blue, with broad, white bands beneath. *Bark* Corky.
• HEIGHT 12–15ft (4–5m).
• SPREAD 5–6ft (1.5–2m).

Abies lasiocarpa
'Arizonica Compacta'

☼ ◑ ❀❀❀   Z 5–6

JUNIPERUS SCOPULORUM
'Springbank'
Habit Narrowly columnar, with drooping branch tips. *Leaves* Aromatic, scale-like, pressed closely to shoots. Intense silvery-blue.
• HEIGHT 12ft (4m).
• SPREAD 3ft (1m).

Juniperus scopulorum
'Springbank'

☼ ◊ ❀❀   Z 3–7

JUNIPERUS SQUAMATA **'Holger'**
Habit Low, prostrate, wide-spreading, with nodding branchlets. *Leaves* Aromatic, needle-like. Steel-blue, turning sulphur-yellow in spring, giving beautiful contrast with older foliage.
• HEIGHT 6ft (2m).
• SPREAD 6ft (2m).

Juniperus squamata
'Holger'

☼ ◊ ❀❀❀   Z 4–8

PICEA OMORIKA 'Gnom'

Habit Broadly and irregularly pyramidal. Pendent branches arch out at the tips.
Leaves Slender, needle-like. Dark green, white beneath.
• CULTIVATION Tolerates alkaline soils.
• HEIGHT 5ft (1.5m).
• SPREAD 3–6ft (1–2m).

Picea omorika 'Gnom'

☼ ◐ ❀❀❀   Z 4–7

ABIES CONCOLOR 'Compacta'

Habit Broadly conical.
Leaves Linear, blunt-tipped, upswept. Bright steel-blue.
• OTHER NAMES *A. concolor* 'Glauca Compacta'.
• HEIGHT 6ft (2m).
• SPREAD 6ft (2m).

Abies concolor 'Compacta'

☼ ◐ ❀❀❀   Z 3–7

JUNIPERUS SQUAMATA 'Blue Star'

Habit Low-growing, dense, compact, bun-shaped.
Leaves Crowded, relatively large, awl-shaped. Bright silvery-blue.
• HEIGHT 20in (50cm).
• SPREAD 24in (60cm).

Juniperus squamata 'Blue Star'

☼ ◌ ❀❀❀   Z 4–8

JUNIPERUS VIRGINIANA 'Grey Owl'

Habit Vigorous, low, wide-spreading, with ascending branchlets.
Leaves Soft, silver-gray, tips flushed purple in winter.
• HEIGHT 10ft (3m).
• SPREAD 10–15ft (3–5m).

Juniperus virginiana 'Grey Owl'

☼ ◌ ❀❀❀   Z 2–9

JUNIPERUS HORIZONTALIS 'Douglasii'

Habit Spreading, prostrate, mat-forming.
Leaves Aromatic, with needle- and scale-like leaves. Soft, bright blue-green, tinted plum-purple in winter.
• HEIGHT 12in (30cm).
• SPREAD 6–10ft (2–3m).

Juniperus horizontalis 'Douglasii'
Waukegan juniper

☼ ◌ ❀❀❀   Z 3–9

JUNIPERUS × MEDIA 'Pfitzeriana Glauca'

Habit Spreading, dense. Branches ascending but drooping at the tips.
Leaves Mainly awl-shaped. Gray-blue.
• OTHER NAMES *J. chinensis* 'Pfitzeriana Glauca'.
• HEIGHT 10ft (3m).
• SPREAD 10–15ft (3–5m).

Juniperus × media 'Pfitzeriana Glauca'

☼ ◌ ❀❀❀   Z 3–9

JUNIPERUS SQUAMATA 'Chinese Silver'

Habit Dense, bushy, multi-stemmed, with branch tips nodding.
Leaves Awl-shaped. Intense blue-green, bright silver beneath.
• HEIGHT 10–12ft (3–4m).
• SPREAD 10–12ft (3–4m).

Juniperus squamata 'Chinese Silver'

☼ ◌ ❀❀❀   Z 4–8

JUNIPERUS SABINA 'Mas'

Habit Low-growing, with ascending branches.
Leaves Mainly awl-shaped. Blue above, green below, purple-tinted in winter. Fetid when crushed.
• HEIGHT 24–36in (60–90cm).
• SPREAD 5ft (1.5m).

Juniperus sabina 'Mas'

☼ ◌ ❀❀❀   Z 3–7

JUNIPERUS CHINENSIS 'Stricta'
Habit Compact, conical-columnar, with upright branches. **Leaves** Soft, needle-like. Blue-green.
• HEIGHT 15ft (5m).
• SPREAD 3ft (1m).

Juniperus chinensis 'Stricta'

☼ ◊ ❀❀❀   Z 3–9

JUNIPERUS PROCUMBENS
Habit Spreading, prostrate, shrubby. **Fruits** Globose, fleshy, berry-like. Brown to black. **Leaves** Aromatic, needle-like. Light green or yellow-green.
• HEIGHT 12–18in (30–45cm).
• SPREAD 6ft (2m).

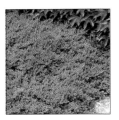

Juniperus procumbens
Creeping juniper

☼ ◊ ❀❀❀   Z 4–9

JUNIPERUS PROCUMBENS 'Nana'
Habit Mat-forming, compact. **Fruits** Globose, fleshy, berry-like. Brown to black. **Leaves** Aromatic, needle-like. Light green or yellow-green.
• HEIGHT 6–8in (15–20cm).
• SPREAD 30in (75cm).

Juniperus procumbens
'Nana'

☼ ◊ ❀❀❀   Z 4–9

THUJA OCCIDENTALIS 'Caespitosa'
Habit Slow-growing, dense, hummock-forming. **Leaves** Congested, irregular, pressed closely to very slender shoots. Dark grayish-green.
• HEIGHT 12in (30cm).
• SPREAD 16in (40cm).

Thuja occidentalis
'Caespitosa'

☼ ◑ ❀❀❀   Z 2–7

MICROBIOTA DECUSSATA
Habit Prostrate, shrubby, with wide-spreading branches. **Fruits** Small, globose, berry-like cone. Yellow-brown. **Leaves** Small, mostly scale-like, in flat sprays. Yellow-green, bronze in winter.
• HEIGHT 20in (50cm).
• SPREAD 6–10ft (2–3m).

Microbiota decussata

☼ ◊ ❀❀❀   Z 3–8

JUNIPERUS SCOPULORUM 'Skyrocket'
Habit Very narrowly columnar. **Leaves** Tiny, scale-like, closely pressed to slender shoots. Glaucous blue.
• OTHER NAMES
J. virginiana 'Skyrocket'.
• HEIGHT To 25ft (8m).
• SPREAD 30in (75cm).

Juniperus scopulorum
'Skyrocket'

☼ ◊ ❀❀❀   Z 3–7

JUNIPERUS HORIZONTALIS 'Turquoise Spreader'
Habit Vigorous, dense, mat-forming.
Leaves Needle-like, sharp pointed. Rich jade-green.
• CULTIVATION Very tolerant of hot, dry sites.
• HEIGHT 12in (30cm).
• SPREAD 6ft (2m).

Juniperus horizontalis 'Turquoise Spreader'

☼ ◐ ❄❄❄   Z 3–9

ABIES LASIOCARPA 'Roger Watson'
Habit Compact, conical.
Leaves Linear, forward-pointing on top of the shoots, spreading below. Silvery-gray, with broad, white bands beneath.
• HEIGHT 30in (75cm).
• SPREAD 30in (75cm).

Abies lasiocarpa 'Roger Watson'

☼ ◐ ❄❄❄   Z 5–6

ABIES BALSAMEA 'Nana'
Habit Dense, globose.
Leaves Aromatic, linear, flattened. Dark green above, yellow beneath, with 2 white bands.
• OTHER NAMES
A. balsamea var. *nana*.
• HEIGHT 3ft (1m).
• SPREAD 3ft (1m).

Abies balsamea 'Nana'

☼ ◐ ❄❄❄   Z 3–5

PICEA MARIANA 'Nana'
Habit Compact, rounded, mound-forming. *Leaves* Short, soft, slender, needle-like. Blue-gray.
• HEIGHT 20in (50cm).
• SPREAD 20–32in (50–80cm).

Picea mariana 'Nana'

☼ ◐ ❄❄❄   Z 2–6

ABIES CEPHALONICA 'Meyer's Dwarf'
Habit Slow-growing, spreading, forming a flat-topped mound.
Leaves Sharp, stiff, linear. Dark green above, white beneath.
• OTHER NAMES
A. cephalonica 'Nana'.
• HEIGHT 20in (50cm).
• SPREAD 5ft (1.5m).

Abies cephalonica 'Meyer's Dwarf'

☼ ◐ ❄❄❄   Z 5–6

PODOCARPUS NIVALIS
Habit Rounded, dense, spreading, shrubby.
Leaves Rigid, lance-shaped, leathery. Olive green.
• CULTIVATION Tolerant of alkaline soils.
• HEIGHT 6ft (2m).
• SPREAD 10–15ft (3–5m).

Podocarpus nivalis

☼ ◐ ❄❄❄   Z 9–11

PSEUDOTSUGA MENZIESII 'Fretsii'
Habit Slow-growing, broadly conical, with twisted, ascending branches.
Leaves Aromatic, short, needle-like. Dull dark green, with white bands beneath.
• HEIGHT 6m (20ft) or more.
• SPREAD 10–12ft (3–4m).

Pseudotsuga menziesii 'Fretsii'

☼ ◐ ❄❄❄   Z 4–7

JUNIPERUS SABINA 'Cupressifolia'
Habit Spreading, with horizontal or ascending branches. Free-fruiting.
Fruits Rounded, berry-like cones. Blue-black.
Leaves In pairs, mostly scale-like. Dark blue-green.
• HEIGHT 6ft (2m).
• SPREAD 12ft (4m).

Juniperus sabina 'Cupressifolia'

☼ ◐ ❄❄❄   Z 3–7

JUNIPERUS RECURVA 'Densa'

Habit Low, spreading, with drooping branchlets.
Leaves Aromatic, awl-shaped, in sprays that are erect at the tips. Dark green.
• HEIGHT 12in (30cm).
• SPREAD 3ft (1m).

Juniperus recurva
'Densa'

☼ ◊ ❀ ❀ ❀   Z 8–9

PINUS SYLVESTRIS 'Nana'

Habit Slow-growing, dense, bushy, broadly conical. **Leaves** In pairs, needle-like, sometimes twisted, widely spaced. Dark blue-green or yellow-green.
• HEIGHT 20in (50cm).
• SPREAD 20in (50cm).

Pinus sylvestris 'Nana'

☼ ◊ ❀ ❀ ❀   Z 2–8

JUNIPERUS SABINA 'Tamariscifolia'

Habit Low-growing, compact, spreading, with horizontal branches.
Leaves Mainly needle-like, carried in tiered sprays. Bright green or blue-green.
• OTHER NAMES
J. sabina var. *tamariscifolia.*
• HEIGHT 3ft (1m).
• SPREAD 6ft (2m).

Juniperus sabina
'Tamariscifolia'

☼ ◊ ❀ ❀ ❀   Z 3–7

PINUS MUGO 'Gnom'

Habit Dense, globose, with stout, twisted branches.
Leaves In pairs, needle-like, crowded. Dark green.
• HEIGHT 6ft (2m).
• SPREAD 6ft (2m).

Pinus mugo 'Gnom'

☼ ◊ ❀ ❀ ❀   Z 3–8

PICEA ABIES 'Ohlendorfii'

Habit Slow-growing, dense. Globose when young, later conical.
Leaves Rigid, slender, needle-like, sharp-pointed. Dark green.
• HEIGHT 3ft (1m).
• SPREAD 3ft (1m).

Picea abies
'Ohlendorfii'

◐ ◊ ❀ ❀ ❀   Z 2–8

PSEUDOTSUGA MENZIESII 'Oudemansii'

Habit Very slow-growing, broadly conical, with ascending branches.
Leaves Aromatic, short, needle-like. Glossy dark green above, light green beneath.
• HEIGHT 20ft (6m) or more.
• SPREAD 10–12ft (3–4m).

Pseudotsuga menziesii
'Oudemansii'

☼ ◊ ❀ ❀ ❀   Z 4–7

PICEA ABIES 'Reflexa'

Habit Prostrate, creeping, dense.
Leaves Rigid, slender, needle-like, sharp-pointed. Dark green.
• CULTIVATION May be trained up a stake to form a mound of weeping foliage.
• HEIGHT 12in (30cm).
• SPREAD 15ft (5m).

Picea abies 'Reflexa'

◐ ◊ ❀ ❀ ❀   Z 2–8

CHAMAECYPARIS LAWSONIANA 'Gnome'

Habit Compact, bun-shaped.
Leaves Aromatic, very small, scale-like, in flattened sprays. Blue-green.
• HEIGHT 20in (50cm).
• SPREAD 20in (50cm).

Chamaecyparis lawsoniana 'Gnome'

☼ ◊ ❀ ❀ ❀   Z 5–8

*CHAMAECYPARIS
LAWSONIANA*
'Minima'
Habit Compact, dense,
globular.
Leaves Aromatic, very
small, scale-like, in
flattened sprays. Light
green.
• HEIGHT 3ft (1m).
• SPREAD 3ft (1m).

*Chamaecyparis
lawsoniana* 'Minima'

☼ ◐ ❀❀❀   Z 5–8

*CHAMAECYPARIS
OBTUSA* **'Intermedia'**
Habit Open, globular.
Leaves Aromatic, tiny,
scale-like, in downward-
spreading, flattened
sprays. Light green.
• HEIGHT 12in (30cm).
• SPREAD 16in (40cm).

Chamaecyparis obtusa
'Intermedia'

☼ ◐ ❀❀❀   Z 4–8

PICEA ABIES
'Gregoryana'
Habit Slow-growing,
dense, globose.
Leaves Rigid, slender,
needle-like, sharp-
pointed. Dark sea-green,
arranged radially around
the shoot.
• HEIGHT 24in (60cm).
• SPREAD 24in (60cm).

Picea abies
'Gregoryana'

☼ ◐ ❀❀❀   Z 2–8

JUNIPERUS × MEDIA
'Pfitzeriana'
Habit Spreading, dense.
Branches ascending,
drooping at the tips.
Leaves Mainly awl-
shaped. Gray-green.
• HEIGHT 10ft (3m).
• SPREAD 10–15ft
(3–5m).

Juniperus × media
'Pfitzeriana'
Pfitzer juniper

☼ ◌ ❀❀❀   Z 3–9

*CHAMAECYPARIS
OBTUSA* **'Nana
Pyramidalis'**
Habit Slow-growing,
dense, conical.
Leaves Aromatic, tiny,
scale-like, in horizontal,
cupped sprays. Dark
green.
• HEIGHT 24in (60cm).
• SPREAD 24in (60cm).

Chamaecyparis obtusa
'Nana Pyramidalis'

☼ ◐ ❀❀❀   Z 4–8

PINUS HELDREICHII
var. *LEUCODERMIS*
'Schmidtii'
Habit Very slow-
growing, dense, ovoid,
mound-forming.
Leaves In pairs. Rigid,
needle-like, sharp- and
forward-pointing. Bright
green.
• HEIGHT 20in (50cm).
• SPREAD 20in (50cm).

Pinus heldreichii var.
leucodermis 'Schmidtii'

☼ ◐ ❀❀❀   Z 6–7

PICEA GLAUCA var.
ALBERTIANA **'Conica'**
Habit Slow-growing,
neat, pyramidal, dense,
and firm. *Leaves* Short,
slender, rigid, needle-
like. Blue-green.
• OTHER NAMES
P. glauca 'Albertiana
Conica'.
• HEIGHT 6–15ft (2–5m).
• SPREAD 3–6ft (1–2m).

Picea glauca var.
albertiana 'Conica'

 ☼ ◐ ❀❀❀   Z 2–6

JUNIPERUS COMMUNIS 'Hibernica'
Habit Neatly columnar.
Leaves Aromatic, needle-like. Mid- to yellowish-green.
• OTHER NAMES
J. communis 'Stricta'.
• HEIGHT 10–15ft (3–5m).
• SPREAD 12–20in (30–50cm).

Juniperus communis
'Hibernica'
Irish juniper

☼ ◊ ❀❀❀   Z 2–7

THUJA ORIENTALIS 'Aurea Nana'
Habit Ovoid, round-topped. **Leaves** Small, triangular, blunt-pointed, overlapping, held in vertical sprays. Yellow-green, bronze in winter.
• OTHER NAMES *Biota orientalis* 'Aurea Nana', *Platycladus orientalis* 'Aurea Nana'.
• HEIGHT 24in (60cm).
• SPREAD 24in (60cm).

Thuja orientalis 'Aurea Nana'

☼ ◊ ❀❀❀   Z 5–9

CEDRUS LIBANI subsp. LIBANI 'Sargentii'
Habit Rounded, bushy, with horizontal, then weeping, branches.
Leaves Slender, needle-like, sharp-pointed, in dense whorls. Gray-green.
• HEIGHT 3–5ft (1–1.5m).
• SPREAD 3–5ft (1–1.5m).

Cedrus libani subsp. *libani* 'Sargentii'

☼ ◊ ❀❀❀   Z 5–7

THUJA ORIENTALIS 'Semperaurea'
Habit Vigorous, ovoid, with a rounded top.
Leaves Small, triangular, blunt-pointed, overlapping, held in vertical sprays. Golden-yellow.
• OTHER NAMES *Biota orientalis* 'Semperaurea, *Platycladus orientalis* 'Semperaurea'.
• HEIGHT 10ft (3m).
• SPREAD 6ft (2m).

Thuja orientalis 'Semperaurea'

☼ ◊ ❀❀❀   Z 5–9

PINUS HELDREICHII var. LEUCODERMIS 'Compact Gem'
Habit Very slow-growing, dense, broadly conical, with upright branches. **Leaves** In pairs, rigid, needle-like, sharp- and forward-pointing. Very dark green.
• HEIGHT 10–12in (25–30cm).
• SPREAD 10–12in (25–30cm).

Pinus heldreichii var. *leucodermis* 'Compact Gem'

☼ ◊ ❀❀❀   Z 6–7

THUJA OCCIDENTALIS 'Filiformis'
Habit Loose, open, mound-forming.
Leaves Tiny, scale-like, on very slender, whip-like shoots pendent at the tip. Light green.
• HEIGHT 5ft (1.5m).
• SPREAD 5–6ft (1.5–2m).

Thuja occidentalis 'Filiformis'

☼ ◊ ❀❀❀   Z 2–7

THUJA PLICATA 'Hillieri'

Habit Slow-growing, dense, rounded.
Leaves Moss-like, in irregular clusters, on stiff, stout branchlets. Rich green.
• CULTIVATION Cut back any long, untidy, or protruding branchlets when young.
• HEIGHT 3ft (1m) or more.
• SPREAD 3ft (1m).

Thuja plicata 'Hillieri'

☼ ◐ ❀❀❀   Z 5–7

CRYPTOMERIA JAPONICA 'Spiralis'

Habit Slow-growing, dense, spreading.
Leaves Slender, needle-like, incurved, flattened at the base. Spirally twisted around the stem. Bright green.
• HEIGHT 6–10ft (2–3m).
• SPREAD 6–10ft (2–3m).

Cryptomeria japonica 'Spiralis'

☼ ◐ ❀❀❀   Z 6–9

JUNIPERUS CHINENSIS 'Expansa Variegata'

Habit Mound-forming, with horizontal or ascending branches.
Leaves Aromatic, scale- and needle-like, in dense sprays. Bluish-green, with some sprays creamy-white.
• OTHER NAMES *J. davurica* 'Expansa Albopicta'.
• HEIGHT 30in (75cm).
• SPREAD 5–6ft (1.5–2m).

Juniperus chinensis 'Expansa Variegata'

☼ ◐ ❀❀❀   Z 3–9

JUNIPERUS × *MEDIA* 'Blue and Gold'

Habit Compact, spreading, with ascending branches.
Leaves Mainly scale-like. Variegated soft gray-blue and creamy-gold.
• OTHER NAMES *J.* 'Blue and Gold'.
• HEIGHT 3ft (1m).
• SPREAD 3ft (1m).

Juniperus × *media* 'Blue and Gold'

☼ ◐ ❀❀❀   Z 3–9

JUNIPERUS × *MEDIA* 'Pfitzeriana Aurea'

Habit Spreading, dense, with ascending branches that droop at the tips.
Leaves Mainly scale-like. Dark yellow-green. Shoot tips golden-yellow in spring.
• OTHER NAMES *J.* 'Pfitzeriana Aurea'.
• HEIGHT 10ft (3m).
• SPREAD 10–15ft (3–5m).

Juniperus × *media* 'Pfitzeriana Aurea'

☼ ◐ ❀❀❀   Z 3–9

TAXUS BACCATA 'Dovastonii Aurea'

Habit Slow-growing, wide-spreading, with horizontally tiered branches that weep at the tips.
Leaves Linear, pointed. Dark green, margined golden-yellow, on yellow shoots.
• CULTIVATION Tolerates most acid or alkaline soils.
• HEIGHT To 20ft (6m).
• SPREAD To 25ft (8m).

Taxus baccata 'Dovastonii Aurea'

☀ ◐ ❀❀❀   Z 6–7

JUNIPERUS CHINENSIS 'Plumosa Aurea'

Habit Low-growing, spreading, with ascending branches that arch at the tips.
Leaves Tiny, scale-like, in crowded, plume-like sprays. Golden-green, bronzed in winter.
• HEIGHT 3ft (1m).
• SPREAD 6–10ft (2–3m).
• OTHER NAMES *J.* × *media* 'Plumosa Aurea'.

Juniperus chinensis 'Plumosa Aurea'

☼ ◐ ❀❀❀   Z 3–9

CHAMAECYPARIS OBTUSA 'Nana Aurea'

Habit Slow-growing, flat-topped, broadly and irregularly columnar.
Leaves Aromatic, tiny, scale-like, in horizontal, cupped sprays. Golden-yellow.
• HEIGHT 6ft (2m).
• SPREAD 6ft (2m).

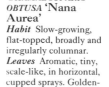

Chamaecyparis obtusa 'Nana Aurea'

☼ ◐ ❀❀❀   Z 4–8

CHAMAECYPARIS PISIFERA
'Filifera Aurea'
Habit Broadly conical, with thread-like, pendulous shoots. **Leaves** Aromatic, tiny, scale-like, closely pressed to whip-like shoots. Golden-yellow.
• CULTIVATION Foliage will scorch in full sun.
• HEIGHT 12–15ft (4–5m).
• SPREAD 10ft (3m).

Chamaecyparis pisifera 'Filifera Aurea'

☼ ◑ ❀❀❀   Z 4–8

PINUS SYLVESTRIS
'Gold Coin'
Habit Slow-growing, rounded. A dwarf form of *P. sylvestris* 'Aurea'. **Leaves** In pairs, slender, stiff, needle-like, carried in dense bundles. Blue-green, turning intense golden-yellow in winter and spring.
• HEIGHT 6ft (2m).
• SPREAD 6ft (2m).

Pinus sylvestris 'Gold Coin'

☼ ◔ ❀❀❀   Z 2–8

CRYPTOMERIA JAPONICA 'Sekkan-sugi'
Habit Rounded, broadly pyramidal, with semi-pendulous branchlets. **Leaves** Slender, needle-like, flattened at the base Pale creamy-yellow.
• HEIGHT 30ft (10m).
• SPREAD 10–12ft (3–4m).

Cryptomeria japonica 'Sekkan-sugi'

☼ ◑ ❀❀❀   Z 6–9

ABIES NORDMANNIANA
'Golden Spreader'
Habit Slow-growing, flat-topped, spreading. **Leaves** Linear, slightly curved, flattened. Bright golden-yellow, intensely so in winter, paler beneath.
• HEIGHT 3ft (1m).
• SPREAD 3ft (1m).

Abies nordmanniana 'Golden Spreader'

☼ ◑ ❀❀❀   Z 4–6

TAXUS BACCATA
Aurea Group
Habit Slow-growing, broadly conical, domed with age. **Leaves** Linear, pointed, flattened. Golden-yellow.
• CULTIVATION Withstands close clipping. Tolerates most acid or alkaline soils.
• HEIGHT 20–30ft (6–10m).
• SPREAD 15–25ft (5–8m).

Taxus baccata Aurea Group
Golden English yew

☀ ◔ ❀❀❀   Z 6–7

THUJA PLICATA
'Stoneham Gold'
Habit Slow-growing, dense, conical. **Leaves** Aromatic, tiny, scale-like, in flattened sprays. Very dark green within the bush, bright golden-orange at the shoot tips.
• HEIGHT 3–6ft (1–2m).
• SPREAD 3ft (1m).

Thuja plicata 'Stoneham Gold'

☼ ◑ ❀❀❀   Z 5–7

TSUGA CANADENSIS
'Aurea'
Habit Broadly conical, often multi-stemmed. **Leaves** Needle-like, flattened, arranged in spirals around the gray shoots. Golden-yellow when young, green with age, with silver bands beneath.
• HEIGHT 15ft (5m) or more.
• SPREAD 6–10ft (2–3m).

Tsuga canadensis 'Aurea'

☼ ◑ ❀❀❀   Z 3–7

CRYPTOMERIA JAPONICA 'Elegans Compacta'
Habit Slow-growing, dense, spreading. **Leaves** Slender, soft, curved, needle-like, in feathery sprays. Green, turning rich bronze-purple in winter.
• HEIGHT 6–15ft (2–5m).
• SPREAD 6ft (2m).

Cryptomeria japonica 'Elegans Compacta'

☼ ◑ ❀❀❀   Z 6–9

ADDITIONAL SPECIES AND CULTIVARS

Numerous variants of plants exist that differ slightly from the normal form of species. Some of these variants exist in the wild and are termed subspecies (subsp.), varieties (var.), or forms (forma or f.). Others are known as cultivars – a contraction of '*culti*vated *var*ieties' – and they exist only in cultivation. The cultivar name is enclosed in single quotes and follows the botanical name, for example *Alnus incana* 'Aurea'. Below are listed some additional trees to those described in the book. A cross-reference is given to the page number of the species or a close relative.

Albizia julibrissin var. *rosea*. A hardier variety. Similar to the species (p.98) but with bright pink flowers in dense, fluffy heads.

Alnus incana 'Aurea'. Similar to the species (p.23) but with orange shoots in winter, yellow leaves, and red-tinted catkins.

Alnus incana 'Laciniata'. Similar to the species (p.23) but with leaves finely divided into narrow lobes.

Arbutus unedo f. *rubra*. A free-fruiting form, similar to the species (p.104) but with pink-flushed flowers.

Betula ermanii 'Grayswood Hill'. An exceptionally graceful form of the species (p.41) but with smooth, creamy-white bark, becoming gray-white and peeling with age.

Betula 'Jermyns'. Vigorous, broadly conical tree, similar to *B. utilis* var. *jacquemontii* (p.76) but with broader leaves and smooth, unmarked, pure white bark.

Catalpa × *erubescens* 'Purpurea'. Deciduous, spreading tree, similar to *C. bignonioides* (p.60). Dark purple, oval or 3-lobed leaves turn deep green when mature. Has bell-shaped white flowers marked with yellow and purple, in mid- to late summer.

Chamaecyparis lawsoniana 'Kilmacurragh'. Narrowly columnar tree to 30–50ft (10–15m), with strongly upright branches bearing sprays of dark green foliage. See *C. lawsoniana* 'Columnaris', p.148.

Chamaecyparis lawsoniana 'Wisselii'. Fast-growing, slender-conical tree to 50ft (15m), with widely spaced, upright branches bearing fern-like sprays of blue-green foliage. See *C. lawsoniana* 'Green Pillar', p.144.

Chamaecyparis pisifera 'Boulevard'. Bushy, slow-growing conical tree to 10ft (3m) or more, with soft, silver-blue foliage, purple-tinged in cold weather. See *C. thyoides*, p.145.

Crataegus laevigata 'Rosea Flore Pleno'. Similar to *C. laevigata* 'Paul's Scarlet' (p.98) but with many double pink flowers in late spring and early summer.

Crataegus mollis. Wide-spreading to 40ft (12m) with broadly oval, lobed, dark green leaves that are white-downy beneath when young. Bears clusters of white flowers, then short-lived, round, red fruit. See *Crataegus flava* p.94 and *C. macrosperma* var. *acutiloba*, p.106.

Cupressus sempervirens 'Swane's Gold'. Similar to the species (p.139). Compact, narrowly columnar tree with gold-tinted foliage.

Davidia involucrata var. *vilmoriniana*. Very similar to the species (p.59) but leaves are smooth, not silky, beneath, and fruits are more elliptic and less russeted.

Eucalyptus globulus. Fast-growing, half-hardy evergreen with peeling bark and narrow, oval-oblong, silvery-blue leaves, turning glossy mid-green with age. See *E. gunnii*, p.42.

Eucryphia × *intermedia* 'Rostrevor'. Similar to *E. lucida* (p.97). Compact, free-flowering, broadly columnar evergreen, with oblong or 3-lobed, glossy dark green leaves, and many single white flowers in late summer.

Fagus sylvatica 'Rohanii'. Similar to *F. sylvatica* var. *heterophylia* 'Aspleniifolia' (see p.38) but with broader leaves that are colored a greenish-purple with red leaf veins and stalks.

Fraxinus angustifolia 'Raywood'. Similar to *F. velutina* (p.65). A vigorous, deciduous, spreading tree of elegant habit. Ash-like leaves have 5–7 narrowly oval leaflets and turn red-purple in autumn.

Halesia carolina. Similar to but smaller than *H. monticola* (p.49). A free-flowering, small tree with masses of white flowers on bare branches in late spring.

Halesia tetraptera. Similar to but smaller than *H. monticola* (p.49). A free-flowering, small tree with masses of pendent, bell-shaped, white flowers on bare branches in late spring.

Hoheria 'Glory of Amlwch'. Tree to 22ft (7m). Semi-evergreen, but can be evergreen given mild winters. Similar to *H. angustifolia* (p.95), bearing many snow-white flowers from mid- to late summer.

Juglans cinerea (Butternut). Related to *J. nigra* (p.29). A fast-growing, deciduous, spreading tree to 80ft (25m), with large, aromatic leaves divided into 7–19 oval, pointed, bright green leaflets.

Juniperus chinensis 'Aurea'. Slow-growing tree to 30–50ft (10–15m), with an oval or conical outline, bearing golden foliage and many yellow male cones. See *J. chinensis* 'Obelisk', p.149.

Liquidambar styraciflua 'Lane Roberts'. Similar to the species (p.36) but produces more reliable autumn colors of deep red-purple.

Liriodendron chinense (Chinese tulip tree). A fast-growing deciduous tree, similar to *L. tulipifera*, (p.34) but its leaves have a narrower 'waist' at the lobe junction and are more blue-white beneath.

Liriodendron tulipifera 'Fastigiatum'. Similar to the species (p.34) but a broadly columnar tree with strongly upright branches.

Malus 'Red Sentinel'. The pink buds open into white flowers 1½in (3cm) across, which set rounded, long-persistent, glossy deep red fruits 1in (2.5cm) across. See *M.* 'Profusion', p.53.

Malus x *robusta* 'Red Siberian'. Vigorous, deciduous, spreading tree with oval, dark green leaves. Has clusters of white or pink-tinted flowers in spring and bright red crab apples in autumn. See *M. prunifolia*, p.109.

Malus x *robusta* 'Yellow Siberian'. Similar to *M.* x *robusta* 'Red Siberian' but with yellow fruits.

Malus 'Van Eseltine'. Deciduous, upright tree to 20ft (6m), bearing clusters of double pink flowers in spring, with small, yellow crab apples in autumn. See *M.* 'John Downie', p.108.

Picea orientalis 'Aurea'. Dense, columnar tree to 70ft (20m), with young foliage of creamy-yellow, later becoming golden yellow before turning green. See *P. orientalis* 'Skylands', p.137.

Picea pungens 'Hoopsii'. Dense, conical tree to 30–50ft (10–15m), bearing sharp, stout, bright silver-blue needles. See *P. pungens* 'Koster', p.138.

Populus x *canadensis* 'Aurea'. A fast-growing tree to 100ft (30m). Similar to *P.* x *canadensis* 'Robusta' (p.22) but with broadly oval leaves that are golden-yellow when young, aging to yellow-green, and borne on red leaf stalks.

Prunus cerasifera 'Pissardii'. A deciduous, round-headed tree similar to *P. cerasifera* 'Nigra' (p.99) but with white or pale pink flowers, and leaves that are red when young, then darker red, then purple.

Prunus 'Kursar'. Deciduous, spreading tree to 25ft (8m), with small, deep pink flowers in early spring, and oval, dark green leaves, turning orange in autumn. See *P.* 'Hokusai', p.87.

Sorbus aucuparia 'Sheerwater Seedling'. Similar to the species (p.72), but a narrowly upright tree, to 12ft (4m), with a compact, ovoid crown, and a profusion of orange-red berries in autumn.

Sorbus commixta 'Embley'. Similar to the species (see p.71), but with more reliable and longer-lasting autumn colors of brilliant red and orange hues. It bears large clusters of bright red fruits in autumn.

Stewartia serrata. Deciduous tree to 30ft (10m) similar to, but smaller than, *S. pseudocamellia* (p.60), with good autumn color and cup-shaped, red-stained white flowers in early summer.

Taxus baccata 'Fastigiata Aureomarginata'. Similar to *T. baccata* 'Fastigiata' (p.145), but leaves have a golden yellow margin.

Tsuga canadensis. Narrowly conical tree 120ft (30m) high. Has bright green, linear leaves, turning dark green above, with 2 broad, white bands beneath. See *T. canadensis* 'Aurea', p.163.

GUIDE TO TREE CARE

ONCE PLANTED, A TREE will remain in position for many years, so it is essential to provide the best possible growing conditions at the outset. Climate, soil type, and the amount of light and shelter available all affect a tree's growth and must be very carefully considered. Attention to soil preparation, planting, and aftercare are also vital for the successful establishment and healthy

CHOOSING TREES FOR PLANTING

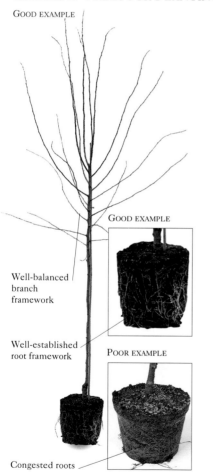

GOOD EXAMPLE

Well-balanced branch framework

Well-established root framework

GOOD EXAMPLE

POOR EXAMPLE

Congested roots

Container-grown tree
Check that roots are not coiled, overcrowded, or protruding from the drainage holes of the pot. It should be easy to remove from the pot, and soil mix should cling to the root ball.

GOOD EXAMPLE

Fibrous 'feeder' roots

Evenly distributed, spreading roots

POOR EXAMPLE

Uneven, 'hockey stick' roots

POOR EXAMPLE

Tightly coiled roots

Bare-root tree
A good root system should be well-balanced, spreading evenly in all directions, and with a mass of vigorous, fibrous roots. Avoid those with uneven or tightly coiled roots.

growth of the tree. Before choosing a tree, check that it will thrive within the temperature, rainfall, and humidity ranges that prevail on the planned site. Consider local factors, such as exposure to wind, which may scorch foliage or cause distortion of the tree's canopy. Even within a species, different cultivars may be more suited to certain conditions.

GOOD EXAMPLE

Balanced shape

Firm root ball with covering intact

Balled-and-burlapped tree
Check that the root ball is firm and has its wrapping and surrounding soil intact. Do not purchase if there are signs of damage or drying out since it will be less likely to establish well.

In areas with late spring frosts, choose trees that leaf out late, since young growth, even of otherwise hardy trees, may be damaged by frost.

Within the garden the microclimate may vary considerably. Ensure that the planting site provides appropriate light levels and wind shelter. On sloping sites bear in mind that the bottom of the slope is more likely to form a frost pocket and the top will be more exposed to wind. A position halfway up is likely to be warmer and more sheltered.

In coastal gardens, shelter from sea-spray and salt-laden winds is vital for some species, although with careful selection certain trees that can withstand these conditions may be used as windbreaks to provide protection for more vulnerable plants.

Avoid planting vigorous species, such as poplars and willows, near buildings and walls, since their wide-spreading roots may cause damage to foundations or drains as they develop. Similarly, do not plant trees where they may interfere with overhead or underground cables.

Selecting a tree
Trees may be bought container-grown, balled-and-burlapped, or bare-root, and in a variety of sizes from seedlings to semi-mature standards. In general, smaller trees establish more quickly, while semi-mature specimens lend immediate impact but need greater attention to aftercare. Whatever the size, check that roots and top-growth are healthy, vigorous, well-developed, and evenly balanced around the stem.

Container-grown trees may be planted at any time, but do not buy them if they are pot-bound: restricted roots seldom establish well and may result in unstable anchorage at maturity. Bare-root trees, with little or no soil on the roots, and balled-and-burlapped trees, with roots and surrounding soil wrapped to keep the root ball intact, must be planted when dormant. Check that roots are free from damage and disease, with no sign of dryness from exposure to wind.

SOIL PREPARATION AND PLANTING

Trees are best planted as soon as possible after purchase, although if kept moist in frost-free conditions, planting of balled-and-burlapped and container-grown trees may be delayed until weather conditions are more amenable. Bare-root trees can be heeled in, if necessary, until weather conditions improve.

When to plant
Container-grown plants can be planted out at any time of the year, except during drought and severe cold. Deciduous bare-root trees should be planted when dormant, between mid-autumn and mid-spring, avoiding frosty weather. Plant hardy evergreens and hardy, deciduous trees with fleshy roots in mid-autumn or mid- to late spring. Half-hardy trees should be planted in mid-spring. Balled-and-burlapped trees should be planted in early to mid-autumn or in mid-spring; deciduous balled-and-burlapped specimens can also be planted during mild spells in winter. Autumn planting, while soils retain residual warmth, allows good root establishment. In cold areas, however, spring planting may be more successful.

Prepare the site in advance to allow the soil to settle. Choose a well-drained site and clear all vegetation to at least 3ft (1m) from the base of the tree to eliminate competition for water and nutrients. Double dig the soil and incorporate well-rotted organic matter in the bottom trench.

Once the planting site has been prepared, dig the planting hole and fork

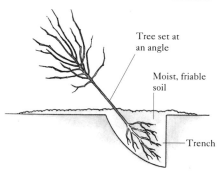

Heeling in
If planting is delayed, the tree will need to be temporarily heeled in. Prepare a trench and set the tree in it at an angle so that the trunk is supported and the roots well covered with soil.

Tree set at an angle

Moist, friable soil

Trench

PLANTING A
CONTAINER-GROWN TREE

1 *Mark out the diameter of the hole at 3–4 times the diameter of the pot. Remove grass and weeds and dig out to 1½ times the depth of the pot.*

2 *Roughen the sides and bottom of the hole with a fork and incorporate well-rotted organic matter into the soil that has been removed from the hole.*

over the sides and base of the hole to break up the surrounding soil. Mix the removed soil with well-rotted organic matter and, for spring planting, incorporate about 4oz (110 g) of slow-release fertilizer. If you are using a single stake (see p.171), drive it into the hole just off center before planting to ensure that the roots are not damaged later.

Container-grown trees need a planting hole 3–4 times the diameter of the root ball. Water thoroughly before removing the tree from the container. Gently tease out the roots by hand and trim away any damaged roots with pruners. Check the planting depth, adding or removing soil as necessary to ensure the final soil level is the same as it was in the container. Backfill the hole, firming gently in stages to avoid air pockets and to ensure good soil contact with the

3 *Add up to 20 percent of the mixed organic matter and soil into the hole. Then insert the stake in a slightly off-center position on the windward side of the tree.*

4 *Place the tree next to the stake and begin backfilling the hole. Using a stake, check and adjust the soil level so that it is eventually the same as it was in the pot.*

5 *Backfill in stages, firming gently as you go. Cut back damaged, over-long sideshoots and lower feathers (inset). Attach tree to the stake and apply mulch.*

Container trees

Plant at the same depth as in the nursery (using the soil mark on the stem as a guide) with the final soil level at about 2in (5cm) below the rim to permit thorough watering. Support standard trees with a stake inserted before planting.

PLANTING A B AND B TREE

Dig a planting hole 2–3 times the diameter of the root ball. Place the tree in the hole, untie the wrapping, and, rocking the plant gently to one side, slide out the material. Backfill the hole, firming gently as you go. Water in thoroughly immediately after planting.

roots. Lightly prune the top-growth to balance it with the root system. Attach the tree to its stake with a tree tie, water thoroughly, and apply a deep mulch to conserve moisture and suppress weeds.

Planting of bare-root and balled-and-burlapped trees is essentially the same as for container-grown specimens, although bare-root trees need a planting hole wide enough to accommodate the roots when fully spread. Balled-and-burlapped specimens need a planting hole 2–3 times the diameter of the root ball.

Small trees may be planted permanently in containers, which must have adequate drainage, a diameter equal to one-sixth to one-quarter of the tree's height, and a depth equal to one and a half times the tree's root ball. Use clean containers, cover the drainage holes with broken crocks, and add a layer of at least 1in (2.5cm) of crocks or coarse gravel. Use a soil-based potting mix with slow-release fertilizer, and a top-dressing of grit 1in (2.5cm) deep.

Keep all young trees irrigated and weed-free for at least the first 2–3 years after planting.

Staking trees

The root system of newly planted trees may take two or more growing seasons to establish well enough to provide firm anchorage against strong winds.

Transplants (3–4ft/60–120cm tall) and whips (unbranched, single-stemmed young trees 3–6ft/1–2m tall), seldom need staking. However, standards need the initial support of a stake to prevent wind rock at the roots. There is good evidence to show that the movement of a tree's trunk and crown in the wind helps promotes good rooting and encourages the stem to thicken. Stakes are needed to secure the root only, so short stakes are generally preferable. The exception is with slender, flexible-stemmed trees with a densely branched crown, such as crab apples. These are best given the support of a high stake in the first year which is then cut down to a lower level in the second year before

STAKING TREES

LOW ANGLED STAKE

Drive in stake after planting at an angle of about 45°, with it leaning into the prevailing wind.

LOW SINGLE STAKE

Low stakes allow stems to move. Drive in before planting, with 20in (50cm) of stake above the soil.

HIGH SINGLE STAKE

Drive in a long stake before planting and secure with ties positioned at both top and bottom.

LOW DOUBLE STAKES

Drive in two stakes after planting on opposite sides. Secure with heavy-duty rubber ties.

removing it in the third. Most trees will be sufficiently well established by the end of the second growing season for the stakes to be removed.

Stakes should be driven in to a depth of about 24in (60cm) below soil level to ensure stability. A single low stake is suitable for most standard trees on all but the windiest sites. It is best driven into the planting hole before planting the tree to avoid damage to the roots. Make sure that 20in (50cm) of the stake protrudes above soil level. Site the stake on the windward side so that when the tree moves in the wind it does not rub against the stake. For container-grown and balled-and-burlapped trees, especially on windy sites, a short stake, angled into the prevailing wind, is preferable. It can be driven in, clear of the root ball, after planting. Alternatively, two or three short, vertical stakes can be evenly placed around the tree, outside the area of the root ball.

Tree ties

Tree ties should be durable, and adjustable to accommodate the increase in the tree's girth without chafing or cutting into the bark. Commercial ties of the buckle-and-spacer type are available. Ties can also be made from nylon stockings or rubber tubing. These are nailed to the stake and formed into a figure eight to make the spacer. When using two or three stakes, secure the tree to the stakes with strips of heavy-duty rubber or plastic.

In many regions, it may be necessary to protect young trees from rabbits or other animals that strip bark. Enclose the trunk in chicken wire, wire netting, or one of the many types of tree guards available.

Buckle-and-spacer tie
Thread tie through spacer and around tree. Buckle so that it is taut but will not damage the bark.

Rubber tie
If using a rubber or plastic tie without a buckle, nail the tie to the stake to prevent bark damage caused by friction.

ROUTINE CARE

The amount of maintenance a tree needs largely depends on the species and its microclimate, soil type, and site. Once established, most trees need little maintenance, but if they are to establish well, young trees need watering, feeding, and most importantly, a clear weed-free area around the base for the first few years after planting.

Trees grown in containers should be regularly top-dressed and re-potted when they have outgrown their existing pot. Controlling pests and diseases, which can be debilitating to young trees, and removal of suckers from grafted specimens, may also be necessary.

Watering

Most trees need plenty of water to grow well, especially on light, sandy soils and for the first two or three years after planting. In the growing season, during periods of dry weather, apply approximately 10–15 gallons per sq yd (50–75 liters per sq m) each week. Established trees seldom need artificial irrigation, except during periods of prolonged drought. During these conditions, however, restrictions are often in place, and measures should be taken to conserve available soil water.

Mulching

Mulching reduces water loss from the soil surface and, in addition, keeps down weeds and reduces the effects of temperature extremes around the roots. Pulverized bark is effective and attractive, but black plastic or old carpet are also useful where aesthetics are less important. Mulches are best applied in spring, but provided the soil is moist, they can be spread at any time except during severe cold and drought. Cover an area about 12–18in (30–45cm) larger all round than the tree's root system,

TOP DRESSING CONTAINER-GROWN TREES

1 Top dressing should be carried out in spring before the tree starts into growth. Using hands or a trowel, remove any mulch and the top 2in (5cm) of soil mix.

2 Replenish the top of the container with fresh soil mix combined with a slow-release fertilizer. Water thoroughly and add a fresh layer of mulch to the surface.

and replenish it every other year for young trees. Nutrient-rich, organic mulches may be used when trees also require feeding.

Feeding
Young trees, especially on poor, infertile soils, benefit from feeding, particularly during the first few years after planting. Established trees need only occasional feeding. Apply organic fertilizers such as well-rotted manure or compost to a depth of 2–3in (5–8cm) in autumn, or during any frost-free period when the tree is dormant. Leave a clear area immediately around the trunk, and extend the mulch to beneath the outer edge of the canopy. Artificial fertilizers are best applied in spring, according to the manufacturers' recommendations. Trees grown for their flowers and fruit need more potash and phosphate, while those grown for their foliage will need more nitrogen.

Weeding
During the early years of the tree's life, keep the area beneath its canopy free of grass and weeds since these will compete with the tree for any available water and nutrients.

Hand weeding, mulching, or covering the soil with black plastic will help to control the weeds. If this does not work adequately, specific weedkillers that do not affect the tree roots may be used.

If a tree's growth is too rapid, retaining or establishing grass around it will help to slow down its vigorous growth by providing competition for food and water.

Tree problems
Provided trees have been properly planted into well-prepared soil, have been adequately fed, carefully watered, and kept free of competing weeds, they should suffer few problems: Healthy, well-grown trees are often less likely to become infested with pests and diseases. Lack of vigor is a reliable sign that something is wrong. Make sure that the

REMOVING SUCKERS

Suckers divert nutrients from the main shoots of the tree. Cut them off close to the base using pruners, then pare over the cut surface with a sharp knife. Rub out new growth as soon as it appears.

tree has not been planted too deeply and that the roots or stems have not been damaged.

Check for pests and diseases. Aphids and spider mites are the most common problems, and on small trees can be treated with appropriate insecticides, preferably before heavy infestations develop. Honey fungus (*Armillaria* spp.) is more serious. White mycelium appears under the bark at the base of the trunk, and black, shoelace-like strands infest the soil around the roots. Yellow or tawny-colored toadstools appear between midsummer and midwinter. Plants will deteriorate over time, and little can be done to treat them. Remove and burn affected plants, stumps, and root systems. Large trees should have their stumps chipped or ground out by a contractor.

Trees may be damaged by strong winds, and young growth may be badly affected by severe frosts. These problems are best avoided by choosing appropriately hardy species, selecting a suitable site, and providing shelter with windbreaks or screens. Cut back any damaged growth to a suitable bud in spring. Frost may also lift newly planted trees, so check after frosty weather and, if necessary, refirm after thawing.

Suckers and water shoots will divert nutrients from the main shoots of the tree if they are allowed to develop unchecked. Remove them as soon as possible. A tree may produce both stem and root suckers. Stem suckers appear just below the graft union on the understock of a grafted tree. Root suckers develop directly from the roots.

Suckers on grafted plants are frequently more vigorous than the desirable, grafted top-growth and, if left, may eventually outgrow or even replace it. Cut the suckers back to the base with pruners, check regularly, and rub out any new growth as soon as it emerges.

Vigorous trees, or those which have their roots close to the soil surface, such as poplars (*Populus*) and ornamental cherries (*Prunus*), often produce root suckers. Although these may be used for propagation, they can become a nuisance if they invade paths or lawns. Cut or pull off the root suckers as close to their base as possible, removing the soil to where

the sucker joins the root, if necessary. For some genera, such as *Prunus*, painting the wounds on the roots with growth retardant usually prevents regrowth and in small quantities will not harm the tree. Epicormic, or water, shoots grow directly out of the trunk and frequently appear around the site of pruning wounds. If allowed to develop, they will grow through and spoil the natural form of the canopy. Cut out at the base with pruners and rub out any new shoots as they emerge.

Transplanting trees

Careful attention to site and species selection should avoid the need for transplanting, but if it becomes necessary, careful preparation and aftercare will enable young trees up to 8ft (2.5m) in height usually to be transplanted successfully. Mature and larger trees are very difficult to move and so are best left to a specialist firm.

Prepare the young tree in the early autumn of the year before transplanting is to take place. Dig a trench around the area just beyond the root ball, with a diameter about one-third of the tree's

---

Transplanting a Young Tree

1 *Dig a trench 1ft (30cm) wide, 2ft (60cm) deep, outside the area of the root ball. Undercut the root ball with a sharp spade. Backfill the trench with soil and well-rotted organic matter.*

2 *The following autumn lift the tree gently first to one side, then the other, sliding burlap or plastic beneath. Carefully tilt the tree the other way and pull the sheeting through underneath the roots.*

height, and undercut to sever any large, coarse roots. Mix the soil taken from the hole with well-rotted organic matter to encourage the production of fibrous feeder roots, and then backfill the trench with the soil. Tie the branches to the central stem with soft twine to avoid damage during transit. Transplant in the following early autumn, replanting to the same depth. In the following 2–3 growing seasons, keep well watered and weed-free. The tree may take several seasons to resume vigorous growth.

Tree felling

Cutting down a tree can be done at any time of year, but trees larger than 15ft (5m) should be tackled by a professional arborist, since felling is a potentially dangerous operation. Also, check that the tree is legally yours and that it is not subject to local ordinances.

Ensure there is a clear space for the tree to fall and for you to move out of the way. Once felled, remove the stump and large roots by digging a trench, loosening the roots, and winching or digging out. If left, the stump may attract wood-boring insects, wood-rotting fungi, and other organisms.

CUTTING DOWN A TREE

Cut out a wedge of about one-third of the trunk diameter, the lower cut horizontal, the upper at 45°, at 3ft (1m) above ground, on the side where the tree will fall. Make the final cut on the opposite side, just above the base of the wedge. Push gently, if necessary, in the direction of fall. Remove the remaining stump by digging a trench around it, loosening the roots and then winching or digging it out.

3 *Tie the burlap firmly but gently around the root ball and transfer the tree to its new planting hole. Unwrap the root ball and place in the hole by reversing the procedure outlined in Step 2. Replant to the soil mark on the stem.*

4 *Support the newly planted tree with guy ropes attached to angled stakes. Water thoroughly and apply a deep mulch to conserve water and suppress weeds. Keep well watered until reestablished.*

PRUNING AND TRAINING

Correct pruning and training helps to maintain a tree's health and vigor, regulates its shape, and in some cases improves flowering and fruiting. The formative pruning of young trees is often vital to ensure a well-balanced and structurally sound framework at maturity. Once their form is established, most trees need little further pruning.

The extent of pruning depends on the type of tree and the desired effects. To form a well-shaped tree usually requires little pruning. A pleached hedge or laburnum arch, however, needs more regular work and expertise.

Most deciduous species are pruned when fully dormant, preferably between autumn and midwinter. Dead wood is removed at any time of year, but is more clearly visible in summer. Most evergreens need little pruning, but if it is necessary, they are best pruned in early spring.

Principles of pruning

First remove any dead, diseased, and damaged wood and cut out weak or straggling growth. Then stand back and carefully assess which branches should be removed or shortened in order to produce a well-balanced framework. Hard pruning stimulates vigorous growth, while light pruning results in limited replacement growth.

All pruning cuts must be accurate and made with clean, sharp tools to minimize damage to the tree. Cut back to a healthy bud or pair of buds, or to a sideshoot pointing in the required direction of growth. When pruning trees with opposite buds, make a straight cut directly above a pair of buds. Cut back those with alternate leaves using a slanting cut just above the bud so that the base of the cut is level with the top of the bud.

When removing entire branches it is essential to cut just outside the branch collar – a slight swelling at the base of

How to prune
For alternate buds, make a slanting cut ⅛–¼in (3–5mm) above the bud (left). For opposite buds, make a straight cut directly above a strong pair of buds (right).

the branch where it joins the trunk. The branch collar constitutes the tree's natural defense against infection, and this is where the callus will form to seal the wound and provide protection against wood-rotting organisms.

Branches less than 1in (2.5cm) in diameter can be removed with a pruning saw or pruners. Larger branches should be removed in sections to avoid tearing the bark on the main trunk.

Formative pruning

The aim of formative pruning is to create trees with a strong, well-balanced framework of evenly spaced branches that are safe and structurally sound when

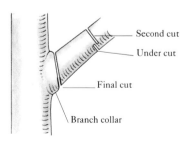

Second cut
Under cut
Final cut
Branch collar

Where to cut
Remove the bulk of the branch with two cuts, as shown. Cut off the stub just outside the branch collar. Do not breach the branch collar when removing a branch.

CUTTING OFF A BRANCH

1 *It is much easier – and safer – to remove the branches in sections. Make an undercut with a pruning saw, 1ft (30cm) away from the trunk, to a depth of one-quarter of the branch diameter. This is important to prevent the bark from tearing back into the branch collar if the branch should break.*

2 *Make a top cut, about 1in (2.5cm) farther away from the trunk, sawing from above. Gently support the free end of the branch with your free hand, so that the cut does not close on the saw and make sawing movements difficult. This also ensures that the branch does not spring upward as it falls.*

3 *Remove the remaining stub, first making a small undercut just outside the branch collar. If the branch collar is not obvious, make this cut at an equal and opposite angle to the ridge of bark which slopes downward from the crotch into the main trunk. Keep supporting the branch with your free hand.*

4 *Make the final cut from the top, just outside the branch collar, angling the saw slightly away from the trunk. If the branch angle is acute, it is easier to make the final cut from below. Leave the cut bare (see inset pic). Do not apply wound paint or dressing, because it can foster wood-rotting organisms or delay healing.*

Training a new leader

1 *Replace a broken or damaged leader with a strong upright lateral. Attach a stake firmly to the top of the main stem and tie the new leader to it.*

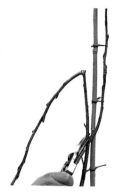

2 *Prune out the old damaged leader, taking care not to damage its replacement. Once the new leader is growing strongly and is clearly dominant, the support stake can be removed.*

they mature. At its simplest, formative pruning enhances a tree's natural shape, requiring only routine removal of dead, damaged, and diseased wood, along with weak, rubbing, or crossing branches. Ornamental garden trees are often pruned to produce a tree form that displays its features to best effect.

Feathered trees form a central leading shoot and have laterals along the length of the stem. They may be allowed to develop naturally, or may have the lower laterals pruned away to produce a central-leader standard – a tree with a clear length of stem below the crown. A branched-head standard has the lower laterals and the leading shoot removed to create an open crown with widely spreading lateral branches, a form commonly seen in small ornamentals such as Japanese cherries (*Prunus*).

Feathered trees need little pruning other than to remove weak or poorly placed laterals (feathers) and any shoots that compete with the central leader, ensuring that the remaining laterals are evenly spaced around the central stem. The lower laterals may eventually die back naturally.

To train a central-leader standard, plant a well-feathered young tree and remove any competing leaders and badly placed laterals. Remove laterals from the lowest third of the stem, and reduce the laterals on the middle third by about one half of their length. In the late autumn

or early winter, cut back the pruned laterals to the main stem, and repeat the procedure over 2–3 years until the stem has been cleared to about 6ft (1.8m). If the leader is lost or damaged, it is essential to select and train in a replacement as soon as possible. Dual or multiple leaders form narrow branch angles (crotches) which lead to structural weakness at maturity.

Branched-head standards are trained initially as central-leader standards, until the desired length of clear stem has been achieved. In mid- to late autumn, remove the central leader, cutting back to a strong, healthy bud and leaving a framework of about five strong, evenly spaced branches. Remove any crossed or badly congested laterals. In subsequent years, remove any branches that cause imbalance or congestion in the crown. Take out any vertical branches that may form secondary leaders, and clear the stem of any laterals that develop below the crown. Some branched-head standards are created in the nursery by top-working as for weeping standards.

Weeping standards are created by grafting one or more sections of a weeping cultivar onto a stock plant with a clear stem of about 6ft (1.8m). Pruning is limited to removing crossed, badly placed, or vertical branches. Some semi-upright stems are left to create tiers of weeping branches.

Removing a competing leader

Prune out the competing leader by cutting it back to its base. Make a clean cut with sharp pruners or loppers, taking care not to damage the remaining leader.

Once the tree is established, it will usually require little further pruning other than the routine removal of dead, damaged, or diseased wood.

Containerized trees need annual pruning to restrict size and spread and to maintain a balanced framework.

Branched-head standards frequently become congested at the center of the crown, so remove inward-growing shoots and any badly placed branches that spoil the balanced framework. The removal of large branches from mature trees is a potentially dangerous operation that should be performed only by a professional tree surgeon.

Coppicing and pollarding

Coppicing is the regular pruning of a tree to ground level to encourage the production of strong basal shoots, while pollarding is the pruning of a tree back to its main stem or branch framework. These are traditional techniques once used to provide a regular supply of firewood or pliable stems for basket-work and fencing, but they are now commonly used for ornamental purposes to enhance leaf color and size, to produce ornamental stems, or to restrict size. Some trees may be coppiced or pollarded on an annual or biennial basis. Coppice in late winter or early spring. Vigorous trees, such as willows (*Salix*) that are grown for their colored stems, may be pruned in midspring just before, or just as, buds break into new growth.

To coppice, cut back all stems to the base with pruning loppers or sharp pruners, leaving the swollen basal wood unpruned, since all new growth will form from this point.

HOW TO COPPICE A TREE

Coppicing may be carried out in order to restrict a tree's size, enlarge its leaves, or enhance the stem color.

Coppicing should be done in late winter or early spring, using tree loppers or a pair of sharp pruners. Cut back all the stems of the tree to 3in (7cm) above the ground. Take care not to

cut into the swollen, woody base of the tree, since all new growth will be produced from this stump.

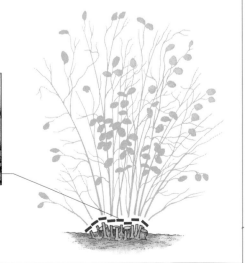

To produce a pollard, plant a young, branched-head standard. When the clear stem has reached the desired height, cut back branches to within 1–2in (2.5–5cm) of the main stem in late winter or early spring. This results in a proliferation of new shoots from the top of the cut stem, which are cut back annually or every other year. Thin to relieve congestion, and completely remove any new shoots that appear on the clear stem.

To produce a pollard with a main branch framework, allow the tree to produce a well-balanced branch system at the desired height. Then, in late winter or early spring, cut back the branches to about 6ft (2m). Cut back the new shoots every two to five years and, once the pollard is established, prune every or every other year.

Renovating old trees

Mature trees that have outgrown their situation or that have been neglected can sometimes be renovated to restore them to full health and vigor. However, renovation demands considerable care and expertise, and it is advisable to consult a professional arborist. An arboricultural association or a local horticultural school may be able to provide a list of approved contractors and consultants who are properly insured and who comply with safe working practices and up-to-date standards of technical competence.

Before inviting contractors to bid, decide exactly what work is required, including the disposal of any debris – which may be the most expensive part of tree surgery operations. Estimates are normally provided free of charge, but a fee may be charged if there is any advisory work involved.

In some cases, a tree may be too old and full of structural defects to make renovation a viable proposition, and if they are large, renovation will also be potentially dangerous. In these cases it is better to remove and replant.

Renovation may be carried out at any time of the year, except in early spring when the sap is rising, since this commonly results in excessive bleeding.

HOW TO POLLARD A TREE

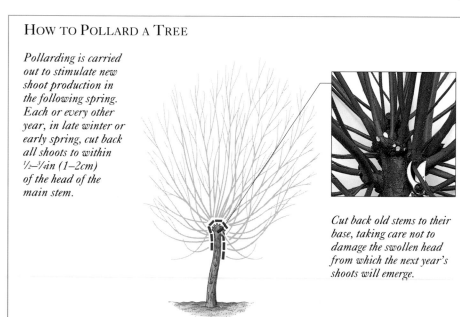

Pollarding is carried out to stimulate new shoot production in the following spring. Each or every other year, in late winter or early spring, cut back all shoots to within ½–¾in (1–2cm) of the head of the main stem.

Cut back old stems to their base, taking care not to damage the swollen head from which the next year's shoots will emerge.

Usually, renovation is best undertaken in late autumn or winter when the trees are fully dormant and the bare branch framework may be clearly seen. Flowering cherries and other *Prunus* species are best treated in early summer to reduce the risk of virus infection. Where the need for renovation is extensive, the process should be carried out in stages over two or three seasons, since drastic pruning inevitably causes shock that may weaken or even kill a tree in poor health.

To renovate, first remove all dead, diseased, and damaged wood, then take out crossing and congested branches and any that spoil the well-balanced framework. In early spring, feed the tree with a general fertilizer and apply a mulch of well-rotted organic matter. Keep the tree well fed and mulched for two to three years.

Hard pruning frequently stimulates the production of a mass of epicormic, or water, shoots. If necessary, select the strongest and best-placed to form replacement framework branches and remove the remainder. Bear in mind, however, that trees renovated in this way are seldom as structurally strong as they would have been if properly trained and pruned when young. The buds of any further water shoots that are produced should be rubbed away before they fully emerge.

Occasionally, you may inherit trees that have been improperly pruned annually, thus producing congested clusters of growth arising from knobby branches, but without the balanced branch framework of a properly pollarded tree. Such "hatrack" pruning is unsightly and reduces flower and fruit production, but, fortunately, corrective pruning is possible. First thin out the knobby stumps at the ends of the main branches. Cut out most of the young shoots on the remaining stumps to leave one or two of the strongest, and cut these back by about one-third of their length. This procedure should be repeated over the following three or four seasons, until a more natural habit of growth has been reestablished.

Renovating a Tree

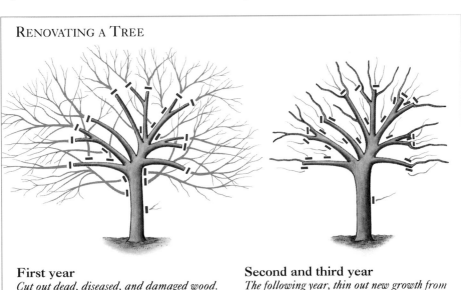

First year
Cut out dead, diseased, and damaged wood. Remove crossing or rubbing branches and any that spoil the balance of the framework.

Second and third year
The following year, thin out new growth from pruning wounds and remove water shoots. If necessary, repeat the following year.

PROPAGATION

Trees may be propagated by seed or vegetatively – by cuttings, layers, or grafting. Most species come true from seed, but some, such as birch (*Betula*), hybridize readily, so offspring may be variable. Cultivars and hybrids seldom come true when grown from seed and are therefore propagated vegetatively.

Many deciduous trees can be propagated from hardwood cuttings. Fast-rooting species, such as willow, are inserted directly into open ground. Slow-rooting species are tied in small bundles, overwintered in sand in a cold frame, and transferred to trenches in the following spring.

Prepare trenches to receive cuttings in early autumn, in friable, well-drained soil. On clay soils, add sharp sand to the base of the trench. Just after leaf fall, select some vigorous shoots of the current season's growth, cutting just above a bud or pair of buds at the junction between the previous and current season's growth.

Cuttings may sometimes be lifted by frost, so check regularly and refirm if necessary. They should root by the following autumn. Many conifers and broad-leaved evergreens can be propagated by semi-ripe cuttings taken in late summer or autumn from the current season's wood. Root in a equal parts mix of grit and peat, in a closed case at 70°F (21°C).

Take heel cuttings of sideshoots or 4–6in (10–15cm) long cuttings from leading or lateral shoots, trimmed just below a node. Remove the lowest two leaves and reduce the remainder by one half. Wound the base and dip in hormone rooting powder or gel. Insert the bottom third of the cutting into a hole in the soil mix, spacing so that leaves do not touch. Water with fungicidal solution and label. Keep just moist until rooted, removing fallen leaves regularly to avoid rot. Cuttings with basal heat should root by the spring.

Cuttings can also be inserted into a cold frame, with frost protection in winter. They may not root until the following autumn and therefore are best left in the frame for another winter, before hardening off and potting up in spring. Mist over in summer and shade from strong sun to avoid drying out and foliage scorch.

PLANTING DEPTHS

Multi-stemmed trees
Insert the cuttings with the top 1–1½in (2.5–3cm) above soil level. This enables the buds in the light to break and form several stems. Space cuttings 12–15in (30–38cm) apart outside, or 4in (10cm) apart in a cold frame.

Single-stemmed trees
Insert cuttings so that the top bud is barely covered by the soil. The lack of light on the stem inhibits the growth of all other buds. Space cuttings 12–15in (30–38cm) apart outside, or 4in (10cm) apart in a cold frame.

FAST-ROOTING HARDWOOD CUTTINGS

1 *Prepare a slit trench by driving a sharp spade vertically into the soil. The trench should be about 7in (19cm) deep, with one vertical side and one sloping side.*

2 *Select strong, straight, and healthy stems of about pencil thickness. Remove approximately 12in (30cm) of stem from the parent plant, just above a bud.*

3 *Remove any leaves. Trim cuttings to about 8in (20cm), with a sloping cut just above the top bud and a straight cut just below the bottom bud.*

4 *Insert into the trench at 4–6in (10–15cm) spacings, so that cuttings are positioned upright against the vertical side of the trench.*

5 *Firm the soil around the cuttings. Space further trenches at about 12–15in (30–38cm) apart. Water in thoroughly and label clearly.*

6 *Lift rooted cuttings during the following autumn and either pot them up individually or transplant them to their final location in open ground.*

Softwood cuttings are taken in spring from the tips of fast-growing shoots. They root easily but wilt rapidly, so prepare and insert them immediately after removal from the parent plant. Fill containers with cuttings soil mix and firm gently. Remove the new growth from shoot tips, cutting just above a node with a sharp knife. Place in an opaque plastic bag to conserve moisture. Trim to 2½in (6cm), just below a node. Remove lower leaves, dip the base in hormone rooting powder, and insert into the soil mix. Water, label, and place in a mist unit or closed case at 70–75°F (21–24°C). Water weekly with fungicide. Once rooted, harden off and pot up individually.

Raising trees from seed

Many trees are propagated easily from seed. Some seed, for example those of crab apples (*Malus*) or mountain ashes (*Sorbus*), should be cleaned of their fleshy coat before sowing. Hard seed

coats, such as those of oaks (*Quercus*), are nicked or rubbed with sandpaper so that they can absorb the water necessary for germination. Leguminous seeds are soaked in hot water for 24 hours.

Many temperate tree seeds exhibit dormancy and must be stored in either warm or cold conditions before they will germinate. Seed sown outside in autumn is chilled naturally during winter, but storing the seed in the refrigerator will produce more reliable results. Mix the seed with moistened vermiculite and place in a clear plastic bag. Store at 33–34°F (0.5–1°C), checking regularly and sowing immediately when signs of germination are seen. Seed chilling requirements vary considerably, from 6–8 weeks for deciduous species, to as little as 3 weeks for conifers. Some seed germinates only after chilling has ceased. Batch sowing over a period – after 4, 8, or 12 weeks of chilling – ensures that at least some seed will germinate.

SLOW-ROOTING HARDWOOD CUTTINGS

For species that do not root easily, tie the cuttings into bundles. Dip the ends of the bundles into a hormone rooting powder. Insert the bundles of cuttings into a sand bed and leave in a cold frame over winter. In spring, insert them individually into a trench at a prepared site outside. The trench should be narrow, with one side vertical, to enable the cuttings to be held securely upright while they take root.

PREPARING SEMI-RIPE CUTTINGS

Cut a shoot 4–6in (10–15cm) long from a leader or sideshoot and trim immediately below a node. Strip off the lower leaves (here of Chamaecyparis obtusa 'Nana Aurea'*) and pinch out the tip if it is soft. Make a shallow wound, about 1in (2.5cm) long, down the side of the cutting and dip it in hormone rooting powder.*

Simple layering

In early spring, cut a 2in (5cm) tongue, 12–18in (30–45cm) behind the growing tip of a vigorous shoot which is still attached to the parent plant. Brush the wound with hormone rooting powder and peg it into a shallow hole. Tie the shoot to a vertical supporting stake and backfill the hole with friable soil mixed together with some leafmold and sand. When it has rooted (after 12 months or so) sever from the parent plant and transplant.

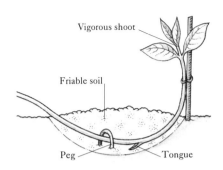

Vigorous shoot

Friable soil

Peg

Tongue

SOWING IN CONTAINERS

1 *Sow fine seed in trays of firmed seed soil mix, making sure it is scattered thinly and evenly. Keep your hand low to prevent the seeds from bouncing on the soil mix as they drop.*

2 *Half-fill a sieve with some seed soil mix, hold it over the seed tray, and tap the sides gently until the seeds are covered to approximately their own depth with mix.*

3 *Carefully apply a ¼in (5mm) layer of horticultural grit or fine vermiculite over the layer of soil mix. Label the seeds, and then water the tray using a watering can fitted with a fine nozzle.*

4 *Once the seedlings are large enough to handle, gently prick them out into individual containers, holding them by the leaves and taking care not to crush their stems and roots. Pot on as necessary.*

GLOSSARY OF TERMS

Italicized words have their own entry.

ACID (of soil). With a pH value of less than 7; see also *alkaline* and *neutral.*

ADVENTITIOUS (of roots). Arising directly from a stem or leaf.

ALKALINE (of soil). With a pH value of more than 7; see also *acid* and *neutral.*

APETALOUS. Having no petals.

APHID. Small, soft-bodied insect that sucks sap from a tree.

AXIL. The angle between a leaf and stem where an axillary bud develops.

BLOOMED. Covered with a bluish-white deposit.

BOLE. The trunk of a tree from ground level to first major branch.

BRACT. A modified leaf at the base of a flower or flower cluster. It may resemble a normal leaf or be reduced and scale-like in appearance.

BUDDING. Bud-grafting, a form of grafting.

CALYX. The outer part of a flower, usually small and green but sometimes showy and brightly colored; it is formed from the sepals and encloses the petals in a bud.

CANKER. A fungal infection that causes bark to darken and sink inward and thus results in a restricted flow of nutrients and water through the tree.

CATKIN. A flower cluster, normally pendulous. Flowers lack petals, are often stalkless, surrounded by scale-like bracts, and are usually unisexual.

CONE. The clustered flowers or woody, seed-bearing structures of a conifer.

COPPICE. To cut back to near ground level each year in order to produce vigorous shoots for ornamental or practical purposes.

COROLLA. The part of a flower formed by the petals.

CROWN. The upper, branched part of a tree above the trunk.

CUTTING. A section of a tree that is removed and used for propagation. See *Guide to Tree Care,* pp.182–4.

DECIDUOUS. Losing its leaves annually at the end of the growing season; semi-deciduous trees lose only some leaves.

ELLIPTIC (of leaves). Broadening at the center and narrowing toward each end.

EPICORMIC. Shoot that grows directly from the trunk of a tree, often around a wound.

EVERGREEN. Retaining its leaves all year round, although losing some older leaves regularly throughout the year. Semi-evergreen trees retain only some leaves or lose older leaves only when the new growth is produced.

FIREBLIGHT. A bacterial infection that attacks blossoms first, then stems and foliage.

FISSURED. Bark that is split or cracked due to age or weathering.

FRIABLE (of soil). Of a good, crumbly texture; capable of forming a soil that can be worked easily.

GLAUCOUS. Bluish-white, bluish-green.

GLOBOSE. Spherical.

GRAFTING. A method of propagation by which an artificial union is made between different parts of individual trees.

HABIT. The characteristic growth or general appearance of a tree.

HEEL. The small portion of old wood that is retained at the base of a cutting when it is removed from the stem.

HONEYDEW. Sticky substance found on foliage, the excrement of pests such as aphids, whiteflies, and mealybugs.

HONEY FUNGUS. An infection caused by the fungus *Armillaria.* It appears as a creamy white mycelium that develops under the bark, and as shoestring-like growths at the base of the tree.

HUSK. The rough outer layer of a fruit or seed.

HYBRID. The offspring of genetically different parents, usually produced in cultivation, but occasionally arising in the wild.

KEY. A winged seed such as that produced by maples (*Acer* species).

LANCE-SHAPED (of leaves). Narrow and tapering at both ends.

LATERAL. A side growth that emerges from a shoot or root.

LEADER. The tip of the main stem of a tree.

LEAF MINERS. The larvae of various flies that tunnel into leaves and destroy them.

LEAFLET. A subdivision of a compound leaf.

LINEAR (of leaves). Very narrow with parallel sides.

LIME. Compounds of calcium; the amount of lime in soil determines whether it is alkaline, neutral, or acid.

LOAM. Well-structured, fertile soil that is moisture-retentive but free-draining.

LOBE. A rounded projecting segment or part, forming part of a larger structure.

MICROCLIMATE. A small, local climate within a larger climate area, such as a greenhouse or a protected area of a garden.

MONOTYPIC. 1. Of a family: containing one genus that contains one species. 2. Of a genus: containing one species.

MULCH. A layer of organic matter applied to the soil over or around a tree to conserve moisture, protect the roots from heaving, reduce the growth of weeds, and enrich the soil.

MYCELIUM. The vegetative part of a fungus, consisting of microscopic, threadlike filaments.

NATIVE. Growing wild naturally in a specific area.

NATURALIZED. Established in the wild and growing as if naturally.

NEUTRAL (of soil). With a pH value of 7, the point at which soil is neither acid nor alkaline.

NODE. The point on a stem from which a leaf or leaves grow.

OPPOSITE (of leaves). Borne two to each node, one opposite the other.

OVATE (of leaves). Egg-shaped in outline, with the broader end at the base, becoming more pointed at the tip.

PALMATE (of leaves). Having four or more leaflets growing from a single point, as in horse chestnut (*Aesculus hippocastanum*).

PANICLE. A compound, branched raceme in which flowers develop on stalks (peduncles) arising from the main stem.

PARASITE. A plant that lives in or on another (the host), from which it obtains nourishment.

PEDUNCLE. The stalk of a flower cluster.

PERFOLIATE (of leaves). Having leaf bases that completely encircle the stem.

PERIANTH. The calyx and corolla, or outer parts of a flower.

PETIOLE. The stalk of a leaf.

PHYLLOCLADE. A flattened stem or branch that functions as a leaf.

PHYLLODE. An expanded leaf stalk, which functions as and resembles a leaf blade.

PINNATE (of leaves). A compound leaf in which the leaflets grow in two rows on each side of the midrib.

PLEACHING. A form of training in which branches from a row of trees are interwoven to form a wall or canopy.

POLLARD. To cut back a tree's main branches in order to encourage abundant growth.

PROP ROOTS. Large roots, found above ground at the base of a trunk, that help to support the tree.

PROSTRATE. With stems growing along the ground. Also called procumbent.

RACEME. An unbranched flower cluster with several or many stalked flowers borne singly along a main axis, the youngest at the apex.

RADIALLY ARRANGED (of leaves). Leaves arranged in a ray pattern around the stem.

RED SPIDER MITE. Tiny insects that drain sap from leaves and cause them to fall prematurely.

REVERT. To return to its original state, as when a plain green leaf is produced on a variegated plant.

ROOT. The part of a plant, normally underground, that functions as an anchor and absorbs water and nutrients. An aerial root is one that emerges from the stem at some distance above the soil level. See also *prop root.*

ROOTBALL. The roots and accompanying soil or soil mix visible when a plant is lifted.

ROSETTE. A group of leaves radiating from approximately the same point, often at ground level at the base of a very short stem.

SCALE. 1. A reduced or modified leaf. 2. Part of the cone of a conifer.

SEPAL. Part of a calyx, usually green. They may be insignificant, but are sometimes showy.

SPIRALLY-ARRANGED (of leaves). Leaves arranged in ascending spiral form around the stem.

STANDARD. A tree with a clear length of bare stem below the lowest branches.

SUCKER. Shoot growing directly from a tree stem, or from below ground level, directly from the root.

TEPAL. A subdivision of the perianth in flowers that have no distinct calyx and corolla.

TOOTH. A small, marginal, often pointed lobe on a leaf.

UPRIGHT (of habit). With vertical or semi-vertical main branches.

VERMICULITE. A lightweight, mica-like mineral that is added to soil mixes to improve moisture retention and aeration.

WATER SHOOT. Shoot growing directly out of a tree stem, frequently around a wound.

WEEPING. With slender branches that hang down.

WHIP. A young tree or grafted seedling without lateral branches.

WINGED (of seeds or fruits). Having a marginal flange or membrane.

INDEX

Each genus name is shown in bold type, followed by a brief description. Species, varieties, and subspecies are given in italics; cultivars are in roman type with single quotes. Common names appear in parentheses.

―――――― A ――――――

Abele see *Populus alba*

Abies (Fir)
Tall-growing conifers with whorled branches. Needle-like leaves are spirally arranged, flattened, often with a silvery band on the underside. Cones are held erect on the branches.
balsamea (Balsam fir)
   'Nana' 158
   var. *nana* see 'Nana'
cephalonica (Greek fir)
   'Meyer's Dwarf' 158
   'Nana' see 'Meyer's Dwarf'
concolor (White fir)
   'Argentea' 124
   'Candicans' see 'Argentea'
   'Compacta' 156
   'Glauca Compacta' see
      'Compacta'
grandis (Giant fir, Grand fir) 135
koreana (Korean fir) 151
lasiocarpa (Subalpine fir)
   'Arizonica Compacta' 155
   'Roger Watson' 158
nobilis 'Glauca' see *A. procera*
   'Glauca'
nordmanniana (Caucasian fir)
   'Golden Spreader' 163
procera (Noble fir)
   'Glauca' 138
veitchii (Veitch fir) 128

Acacia
Evergreen, semi-evergreen, or deciduous trees and shrubs, grown for their attractive flowers and foliage. Many have phyllodes instead of true leaves.
dealbata (Mimosa, Silver wattle) 77

Acer (Maple)
Deciduous or evergreen trees or shrubs, grown for their foliage or decorative bark; many display

brilliant autumn color. Leaves are opposite. Small flowers are followed by 2-winged fruits.
capillipes (Snake-bark maple) 74
carpinifolium (Hornbeam maple) 101
cissifolium
   subsp. *henryi* 73
crataegifolium (Hawthorn maple)
   'Veitchii' 94
davidii (Père David's maple)
   'Madeline Spitta' 70
ginnala (Amur maple) 109
griseum (Paperbark maple) 122
henryi see *A. cissifolium* subsp. *henryi*
japonicum (Full moon maple)
   'Aconitifolium' 108
   'Aureum' see *A. shirasawanum*
      f. *aureum*
   'Vitifolium' 107
laxiflorum 115
lobelii (Lobel's maple) 25
macrophyllum (Big leaf maple, Oregon maple) 19
negundo (Ash-leaved maple, Box elder)
   'Argenteovariegatum' see
      Variegatum'
   'Variegatum' (Variegated box elder) 63
palmatum (Japanese maple) 10
   var. *coreanum* see 'Koreanum'
   'Koreanum' 106
pectinatum subsp. *laxiflorum* see
   A. laxiflorum
pensylvanicum (Moosewood) 81
platanoides (Norway maple)
   'Crimson King' 21
   'Lorbergii' 39
pseudoplatanus (Sycamore maple)
   'Brilliantissimum' 92
   'Erythrocarpum' 36
   'Simon Louis Frères' 63
rubrum (Scarlet maple, Red maple, Swamp maple) 37
   'Columnare' 11, 71
   'Scanlon' 35
   'Schlesingeri' 37
rufinerve (Snake-bark maple) 72
saccharum (Sugar maple)
   'Monumentale' see 'Temple's Upright'
   'Temple's Upright' 73
shirasawanum
   f. *aureum* 102
striatum see *A. pensylvanicum*
tataricum subsp. *ginnala* see
   A. ginnala
triflorum (Three-flowered maple) 110

Aesculus (Buckeye, Horse-chestnut)
Deciduous trees and shrubs, grown for their leaves and upright panicles or clusters of flowers. Fruits (horse-chestnuts) sometimes have spiny outer casings.
californica (California buckeye) 83
x *carnea* (Red horse-chestnut)
   'Briotii' 19
chinensis (Chinese horse-chestnut) 19
flava (Sweet buckeye, Yellow buckeye) 73
hippocastanum (Common horse-chestnut) 18
indica (Indian horse-chestnut)
   'Sydney Pearce' 62
x *neglecta* (Sunrise horse-chestnut
   'Erythroblastos' 92
octandra see *A. flava*
African tulip tree see *Spathodea campanulata*

Agonis
Frost tender. Evergreen trees and shrubs, grown for their leaves, flowers, and overall appearance.
flexuosa (Willow myrtle, Willow peppermint) 94

Ailanthus
Deciduous trees, grown for their foliage and attractive, 3–5 winged fruits in autumn.
altissima (Tree of heaven) 34
glandulosa see *A. altissima*

Albizia
Deciduous or semi-evergreen trees with feathery foliage and flower heads that resemble bottle-brushes.
distachya see *A. lophantha*
julibrissin (Silk tree) 98
lophantha (Plume albizia) 103
Alder see *Alnus*
Alexandra palm see
   Archontophoenix alexandrae
Almond see *Prunus dulcis*

Alnus (Alder)
Deciduous trees and shrubs that thrive in wet situations. Male catkins are more attractive than female ones, which are followed by persistent, woody fruits.
cordata (Italian alder) 24
glutinosa (Black alder, Common alder)

ACKNOWLEDGMENTS

Key: l = left, r = right, t = top, c = center, a = above, b = below

Photography by:

A–Z Botanical Collection Ltd 11tr, 192br

Gillian Beckett 72tr

Biofotos/Heather Angel 35bl, 132l

Christopher Brickell 92tr, 120tl

Eric Crichton 11cl, 20tr, 113bl, 150

Michael A. Dirr/The University of Georgia 64br

The Garden Picture Library 34br/John Glover 74br; Robert Estall 133c

Derek Gould 85tr, 111br

Neil Holmes 39br

Oxford Scientific Films/Deni Bown 114l, 154

Photos Horticultural 11tl, 88r, 127c, 159cra, 192tl

Savill Garden, Windsor 153r, 163cla

A. D. Schilling 78

Harry Smith Collection 11c, 11bl, 14t, 14b, 35tl, 51br, 55tr, 69tr, 73br, 74l, 77tr, 77b, 92br, 98br, 101tl, 103l, 103br, 104tr, 104br, 108tr, 113br, 113tr, 126, 132tr, 132br, 135tr, 137bl, 143tl, 148r, 149r, 152b

Additional photographs by:

Christopher Brickell

Eric Crichton

Geoff Dann

Steve Wooster

Picture Research:

Fiona Watson

Every effort has been made to trace the copyright holders. Dorling Kindersley apologizes for any unintentional omissions and would be pleased, in such cases, to add an acknowledgment in future editions.

Abbreviations			
C	centigrade	in	inch, inches
cm	centimeter	m	meter
cv.	cultivar	mm	millimeter
F	fahrenheit	oz	ounce
f.	forma	sp.	species
ft	foot, feet	subsp.	subspecies
g	gram	var.	variant

at Sheila Franklyn - Daphne

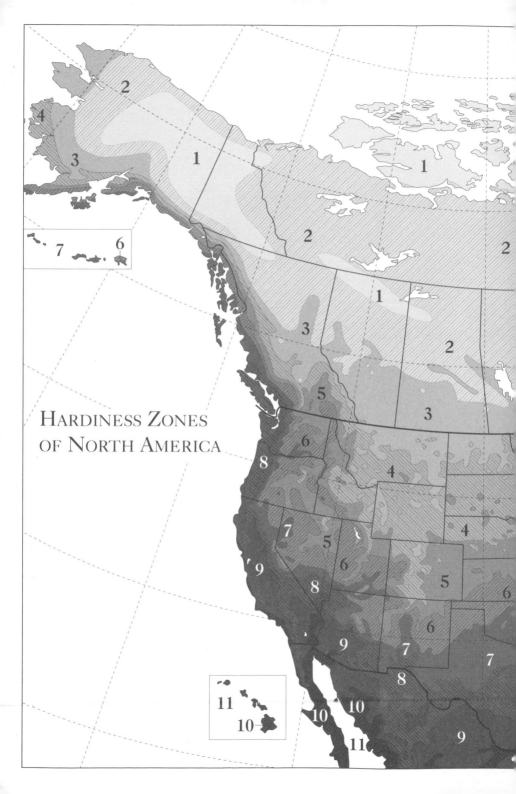

HARDINESS ZONES
OF NORTH AMERICA